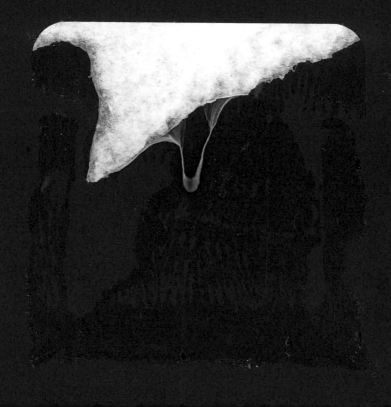

In 1939, the famous political cartoonist Herbert Block, widely known as "Herblock," created this cartoon to make a play on words regarding the Texas nickname of "the Lone Star State" to illustrate the rising power of Texans in Congress. Caricatures are of Texans (top row from left) Sam Rayburn, Tom Connally, John Nance Garner, (second row from left) Wright Patman, Maury Maverick, Morris Sheppard, (third row from left) Martin Dies, Hatton Sumners, and W. Lee O'Daniel. All were high profile leaders at the time. Used by permission of the Herb Block Foundation.

Lone Star Leaders

Power and Personality

in the

Texas Congressional Delegation

James W. Riddlesperger Jr. *and* Anthony Champagne

A Joint Project of
The Center for Texas Studies at TCU *and*
TCU Press
Fort Worth

Copyright © 2011 by The Center for Texas Studies

Library of Congress Cataloging-in-Publication Data

Riddlesperger, James W., Jr.

Lone Star leaders : power and personality in the Texas congressional delegation / James W. Riddlesperger Jr.,

Anthony Champagne.

p. cm.

A joint project of The Center for Texas Studies at TCU and TCU Press.

Includes bibliographical references and index.

ISBN 978-0-87565-418-8 (cloth : alk. paper)

1. Legislators--Texas--Biography. 2. Politicians--Texas--Biography. 3. United States. Congress--Biography.

4. Texas--Politics and government. 5. United States--Politics and government. I. Champagne, Anthony.

II. Texas Christian University. Center for Texas Studies. III. Title.

F385.R53 2011

328.73'073--dc22

2010035092

TCU Press

P. O. Box 298300

Fort Worth, Texas 76129

817.257.7822

http://www.prs.tcu.edu

To order books: 800.826.8911

Designed by Barbara Mathews Whitehead

Contents

Acknowledgments vii
Foreword, Mary L. Volcansek ix
Preface, The Honorable Jim Wright xi

1 Introduction *3*
2 Joseph Weldon Bailey *9*
3 Morris Sheppard *17*
4 John Nance Garner *25*
5 Sam Rayburn *33*
6 Hatton W. Sumners *39*
7 Thomas Connally *49*
8 Wright Patman *57*
9 Martin Dies Jr. *63*
10 George Mahon *71*
11 Lyndon Baines Johnson *81*
12 Bob Poage *89*
13 W. Lee O'Daniel *95*
14 Lloyd Bentsen *105*
15 Jack Brooks *113*
16 Price Daniel *121*
17 Bruce Alger *129*
18 Jim Wright *135*
19 Ralph W. Yarborough *145*
20 Henry B. González *153*
21 John Goodwin Tower *159*

22 George H.W. Bush *169*

23 Bill Archer *177*

24 Barbara Jordan *183*

25 Charles Wilson *191*

26 Phil Gramm *197*

27 Richard Armey *203*

28 Tom DeLay *209*

29 Kay Bailey Hutchison *217*

Notes 224

Index 244

Acknowledgments

THE AUTHORS ARE GRATEFUL to the many people who helped us in completing this book.

We have been lucky to have the assistance of a number of former students. Professor Champagne wishes to acknowledge University of Texas at Dallas students Benjamin Casey, Farhan Charania, Borna Danesh, Kimberly Miller, Shivangi Pokharel, Tony Seagroves, Sarah Strathearn, and Hung Vu. Professor Riddlesperger thanks former TCU students Alex Harrell, Mark Jones, Susan Keitges, Karen Luong, and Brandon Ortiz.

The authors are grateful to The Center for Texas Studies at TCU, under the able leadership of Mary Volcansek, as well as the Lowe Foundation of Austin, Texas, for its financial support. Research was supported, in part, through a grant from the University of Texas at Dallas.

We are also beholden to the staffs at the East Texas Research Center at Stephen F. Austin State University, the Dallas Historical Society, the Dallas Public Library, the Dolph Briscoe Center for American History, the A. Frank Smith Jr. Library Center at Southwestern University in Georgetown, Texas, the Lyndon Baines Johnson Library, the Poage Legislative Library at Baylor University, the Sam Houston Library and Research Center at Liberty, Texas, the Southwest Collection at Texas Tech University, the Texas State Archives, and the Jim Wright Collection at the Mary Couts Burnett Library at TCU.

Finally, the authors wish to thank the staff at the TCU Press, and especially former director Judy Alter, Susan Petty, and Melinda Esco.

Foreword

The Center for Texas Studies at TCU proudly offers *Lone Star Leaders: Power and Personality in the Texas Congressional Delegation* as part of its ongoing commitment to public education about the special place of Texas in our national life and character. *Lone Star Leaders* joins the Texas Biography Series, *Going to Texas: Five Centuries of Texas Maps,* and *A Century of Partnership: Fort Worth and TCU,* as projects undertaken in partnership with the TCU Press. Tony Champagne and Jim Riddlesperger's *Lone Star Leaders* allows readers to appreciate the Texas-size imprint that Texans made on national politics, particularly during the twentieth century, and does so by bringing together images and stories that come to life, in a playful but respectful fashion, the Texas congressional leaders and the times in which they led the country.

The Center for Texas Studies gratefully acknowledges a grant from the Lowe Foundation that made this project possible, as well as support from the Amon G. Carter Foundation, The Burnett Foundation, the Jane & John Justin Foundation, the Summerlee Foundation, the Summerfield G. Roberts Foundation, and the many individuals who have underwritten center projects. Their generosity enables the center to continue its mission of "celebrating all that makes Texas distinctive." We are most appreciative.

Mary L. Volcansek
Executive Director,
The Center for Texas Studies at TCU

Preface

IT WOULD BE HARD to assemble so heterogeneous a collection of colorful individualists as the men and women who have served the state of Texas in the United States Congress. As varied as they were in backgrounds, vocations, habits, and political leanings, many of them made highly significant historic contributions to our nation's growth and strengths.

Two of them (Lyndon Johnson and George H. W. Bush) ascended to the presidency. A third, John Nance Garner, preceded those two in serving as vice president. Three of us (Garner, Sam Rayburn, and I) were selected by our congressional colleagues to serve as Speaker of the US House of Representatives, while Lyndon Johnson served the Senate as majority leader. Richard Armey and Tom DeLay served as majority leader of the House of Representatives, and Joseph Weldon Bailey was minority leader.

Perhaps a fitting precursor to twentieth-century Texans was Sam Houston, citizen of three nations (the United States, the Cherokee nation, and the Republic of Texas). He was elected governor of Tennessee as well as of Texas, earlier serving Tennessee in the US House and later representing Texas in the US Senate. In between, he commanded the forces that won Texas's battle for independence from Mexico and did a stint as president of the Republic of Texas.

Less spectacular but intensely interesting and similarly impressive have been the lives and exploits of a number of others. Some have made enormous contributions to America in their respective fields of law. Their stories cry out to be read.

Here, for the first time, is a major compilation of these fascinating life tales. Two noted political science professors, James Riddlesperger and Anthony Champagne, have devoted years to the compilation and personal verification of the intriguing events that propelled the lives of these accomplished politicians and public servants.

For nearly thirty years, the authors have pursued and conducted literally hundreds of personal, one-on-one interviews with members and former members of the Texas congressional delegation and with friends, former colleagues, and staff to learn the pertinent and sometimes little known facts of these careers.

These are and were real people of whom the authors write. Their careers—some illustrious, some lengthy, some briefer but pithy with public consequence—are the very stuff from which our nation has attained its pinnacle of prominence.

During most of the twentieth century, the Texas delegation was continually increasing in congressional power and influence. This had to do, in part at least, with the relatively longer tenures in the lawmaking arena with which Texas voters were prone to reward their local favorite sons. In an age when powerful committee chairmanships—particularly in the House—were awarded to individual members on the basis of seniority, length of service became a coveted tool.

Sam Rayburn once was asked to explain why Texas so frequently led all the other states in its number of important committee chairmen. Rayburn's reply was to the point: "We pick 'em young, and we pick 'em honest. We send 'em there, and we keep 'em there!"

But it isn't longevity alone that has explained and sometimes empowered this variegated lot of Texas political practitioners. Here the authors explore their strengths and weaknesses. In some cases, you may be alternately admiring and appalled. Their stories, as told by these two superb researchers, will help you understand who they were and are, what they've done to applaud or regret, and sometimes why.

The Honorable Jim Wright
May 12, 2010

Lone Star Leaders

I

Introduction

TEXAS HAS produced members of Congress who have wielded enormous power as chairs of committees and as party leaders. When, for example, effective Senate leaders are discussed, Lyndon Johnson always is spoken of as one of the masters of the Senate. Similarly, when House leaders are discussed, Sam Rayburn is usually identified as one of history's most successful legislators and as the longest serving and most effective Speaker of the US House of Representatives.

Two Texans who served as members of Congress have gone on to serve as president of the United States—Lyndon Johnson and George H. W. Bush. Lyndon Johnson served as senate minority and majority leader. Sam Rayburn, John Nance Garner, and Jim Wright served as Speakers of the House of Representatives. Richard Armey and Tom DeLay (along with Rayburn and Wright) served as majority leaders. Joseph Weldon Bailey, John Nance Garner, and Sam Rayburn all served as minority leaders in the House.

Numerous Texans have served as chairs of Senate and House committees. Indeed, in the New Deal era and its aftermath, so many Texans served as chairs of important committees that a complete listing would have made this volume far too lengthy. Important committee heads such as Marvin Jones, who chaired the Agriculture Committee; James Buchanan, who chaired the Appropriations Committee; and John Mansfield, who chaired the Rivers and Harbors Committee, are excluded from this book. Among the many Texans who did serve as committee chairs and who made important contributions to public policy, these are included in this book: George Mahon, who served as chair of the Appropriations Committee; Bob Poage, who served as chair of the Agriculture Committee; Wright Patman, who chaired the Banking and Currency Committee; Jack Brooks, who chaired the Judiciary Committee; and Bill Archer, who chaired the Ways and Means Committee. Still other Texans—Joseph Weldon Bailey, for example—became important congressional figures, not necessarily because of formal offices held, but because of their overpowering personalities. Other Texans were pioneers: Barbara Jordan was the first black congresswoman from the South and a masterful public speaker; Henry B. González was an activist for civil rights for Latinos and one of the first Latinos in Congress; and Kay Bailey Hutchison was the first woman US senator from Texas.

Not all Texans in Congress have been pioneers or effective political leaders, however. Texas has had its share of buffoons and characters in Congress. Notable among this group would be W. Lee (Pappy) O'Daniel, who left the governorship of Texas to become one of the state's most ineffective senators. Another in this group was Martin Dies, whose publicity-seeking and fanatic anti-communism destroyed his chances to advance in the congressional hierarchy, and who helped make the House Committee on Un-American Activities one of the most despised committees in congressional history. Bruce Alger was a far-right ideologue who, although he held a seat on one of the premier committees of the House—the Ways and Means Committee—was largely ineffective because of an inability to compromise or to work with others holding more moderate views.

Congressman Charlie Wilson shows that it is possible to play dual roles—to be an entertaining character in Texas politics and to have an important policy impact—to the point of being a major figure in bringing about the Soviet Union's defeat in Afghanistan. Wilson's flaws can be overlooked in light of his amazing policy effectiveness, and the buffoons like O'Daniel, Dies, and Alger have been quite rare. When one thinks of Texans in Congress, it is easy to identify a substantial number of members who wielded vast power on the congressional stage.

Texas political power really began in the late nineteenth century. Texans Roger Q. Mills served as chair of the Ways and Means Committee from 1887-1889, and Joseph Weldon Bailey was minority leader in the House from 1897-1899. Bailey served as a mentor and political ally to future Speakers of the US House John Garner and Sam Rayburn.

In the era of Woodrow Wilson, Texas power greatly expanded. Senator Morris Sheppard's influence extended far beyond the Prohibition legislation with which his name is associated today. Sheppard was an advocate for progressive legislation in general and a supporter of defense spending. John Nance Garner's political influence was first felt in the Wilson administration, particularly as a liaison on war matters between the administration and the House. Garner's influence was to continue, especially in the Hoover era, when he rose to minority leadership to become a major critic of Hoover administration policies. And, with Democratic control of the House in the aftermath of the 1930 elections, Garner became Speaker of the House of Representatives and a presidential contender.

With the Franklin Roosevelt administration, Texas's influence increased. Texas was a Democratic state, and with Democratic control of Congress and a Democratic president, the state's power grew. John Garner became vice president in 1933, and Texans chaired six committees in the House—Agriculture, Interstate and Foreign Commerce, Judiciary, Public Buildings, Rivers and Harbors, and Territories. Morris Sheppard and Tom Connally were Texas powerhouses in the US Senate in that era. Sam Rayburn, chair of the Interstate and Foreign Commerce Committee and a workhorse of the New Deal, became majority leader in 1937. William Bankhead, the Speaker, suffered from a serious heart ailment that limited his effectiveness in that role. The result was that Rayburn often combined the roles of Speaker and majority leader. With Bankhead's death in 1940, Rayburn became Speaker for the longest time in American history. He served as Speaker from 1940 until his death in 1961, with the exception of the four years when Republicans controlled the House, and he served as minority leader during that period.

With the Eisenhower era, Lyndon Johnson, Sam Rayburn's protégé, became minority leader and then majority leader of the Senate. It was an extraordinary time with Texans in the top leadership of both the House and the Senate.

Even after Rayburn's death in 1961, Texas's power continued. The state retained major committee chairs, and Lyndon Johnson became president in 1963 when John Kennedy was assassinated. Texas was changing as well. Republicans were becoming more influential in state politics. John Tower, a Republican, replaced Lyndon Johnson in the Senate in a freak election where the sheer number of Democratic candidates seeking to replace Johnson gave the seat to John Tower. Tower gained influence in the Senate, becoming one of its most conservative voices. Meanwhile, Ralph Yarborough, who had been a rival of Lyndon Johnson's, was one of the most liberal voices in the Senate. Republicans hoped that Houston's Republican congressman, George H. W. Bush, would pick off Yarborough, who was seen as too liberal in an increasingly conservative state. But that plan was foiled when conservative Lloyd Bentsen defeated Yarborough in the Democratic primary, went on to defeat Bush in the general election, and became in his own right one of the Senate's most effective members.

The aftermath of Watergate brought many changes in politics, one of which was a decline in the sanctity of congressional seniority as the road to advancement in

Congress. The Democratic Caucus began to challenge senior Democrats whom they saw as out-of-touch or too dictatorial in their control of committees. Texans Bob Poage and Wright Patman were removed as the chairs of Agriculture and of Banking and Currency. The Watergate investigations pushed Jack Brooks, a master investigator and interrogator, into the public eye, and Brooks eventually became chair of the Judiciary Committee.

Texas was not just becoming more conservative and more Republican. African Americans, Latinos, and women were also gaining in political power. With their rise, Henry B. González and Barbara Jordan gained political influence in the Congress. Jordan was thrust into the public eye by the Nixon impeachment hearings. Her extraordinary speaking skills and her commitment to justice made her a major figure in congressional politics and on the national political stage. Kay Bailey Hutchison was the first woman elected as US senator from Texas.

In 1976, Jim Wright was elected majority leader by a one-vote margin, became Speaker in 1987, and resigned as Speaker in 1989. George H. W. Bush's career did not come to an end with his defeat by Lloyd Bentsen in 1970. He was to serve as Ronald Reagan's vice president and then rise to the presidency. Republican Bill Archer replaced Bush as a member of Congress and Archer was to become chair of the Ways and Means Committee, one of the most powerful committees of the House. With the Reagan era, Phil Gramm burst on the political scene, first as a Democratic member of the House, then as a Republican, and then as a Reagan Republican US senator.

Dick Armey was elected due to Reagan's popularity in Texas. Armey would eventually become majority leader of the House of Representatives after the Republican return to power in the House in 1994. With Armey's retirement from the House, Tom DeLay would become majority leader.

It looked like Texas power would never end. From the late 1800s through the twentieth century, Texas was producing party leaders in Congress and chairs of major committees. But that suddenly came to a halt after the 2008 elections. Tom DeLay had arranged for the Republicans in the Texas legislature to reapportion the state's congressional districts to their party's advantage, but Republicans lost control of both the administration and the House and Senate. Additionally, DeLay, the Texas member of Congress with the greatest power in his position of majority leader, was indicted and resigned from Congress. Suddenly Texas—a state known for producing congressional powerhouses—had none. In the House, it had no party leader and no chair of a standing committee. Its only claim to power was the chair of a select committee. In the Senate, Republicans John Cornyn and Kay Bailey Hutchison were in the minority, and Hutchison was planning to leave the Senate to run for governor of Texas. At least for a while, the glory days of Texans in Congress were gone. With the 2010 elections, Republican members of the House from Texas again rose to power in the hierarchy of the House. Texas will continue to produce congressional leaders, although in the near future at least, that will only happen when Republicans control the House or Senate since Texas has become so overwhelmingly a Republican state.

This book is the story of the men and women who represented Texas in Congress. For a century and a quarter they were masters of congressional politics and represented Texas on the national stage. The characters, the ideologues, and the buffoons are also part of the Texas story in Congress. But they are a much smaller part of the story compared to the party leaders and committee chairs and the political pioneers that made Texas a major player in congressional politics for the past 125 years.

Joseph Weldon Bailey was one of Texas's most charismatic and controversial political figures. After serving in the House of Representatives, including two years as minority leader, Bailey served in the US Senate. Photograph in Joseph Bailey Papers, Dallas Historical Society. Used by permission.

2

Joseph Weldon Bailey

US Representative 1891-1901
(Minority Leader 1897-1899);
US Senator 1901-1913

ISTORY has largely forgotten Joseph Weldon Bailey. He was born in Mississippi in 1862 and moved to Gainesville, Texas, in 1885. Gainesville was across the Red River from Indian Territory and seemed an ideal trading center. Bailey opened a law office there and soon entered the political fray. In 1890, at the age of twenty-seven, he successfully challenged the incumbent congressman, Silas Hare, and became the youngest member of the House of Representatives. He associated himself with the Farmer's Alliance and became a spokesman for Silver Democrats in the House. Soon, he was proclaiming himself an expert on the US Constitution.[1] His oratorical skills were compared to those of William Jennings Bryan, and Bailey made such a mark, even in his first term in the House of Representatives, that future Speaker Champ Clark pointed to him as proof that a freshman congressman could have an impact within the House.[2] By 1897, Bailey was the Democratic leader in the House, and was nominated as the Democratic candidate for Speaker against Republican Thomas Reed. Bailey was handily defeated, of course, by a party vote where the Republicans overwhelmingly outnumbered the Democrats. It was not long before Bailey grew frustrated with the House. Champ Clark wrote:

It is interesting to note that Bailey, young, brilliant, able, enthusiastic, and aggressive, became minority leader of the Fifty-Fifth Congress, and with all his splendid ability was so pestered by Democratic kickers that he followed

Crisp's example, declined to stand for reelection, and went over to the Senate, where he developed into one of the most powerful debaters of this generation.[3]

Bailey served as a US senator from Texas from 1901-1912. Interestingly, Bailey changed as he moved to the Senate. Although he was an agrarian Silver Democrat in the House, where he had voted with Southern Democrats and agricultural interests, in the Senate he supported the regulation of railroads and railroad service, was an early supporter of the income tax, and opposed American expansionism. In fact, he became more conservative and often voted with Northern Democrats. Most importantly he became increasingly involved in business schemes to increase his personal wealth.[4]

Bailey was probably insolvent as late as 1899, but by early 1903 he was buying property and soon, claimed his political opponents, he was probably a millionaire.[5] One critical magazine article claimed that "Mr. Bailey spent money like water, as men of fancy, appetite, and imagination ever do; and since his needs were forever outrunning his resources, he was perennially 'hard up.'"[6] Then, claimed another critic, "Once in the Senate, Bailey began to think of and long for money. He had tastes, and while they were not elevated, they were expensive. He liked horses, he liked cards, and horses and cards are not within the wages of a senator."[7]

Though Bailey, with his typical rhetorical flourishes, claimed that "In all the long and glorious history of our and other Southern States, there never lived and served a man whose record is as much above suspicion of unselfish men as mine,"[8] Bailey's rapid economic success came largely through controversial business deals—one of which led Bailey into enormous political difficulties. The Waters-Pierce Oil Company was the major supplier of lighting fuel in Texas. In 1895, charges were filed against the company alleging that as a marketing company for Standard Oil, it was in violation of the anti-trust laws of Texas, and in 1900, the state won its suits. This required the company to forfeit its charter to do business in Texas. Waters-Pierce Company president Henry Clay Pierce then hired Bailey to assist the company's efforts to regain its license. Bailey then borrowed a substantial amount of money from Pierce to settle a debt. Afterward, he met with the governor of Texas about relicensing the company, although when the Texas attorney general objected, it was necessary to dissolve the company, reorganize, and apply for a new license. That effort to assist Waters-Pierce became controversial, and Bailey did not admit that he had borrowed the money from Pierce. The result was that the Texas legislature investigated Bailey's role in the relicensing of Waters-Pierce. Although two state

Joseph Bailey defended himself against corruption charges before a packed house in the state capitol in this speech before the Texas legislature on January 27, 1907. Photo in collection of the Dolph Briscoe Center for American History, Austin, Texas. Used by permission.

legislative investigations cleared Bailey of wrong-doing, it was revealed that he had obtained very large legal fees from companies while serving as a Texas senator, and hints of corruption remained to plague Bailey for the remainder of his career.[9] Bailey insisted that "a senator had the right in his spare time to practice law with a view to laying up a competence in his old age,"[10] but his representation of corporations such as Waters-Pierce created great controversy.

Bailey's bigger-than-life personality, his arrogance, vanity, oratorical skill, and brilliance divided the state into pro- and anti-Bailey factions. It was his powerful personality, rather than any policies that he pursued, that created Bailey's political legacy, for two key Bailey men eventually went on to become Speakers of the US House of Representatives. John Nance Garner of Uvalde, Texas, was aligned with Bailey due to a political alliance between Bailey and Jim Wells, one of the major political leaders in the Rio Grande Valley. Bailey was a key political supporter of Sam Rayburn. Sam Rayburn was elected Speaker of the Texas House of Representatives largely because of his political ties to Joe Bailey, and later Rayburn represented a congressional district that was substantially Bailey's district. Rayburn as a young man worshiped Bailey, saying, "This Adonis of a man with a massive brain captured my imagination and became my model."[11]

Joe Bailey must have been an extraordinary man. Champ Clark, who became Speaker in 1911, described Bailey as "young, brilliant, able, enthusiastic, and aggressive."[12] When Sam Rayburn asked him who had been the ablest member of Congress with whom he had served, Clark replied, "If I had to pick one, it would be Joe Bailey." Republican Speaker Joe Cannon echoed Clark's statement.[13] The congressman and New York Central Railroad executive Chauncey Depew said that Bailey was one of "the most brilliant debaters of any legislative body" who "would have adorned and given distinction to any legislative body in the world."[14] Claude Bowers, a historian of that time period, said of Bailey, "no man drew greater crowds to the gallery on the announcement that he would speak. His voice was melodious as a fine organ." Bowers added that Bailey was "domineering, extraordinarily able and eloquent. . . . Tall, powerfully built, with a handsome head and features, he carried himself like a conqueror. His eloquence was both powerful and persuasive. . . . His voice was melodious, and when he finished his peroration his tones lingered in the chamber like the echo of chimes in a cathedral."[15] Bailey adopted the dress of a post-Civil War Southern gentleman and for over twenty-five years wore a broad-brimmed hat, a Prince Albert coat, and long hair.[16] He was also sensitive and hot-tempered. He was once accused of going after a political opponent with a knife and, on another occasion, of pulling a gun from a satchel to silence some enemies on a train.[17] In 1902, his temper created a major political embarrassment for him. He was involved in a controversy with W. L. Penfield, who was solicitor of the State Department. Bailey was interested in a contract dispute between a constituent and Mexican interests. After the constituent lost his case in Mexican court, Bailey insisted that the State Department intervene before the Mexican Supreme Court. When the State Department did not provide enough assistance to satisfy Bailey, he criticized Penfield. This led Senator Albert Beveridge

Joseph Bailey walking near the US Capitol wearing his signature Prince Albert coat.
Photograph in the collection of the Library of Congress.

to rise and defend his fellow Indianan Penfield. Beveridge referred to the Bailey speech as "an unwarranted attack." Offended, Bailey asked that Beveridge withdraw those words and when Beveridge did not do so, Bailey became infuriated and tried to grab Beveridge around the throat. Bailey had to be restrained by the doorkeeper and several senators, and he was removed to the Senate cloakroom.[18] Bailey was sometimes, in other words, simply out of control.

Bailey did not seek his Senate seat again in 1912, possibly because he was facing significant opposition. However, it was also the case that Bailey had another fit of anger. He had attempted to resign over New Mexico and Arizona statehood. He had also resigned from the Committee on Privileges and Elections and the National Monetary Commission. He claimed that he quit politics because he concluded that Prohibition would become the dominant issue for years and that any man who made Prohibition an issue was unworthy of office. It is also the case that he was increasingly unhappy with the progressivism of the Democratic Party.[19] In 1911, he attacked "those populistic heresies known as the initave [sic] referendum"[20] and he resigned when he interpreted a vote of the Democrats in the Senate as supporting those policies. Only after he had been assured that he had misconstrued the vote did he withdraw the earlier resignation.[21] Still, it was clear Bailey wanted out of the Senate. He had changed his trademark dress to an ordinary suit and a black derby hat, and he announced that he was building a home in Washington that would cost between $30,000 and $50,000. He gave a speech on September 5, 1911, announcing that he would leave the Senate, and he did so on January 3, 1913. [22]

However, this was not the end of Joe Bailey. He contemplated running for Senator Charles Culberson's Senate seat in 1914, but then changed his mind.[23] Moving back to Texas in 1920, Bailey entered the race for governor, declaring that he would "redeem Texas and Democracy." Even though he had not lived in Texas for years, he was greeted by huge crowds who heard him promise to cut state appropriations in half and pursue an anti-labor agenda. He wanted to improve education, separate church and state, and have less control from Washington. He was opposed to Prohibition, women's suffrage, the League of Nations, and class legislation. He preferred the old church organs to pipe organs and square dancing to the "fox trot." He liked "Sewanee River" and "My Old Kentucky Home" rather than songs like "Oh, You Beautiful Doll" or "I Love My Wife, But Oh You Kid." Pat Neff, one of Bailey's opponents, said of Bailey, "He is the only living statesman; all others are dead. He walks with his face to the past and his back to the future. He is satisfied with everything except the League of Nations, the national administration, the state administration, the Democratic Party, the president of the United States, Congress, the two Texas senators, the eighteen Texas congressmen, the state legislature, Prohibition, women's suffrage and the enforcement of Prohibition laws. However, Joe is highly pleased with himself."[24] Neff defeated Bailey in a runoff election.

In 1927, Sam Rayburn, Joe Bailey's protégé, wrote his sister Kate about Bailey, "When he is animated as he always is when he talks, he is something of the old Bailey, but in repose he is saggy and sad looking—He is a mighty old man for 63."[25] Two years later, on April 13, 1929, Bailey died while arguing a case in a Sherman court.

Senator Morris Sheppard working at his desk, November 14, 1937. Photograph from the collection of the Library of Congress.

3

Morris Sheppard

US Representative 1901-1913;
US Senator 1913-1941

IF MORRIS SHEPPARD is remembered at all, it is because of his support and his leadership in the fight for ratification of the Eighteenth Amendment—the National Prohibition Amendment. In fact, Sheppard considered the Eighteenth Amendment to be the greatest accomplishment of his career.[1] Sheppard, however, was far more than an ardent "dry" in the debate over Prohibition, although he became known as the "driest of the dries." This small man—he was only five feet four inches—was tenacious, witty, and charming. He was a talented orator, a friend and supporter of William Jennings Bryan, an enthusiastic Wilson Democrat, and—with the exception of the Prohibition issue—a dedicated supporter of Franklin Roosevelt's policies. In short, he was, throughout his long political career, a National Democrat who supported Progressive causes.[2]

Morris Sheppard was born in Morris County, Texas, in 1875, attended The University of Texas for undergraduate and for law school, and then received additional legal training at Yale University. He began practicing law in Pittsburg, Texas, in 1898, and then moved to Texarkana in 1899 where he continued his legal practice. His father, John Sheppard, had been a district attorney, a judge, and a congressman, and when John died Morris was elected as his successor. Morris served in the US House of Representatives from 1902-1913, when he was elected a US senator in a hotly contested election created by the resignation of Joseph Weldon Bailey. Sheppard served as a US senator from 1913 until his death in 1941. Although he was not quite sixty-six years of age when he died, he served thirty-nine years in Congress and, at the time of his death, he had the longest congressional service of any serving member. With the exception of his position on the Military Affairs Committee, which he chaired late in his Senate career, he served on no major committees. However, his support for defense measures as World War II was approaching was crucial to the security of the United States. He did have a leadership role in the Senate when he served from 1929-1933 as Democratic whip, the position directly behind that of Democratic leader.[3]

Sheppard was only twenty-seven years old when he was elected to his father's old congressional seat. He was so young that some of his colleagues thought he was a page when he took the oath of office. His years in the House were frustrating—he was in the minority party, and during most of his House years the Speaker was Joseph Cannon, a Republican from Illinois who was a notoriously dictatorial leader and who was unwilling to favor a junior Texas Democrat. Sheppard labored on unimportant committees and then fumed when Cannon would refuse to recognize him. Yet, even in those early years, Sheppard's dedication to Prohibition was evident as was his Progressivism. He introduced legislation to prohibit the shipment of alcohol into "dry" areas and proposed insuring bank deposits.[4]

One of the lasting issues in the politics of that era (and earlier) was the tariff. Typically, Republicans favored high tariffs or taxes on imported goods and Democrats tended to favor low tariffs. In part, this difference reflected the regional divisions of the two parties, as Democrats tended to come from Southern, less industrialized states, while Republicans tended to come from Northern, industrialized states which benefited from taxes on imported goods that helped protect domestic industries but raised prices for consumers. Sheppard developed a reputation for his knowledge of tariff policies. He was—as one would expect from a Southern Democrat—a tariff reformer who sought lower taxes on imports. Sheppard's rhetorical skills were evident when he denounced Republicans for their "stand pat" tariff policies. "Stand pat," said Sheppard, "is merely another expression for dry rot. Swollen with the spoils of office, corpulent with the wine of power, distended with the dropsy of corruption, the Republican Party drags its huge inflated body across the halls of state... while its coward lips wail out, 'stand pat.'"[5]

While a member of the House of Representatives, Sheppard was able to pass a bill establishing the National Archives,[6] but it was only when he went to the Senate in the wake of Woodrow Wilson's presidential victory in 1912 and the corresponding Democratic control of Congress that Sheppard began to have a significant policy effect.

As a senator, Sheppard increasingly focused on Prohibition, ultimately achieving success with the ratification of the Eighteenth Amendment. Prohibition was not an

A youthful Morris Sheppard on the Capitol steps. Photograph from the collection of the Library of Congress.

issue created by Sheppard, but he was its outspoken supporter in the Senate and was so deeply involved in Prohibition legislation that he will be forever identified as one of its leading advocates. There are several possible explanations for his commitment to this issue. One is that he had seen biology books that showed the effects of alcohol on a body's internal organs; another was that as a leader of the fraternal organization, the Woodmen of the World, he had seen the effects of alcohol on many of his fellow Woodmen. Sheppard was from East Texas, which at the time had a large Methodist and Baptist population that supported temperance, even though Texas as a whole was divided on the Prohibition issue. Sheppard himself was a dedicated Methodist, and as a Progressive, he believed that government could improve people's lives—and that included protecting people from the destruction associated with alcohol and the saloon.[7] When, for example, the Senate was debating his Prohibition bill in July, 1917, Sheppard defended his stand against the argument that national Prohibition interfered with the rights of states to make choices as to whether alcohol should be legal, and also interfered with the right of individuals to choose whether to drink. "The issue," claimed Sheppard, "is the right of the community to override the individual tastes of a man who wishes to do that which is not good for the community. . . . This is not a question of states' rights, but a question of safeguarding the health and morals of the nation."[8] Illustrative of Sheppard's pride in the passage of the Eighteenth Amendment, he gave a speech every year on the anniversary of the amendment's ratification.[9]

Sheppard fought repeal of the Eighteenth Amendment, even to the point of attempting to filibuster the repeal resolution.[10] He was not without humor in his support, however. In 1938, Sheppard was at a party when Sol Bloom, a Jewish congressman from New York, arranged to have a cocktail sent to him. To give the "Father of Prohibition" an alcoholic drink could, of course, have led to an embarrassing scene. Sheppard, however, quickly responded by having a ham sandwich sent to Bloom. This story, so characteristic of Sheppard's wit and good humor, has become a part of congressional folklore.[11]

Prohibition did bring some personal embarrassment to Sheppard. A large moonshine still was found on land owned by Sheppard. For the "driest of the dry" to have a still on his property was, of course, politically harmful to Sheppard, but it was soon determined that the still was being operated by Sheppard's cousin without his knowledge.[12] A much more serious issue was the conflict Sheppard faced between his support of Prohibition and support for Democratic presidential nominees who advocated repeal. In 1928, the Democratic nominee was Al Smith of

John Nance Garner and Senator Morris Sheppard. Photograph from the collection of the Library of Congress.

New York, a Tammany Hall-Catholic-wet. Many in Texas and the South would not support Smith. He was too urban, too Catholic, and too opposed to Prohibition. However, in the conflict between party and Prohibition, Sheppard supported the party and stayed loyal to the Democratic ticket.[13]

That remained the case in 1932 when Franklin Roosevelt supported repeal of Prohibition. Although Sheppard opposed Roosevelt's repeal efforts, he was an avid proponent of Roosevelt's election and of the New Deal. Sheppard even supported Roosevelt's court-packing plan in 1937 that would increase the size of the Supreme

*Senators Morris Sheppard, of Texas (right) and Hattie Caraway of Arkansas ride from their offices to the Capitol on the senate
subway to vote on the nomination of Senator Hugo Black as a Supreme Court Justice, August 17, 1937.
Photograph from the collection of the Library of Congress.*

Court and, of course, einsure a pro-New Deal. That attack on the court was too
much for many, including influential Texans such as Vice President John Nance
Garner, Texas's other senator, Tom Connally, and Congressman Hatton Sumners of
Dallas, who was chair of the House Judiciary Committee. However, Sheppard
backed the court-packing plan.[14] His pro-Roosevelt leanings were also evident in a
Senate battle for the majority leadership between Senator Pat Harrison of
Mississippi and Senator Alben Barkley of Kentucky. Generally, the election of a
majority leader is considered a matter internal to the Senate where the senators of
the majority party make their own political and personal judgments in choosing
their leader. Pat Harrison, however, was the more conservative of the two candidates
and President Roosevelt, although he had promised to be neutral in the race, wrote
a lengthy letter to Barkley that seemed to signal a preference of Barkley over
Harrison. Morris Sheppard had promised Pat Harrison that he would support him

for majority leader. However, one hour after President Roosevelt's letter to Barkley became public, Sheppard switched his vote to Barkley, saying to Harrison, "I am sorry, Pat, but the President's wishes come first with me."[15]

Sheppard's legislative skills were great enough and his Progressivism strong enough that supporters of women's suffrage approached him for assistance in securing the legislative support of fifty-six senators who voted for the amendment (twenty-five senators opposed it).[16]

A hallmark of Morris Sheppard's career was his loyalty to the Democratic Party and to Democratic presidents along with support for Progressive policies. Sheppard was a Wilson supporter and backed the president on tariffs and on border disputes with Mexico that arose as a result of the 1910 Mexican Revolution. He supported military preparedness and was an advocate for the League of Nations.[17] His 1921 speech in support of the League of Nations shows his skill with words, his opposition to American isolationism, and an idealism that rivals that of Woodrow Wilson:

> . . . I believe it is the duty of this Nation to ratify the Treaty of Versailles and join the League of Nations. . . . Believing that the issue of issues before the United States and all mankind is the League of Nations created by the Treaty of Versailles, ... that this league, slow though may appear its processes and numerous the difficulties which surround it, offers to this generation and to the century the only hope of the final establishment of organized right and justice among the nations, I can not vote for any enactment in which, once more asserting our isolation from the league, we emphasize our desertion of humanity.[18]

With the presidency of Franklin Roosevelt, Sheppard the Wilson Progressive became an ardent supporter of the New Deal. He became chair of the Military Affairs Committee in 1933 and was a key voice supporting military preparedness as World War II approached. Perhaps his greatest contribution to the national defense was his support of the Selective Service Act, for which he helped secure Senate passage only a little more than a year before the attack on Pearl Harbor. Sheppard also was a key legislator for the Lend-Lease Act that greatly benefited England's war effort.[19]

Sheppard suffered a brain hemorrhage and died on April 9, 1941. One obituary stated that he "has literally worked himself to death in the service of his country."[20]

Young Congressman John Nance Garner poses for a photograph. Photograph from the collection of the Library of Congress.

24

4

John Nance Garner

US Representative 1903-1933
(Speaker 1931-1933);
President, US Senate 1933-1941

ISTORY has not treated John Garner favorably. Joe Frantz, for example, wrote of Garner, "It could be questioned whether Garner brought any affirmative qualities to either the speakership or the vice presidency except a certain wiliness and the ability to keep his mouth shut. . . ."[1]

Today John Nance Garner is probably best known as Franklin Roosevelt's vice president for two terms, as a vice president who rebelled against what he believed was a left-leaning tendency on Roosevelt's part, and as a man who John L. Lewis described as "a labor-baiting, poker-playing, whiskey-drinking, evil old man."[2] Garner, however, had a remarkable career in the House of Representatives prior to being vice president. He was elected to the House of Representatives in 1902 and served until 1933 when he became vice president. Those three decades in the House ultimately led him to the speakership in 1931 and, for a while, he was believed to be presidential timber.

Born in northeast Texas in 1868, Garner was elected from a large South Texas district with the support of rural political bosses who controlled Mexican American voters. The bosses, most notably Jim Wells, kept Garner in office and, in turn, Garner funneled government projects to the district and provided the bosses with political patronage. Support from these bosses generally meant that Garner was secure in his district, and he steadily built seniority in the House of Representatives and gained power. Elected to the House in 1902, in 1910 Garner was elected Democratic whip. In 1913, Garner moved from the Foreign Affairs Committee to the Ways and Means Committee. Not only was the Ways and Means Committee exceptionally important, it was the tax-writing committee of the House, and in those days, the Democratic members of the committee also served on the Democrats' Committee on Committees. Ways and Means was therefore an important source of power for Democrats in the House. It was Garner who steered through the House President Wilson's controversial legislation establishing the Federal Reserve, and it was Garner who became President Wilson's liaison with the House regarding World War I legislation.

In 1928, Garner was elected Democratic minority leader in the House where he led the opposition to Hoover administration policies. He opposed the high Smoot-Hawley Tariff, supported lower tariffs, and expanded public works. With Democratic control of the House by a bare majority, Garner was elected Speaker in 1931 and pushed for greater public works projects. Garner was a candidate for the Democratic nomination for president in 1932 and controlled delegates from Texas and California. He made a deal with Franklin Roosevelt that prevented Roosevelt's nomination from being blocked at the convention, and Roosevelt was nominated for president with Garner as his vice president.[3]

Garner was notoriously thrifty, to a point that his thrift was a joke among his companions. Congressman John McDuffie of Alabama recalled, for example, talking with one of Garner's fishing partners:

> I said to him one day, "I bet Mr. Garner has 90 cents out of every dollar he made." Mr. Schwartz said, "You are wrong." I said, "Why?" He said, "Because he has 99 cents out of every dollar he ever made."[4]

For years the Garners lived in the Washington Hotel. Admirers frequently gave them large quantities of food such as venison, bear, and beef because of Garner's well-known love of hunting and the outdoors. Large amounts were allowed to spoil in the hotel iceboxes because Garner and Ettie, his wife, could not bear to give it away.[5]

Yet Garner was wealthy. At one time he owned two banks, a large number of mortgages on homes in Uvalde, and many acres of South Texas farmland, ranchland, and pecan orchards, including a 23,000 acre ranch with the largest goat herd in the world. He also held a large amount of stock in a coffin company.[6]

Garner had an enormous capacity for making friends, but he had few intimate friends. He tended to keep his own counsel, sometimes not even telling until the last moment his closest protégés such as Sam Rayburn about his presidential plans.[7]

Once he had established his value to the political bosses in his district, he paid little attention to what most politicians would consider fundamental political concerns such as elections, even though he often had Democratic primary opposition and, unlike many Southern congressmen, fairly significant Republican opposition.

Arthur Schlesinger Jr. described Garner as having a "bright, ruddy face, short-cropped white hair, cold blue eyes, and a tight small mouth." He presented, wrote Schlesinger, an appearance of "an infinitely experienced sage and of a newborn baby."[8] He was tough-talking and hard-hitting. There was, D. B. Hardeman and Donald C. Bacon wrote, a quality of the frontier about him, and he was "painfully truthful, even blunt, ambitious, and felt satisfaction in dealing with national problems." He was rough with people, telling Sam Rayburn, "You've got to bloody your knuckles."[9]

Whiskey, perhaps some poker, and some conversation were Garner's way of doing business. He frequently met during the speakership of Republican Nicholas Longworth in what was called the "Bureau of Education" where he would "strike a blow for liberty" (i.e., drink whiskey) and arrange political compromises. For Garner, politics and alcohol spiced with some poker were the necessary prerequisites of public policy making

Historian Jordan Schwarz has written, "Notwithstanding the desperate condition, the Democratic Party offered few alternatives to the policies of the party in power."[10] The major focus of disagreement between Garner and the Hoover administration was that Garner was somewhat more sensitive to the human needs created by the Depression and more aware than Hoover that the 1930 elections were a demand by voters for greater governmental involvement in the economy.[11]

Garner had a somewhat more inflationary approach than did Hoover, but he was a disappointment to liberals. Reporter Robert Allen considered Garner to be a Democratic Calvin Coolidge.[12] Rexford Tugwell saw Garner as a "confused Texan" who was "so conservative and so lacking in imagination that nothing had occurred to him that Hoover had not thought of first. . . . And anyway Garner was known to be more worried about balancing the budget than about unemployment. He was hopelessly sterile as a leader. . . ."[13] While Tugwell's evaluation of Garner is very harsh, Garner did not offer, indeed could not offer, given his minute majority in the House, a clear alternative to Hoover's policies.

As vice president, Garner was a valuable advocate for the administration in the Congress. It was not until about 1937 that his disagreements with administration policy turned him into a hindrance for the administration. Until 1937, he was a useful legislative tactician for the New Deal and he was valuable in passing New Deal legislation. Garner, after all, had thirty years in Congress and two years as Speaker. He had a vast network of friends in Congress and vast knowledge of the legislative process.

Garner was more involved in leadership battles in the House of Representatives than any other vice president. He quite openly backed his whip, John McDuffie of Alabama, over his majority leader, Henry Rainey of Illinois, in the election to choose his successor as Speaker. Unable to defeat Rainey for Speaker, Garner then backed Sam Rayburn for Speaker in 1934 over Joseph Byrns of Tennessee, Rainey's majority leader. Again Garner was unsuccessful, but in 1937 he succeeded in a struggle to elect Sam Rayburn majority leader over John O'Connor of New York.[14] Such overt interference in a House leadership race by a vice president was unprecedented, but Garner was finally able to place a protégé in the leadership of the House.

Garner had enormous support within the powerful Texas delegation and an especially close relationship with Sam Rayburn, chairman of the Interstate and Foreign Commerce Committee and a major figure in early New Deal legislation. Texans held numerous committee chairs and one special committee. In working with the Senate, Garner had nineteen Senate members with whom he had served in the House, and almost every one of them was a personal friend of his. Although Garner did not like some of the early New Deal, he was loyal to the administration and he became one of the most powerful vice presidents in history.[15] Lionel V. Patenaude wrote of Garner's early years as vice president:

> Operating from his vice presidential room just off the Senate Lobby, Garner would gather his friends and spin a few yarns, which were highlighted by pertinent suggestions. The president regularly used him to pass the word to Congress on priority legislation. But he was not just a messenger, he was the New Deal's "mid-wife." In the process he "worked wonders on law makers. . . . " In his inner sanctum, or in his Bureau of Education, over branch water and bourbon, many an important decision was made which affected New Deal legislation.[16]

Still, Garner was fundamentally conservative. There were hints of tension between Roosevelt and Garner as early as 1935.[17] In March, 1935, Garner complained that cabinet meetings, which he attended, were not useful for the discussion

Vice President Garner backed his protégé Sam Rayburn during Rayburn's successful campaign for the house majority leadership in 1936. Originally published in the Washington Evening Star.
Clifford Berryman cartoon in the collection of the National Archives. Used by permission.

of policy, and by 1935 Garner was thinking the economic emergency was over and that some of the policy experiments could be ended.[18]

In 1937, that fundamental conservatism began to create a break between Garner and Franklin Roosevelt. It was not long until it was clear that Garner had set out to sabotage the New Deal. By 1938, Garner and Roosevelt were barely on speaking terms. They disagreed on the sit-down strikes, deficit spending, packing the Supreme Court, the battle over the majority leadership in the Senate between Pat Harrison and Alben Barkley, the Wages and Hours Bill, and the effort to purge the Democratic Party of anti-Roosevelt members of Congress.[19] Garner was also opposed to a third term for Roosevelt.

Finally, on December 17, 1939, Garner officially announced his candidacy for president.[20] Garner had tremendous financial backing for his campaign.[21] But everything awaited the president's decision on what he would do.[22] With the declining

WATCH YOUR STEP

international situation and Roosevelt's decision to seek a third term, Garner's presidential prospects ended. He returned to Uvalde where he was apparently content. He lived to be almost ninety-nine years of age and died in 1967.

Garner was a master of the legislative process and in FDR's first term, he had served Roosevelt well as a legislative strategist and lobbyist. A Democratic Party loyalist, Garner ultimately choked over the economic policies of Roosevelt's second term. The result led to the most public break between a president and vice president in the twentieth century.

Opposite: *Former Vice President John Nance Garner stepping from a train in Uvalde, Texas. Photo in collection of the Dolph Briscoe Center for American History, Austin, Texas. Used by permission.*

Sam Rayburn on his ranch near Bonham, Texas, with his trusty and well-dented Dodge pick-up. Photo in collection of the Dolph Briscoe Center for American History, Austin, Texas. Used by permission.

5

Sam Rayburn

US Representative 1913-1961 (Majority Leader, 1937-1940;
Speaker 1940-1947, 1949-1953, 1954-1961;
Minority Leader 1947-1949, 1953-1955)

ORN IN 1882 in Tennessee, Samuel Taliaferro Rayburn was the son of poor farmers who in 1887 migrated with their ten children to northeast Texas in search of a better life. Rayburn was able to obtain a college degree at East Texas Normal College in Commerce, Texas. Attending college and then getting a degree gave the young man the chance to move away from a backbreaking future as a cotton farmer. Late in his life, he was to tell friends that he "missed being a tenant farmer by a gnat's heel."[1] After teaching in several schools, Rayburn chose a political career and was elected a state representative in 1906. In 1908, he was reelected and used his time with the legislature in Austin to take courses at The University of Texas that allowed him to be admitted to the bar.[2]

After joining a law practice in Bonham, Texas, he was far more successful as a politician than as a lawyer. In 1910, Rayburn was elected to a third term in the legislature, and in early 1911, he was elected Speaker of the Texas House of Representatives. The success in his state-level political career was not due solely to his initiative, but also to the efforts of his political mentor, Congressman and later Senator Joseph Weldon Bailey.

As Speaker of the Texas House, he was able to control a reapportionment of the US House seats from Texas that gave him a political district that he liked. Rayburn served in Congress from 1913 until his death in 1961. His district was a rural northeast Texas district that, as the years went by, became increasingly malapportioned and so had an unusually small population. However, Rayburn saw his

33

main role as a representative of rural America. He did not wish a larger and more urban district and, since the US Supreme Court did not require "one person-one vote" during his lifetime, the Texas legislature maintained the district that Rayburn desired.[3]

Rayburn frequently faced significant political opposition in the Democratic primary and was nearly defeated as late as 1944. Indeed, in 1948, he faced a major political threat in the Democratic primary because of his support for Harry Truman, and he found it necessary to publicly oppose Truman's civil rights policies. It was not until the 1950s that Rayburn was politically secure within his district. Early in his career, some of his most important opposition came from anti-Joe Bailey politicians and politicians who capitalized on national economic problems. Later in his career, politicians opposed him who argued that he was more liberal than his district and that national leadership interfered with representation of the district. Rayburn counteracted that opposition with a highly personal approach to his constituents. Throughout his career, he was easily accessible to constituents and very solicitous of their needs. He developed a network of friends and supporters in every community in the district who volunteered their time and energies to campaign on his behalf, and, beginning with the Roosevelt era, he had the power to bring numerous important public works projects to his district. He raised and spent little money for his campaigns, used only some radio in the campaigns, and never used polling, surveys, or constituent newsletters.[4]

When Rayburn was not in Washington, he was usually in his district. He traveled remarkably little. Constituents were always welcome to visit him in his home, either with or without an appointment. He had great interest in helping his and other rural districts through major water projects, rural electrification, farm-to-market roads, and soil conservation programs.[5]

Rayburn first ran for the US House of Representatives in 1912 and was elected with a plurality of the vote.[6] He quickly allied himself with another political mentor, Congressman John Nance Garner. Garner, as a member of the House Ways and Means Committee, was also a member of the Democrats' Committee on Committees. He was able to get Rayburn a prized seat on the Committee on Interstate and Foreign Commerce, one of the most important committees in the House. It was the only committee on which Rayburn served during his long career in the House of Representatives.[7]

In the Wilson era, Rayburn was a new congressman with an activist political agenda. He was interested in the regulation of railroads and he pushed the Rayburn Stock and Bond Bill that gave the Interstate Commerce Commission authority to prevent railroads from issuing stocks and bonds without its approval. The bill was initially supported by the Wilson administration, but was dropped as a Wilson legislative priority when both the elections and war approached.[8]

Rayburn soon had to settle for a long period of inactivity—the Republicans controlled the House from 1919 until 1931. However, in 1931, Rayburn became chair of the Interstate and Foreign Commerce Committee and Rayburn's mentor, John Garner, became Speaker in 1931 and was a contender for the presidency in 1932. Rayburn helped manage Garner's campaign and was one of the people who put together the Roosevelt-Garner ticket at the 1932 Democratic Convention. After the election of Roosevelt, Rayburn became a loyal Roosevelt ally in the House and his committee passed some of the most important legislation of the first New Deal.[9] That legislation included regulation of utility holding companies, the regulation of securities and the creation of the Securities and Exchange Commission, the creation of the Federal Communications Commission, and the creation of the Rural Electrification Administration.[10]

Rayburn had ambitions to move higher in the House hierarchy, however. After some half-hearted attempts to move directly from his committee chairmanship to the speakership, he ran for majority leader in 1936. He was supported openly by his old ally, Vice President Garner, and more subtly by President Roosevelt. His opponent was John O'Connor, a Tammany Hall congressman from New York and chairman of the Rules Committee, who argued that Texas and the South already had too much power in the House and that the North needed more representation in the leadership. However, Rayburn was better liked and had the support of the administration. He became majority leader in 1937.[11]

As majority leader under seriously ill Speaker William Bankhead of Alabama, Rayburn often was in effect both leader and Speaker of the House. In 1940, Bankhead died, and Rayburn was able to become Speaker without opposition.[12] During the Rayburn era, the Speaker's office was institutionally weak. The power of the Speaker had been broken in 1910 as a result of a revolt against Republican Speaker Joe Cannon's exercise of dictatorial power. By the time Rayburn was Speaker, power had been transferred to the chairs of congressional committees. Nevertheless, in spite of the limited formal powers of the speakership, Rayburn was a remarkably strong and effective Speaker. He was a strong supporter of defense in World War II and gained early fame for his parliamentary maneuvers that led to an extension of the military draft shortly before the war's outbreak of war. Overall, in foreign affairs he was deferential to presidential power. Domestically, he grappled with balancing conservative Southern political power in the House—the result of

Sam Rayburn signing the Declaration of War against Japan, the last declaration of war to date. Photo in collection of the Dolph Briscoe Center for American History, Austin, Texas. Used by permission.

The Democratic leadership in Congress, represented by House Speaker Sam Rayburn and Senate Majority Leader Alben Barkley, hoped that reorganization of Congress in 1946 would be politically popular and help Democrats maintain control of Congress. Voters, however, would have a different opinion. In the November elections, the Democrats lost control of both the House and the Senate. Berryman cartoon published July 28, 1946.
From the US Senate Collection, Center for Legislative Archives.

the seniority system—with the numerical strength of Northern Democratic congressmen. Rayburn was a segregationist for political reasons—since he represented a rural Southern district. However, he quietly supported the passage of the 1957 Civil Rights Act, the first civil rights legislation passed by Congress since Reconstruction. At the end of his career, Rayburn engaged in one of the greatest political battles of his career with Howard Smith, then chair of the Rules Committee, who was opposed to the Kennedy administration's political agenda. Rayburn led the successful fight to expand the size of the committee and, therefore, aid the Kennedy programs through the House.

Rayburn served as Speaker from 1940 until his death in 1961, with the exception of the four years when the Republicans were in control of the House. During that time, he served, rather reluctantly because of the reduced power, as Democratic leader of the House.[13] In 1952, Rayburn supported a boomlet for his presidential candidacy after Truman withdrew from the race. In 1940, 1944, and 1956, Rayburn seems to have seriously considered a bid for the vice presidency.[14] However, he also seems to have understood that his chances for either of these offices were slim. He frequently said of his chances, "I was born in the wrong place at the wrong time."[15]

By the 1950s, he had become a political institution. He was admired for his judgment and leadership, although criticized by conservative Southerners for being too liberal and by liberals for being too conservative. He had, however, immense prestige, and held the respect of members. Carl Albert, a protégé of Rayburn's and later a Speaker of the House, explained the sources of Rayburn's power. Albert noted that Rayburn had the longest seniority that anyone in the leadership had ever had. Additionally, Rayburn had strong support from the large and powerful Texas delegation in the House, which during Rayburn's time as Speaker was overwhelmingly Democratic. Finally, over the years, Rayburn had become such a national institution that no one would dare to double-cross him.[16]

Rayburn had benefited from the friendship of Joe Bailey and later John Garner and, as he aged, he became the mentor to younger politicians whom he regarded as talented and able. His close association with Lyndon Johnson is probably the best known of these protégé relationships. Johnson regarded his relationship with Rayburn as so important that he thought the way to become president was through Rayburn.[17] Future Speakers of the House Carl Albert and Jim Wright were also protégés of Sam Rayburn, as was House Majority Leader Hale Boggs and Rules Committee Chair Richard Bolling, all of whom worked closely with Rayburn in forwarding his political agenda. In exchange, Rayburn promoted their political careers.[18]

Rayburn understood the institution so well that he claimed he could feel the sentiments of the House[19]—and he probably could. His death of pancreatic cancer in 1961 was the end of a long and remarkably successful speakership that was based largely on the strength of his personality.

6

Hatton W. Sumners

US Representative 1913-1947

HATTON SUMNERS began as a struggling farmer's son in post-Reconstruction Tennessee. After his move to Texas, he became an earnest lawyer in Dallas and ultimately a powerful leader in Congress. Early in his career he was a handsome, friendly young man with an endearing sense of humor. As he aged, he became notoriously thrifty and developed the bearing of a judge: tall, dignified, retiring, with a kindly, chivalrous manner and with a humorous twinkle in his eye. His colleagues would affectionately refer to him as Judge Sumners because of his intellectual bent, but his famous fight with Franklin Roosevelt over the court-packing plan made such an appointment slip from his grasp. After that fight, his influence within the Democratic Party in Washington declined, and he eventually retired from Congress to end his career in Dallas.

On a farm in Boons Hill, Tennessee, Hatton William Sumners was born to Captain William A. Sumners, former Confederate officer, and Anna Walker Sumners on May 3, 1875, the second of three children. He was named after Tennessee native Confederate General Robert Hatton, who died at the Civil War battle of Fair Oaks.[1]

Sumners's memory of his early life in Tennessee was mainly of wearisome and unending work. His father never fully recovered from his Civil War injuries, and as his health declined, young Hatton assumed more family responsibilities. His family valued education, encouraging Hatton to attend classes in a one-room school near their farm.[2]

By the time Hatton was eighteen, the depression due to the Panic of 1893 was in full swing. The Sumnerses' farm was nearly bankrupt, so the family resettled in

Hatton Sumners was mentioned prominently as a candidate for the US Supreme Court when Justice George Sutherland retired, reflecting the high opinion that Chief Justice William Howard Taft had expressed. By the date of this picture, January 7, 1938, however, Sumners had distanced himself from President Roosevelt and the New Deal. Photograph from the collection of the Library of Congress.

A young Hatton Sumners in his law office. Photograph in the collection of the Dallas Historical Society. Used by permission.

North Texas, where Mrs. Sumners's family had written of their success with the rich, fertile soil and of numerous business opportunities. Hatton went to Garland, Texas, and found the prospects for success "to his liking." He worked in his uncle's small general store and had a trading business in order to raise money. By the time his family had sold their Tennessee farm and joined Hatton in the small farming community of Garland, he had saved nearly enough to purchase a small farm.[3] More often than not, Hatton could be found in his uncle's store hunched over law books. He developed a particular love for public speaking and hoped that by studying law he could help frame laws that would solve the many problems that farmers encountered.[4] Sumners moved to Dallas and got a job with Dallas City Attorney Alfred P. Wozencraft, who also supervised his legal education.

By 1897, Sumners passed the bar examination, and he rented a one-room law office, paying thirteen dollars for a second-hand desk, table, and chairs. Sumners became interested in the political affairs of Dallas and joined the Young Men's Democratic Association in 1899. In 1900, Sumners ran for the office of county attorney, despite worries that he was still "wet behind the ears," winning a decisive victory.[5] In office, Sumners worked relentlessly against the proprietors of gambling houses and he would participate in raids of such establishments with his six-shooter tucked in his pocket. The gambling houses responded with promises of retribution.

Retribution came in 1902 when Sumners lost the Democratic primary to Walter S. Lemmon. He appealed to the Democratic committee to order a recount, and when the committee refused, he filed a restraining order against the committee and Lemmon. Sumners argued that the gambling interests funded a campaign of illegal voting, but the case was dismissed and the election was allowed to stand. Sumners spent the next two years investigating illegal voting in Dallas County and lobbying for a change in the election law. In 1903, working with Texas Representative Alexander Terrell, a law incorporating many of Sumners's recommendations was adopted. The Terrell Election Law provided uniform party nomination primaries and conventions, official ballots, and security to guarantee against various types of election fraud.[6]

Under the new law, Sumners was reelected county attorney in 1904. Again he pursued the gambling houses, and one writer referred to Sumners as "Elijah-like" in his pursuit. Sumners burst into a businessmen's "prayer meeting" of influential Dallas citizens at one point, railing at the group for sitting "here chasing God around," but not lifting "a finger to help me, or Dallas." Before the end of the meeting, he had obtained their cooperation to finish "cleaning up the town."[7] In 1906, Sumners chose not to campaign for reelection, instead working on a proposal for a statewide anti-gambling statute. He also devoted much of his time to an issue that concerned many farmers: the counterfeit futures market or "bucket shops" as they were commonly called. He insisted that these bucket shops were little more than gambling "dives for commodities such as cotton and grain and were run by crooks masquerading as brokers preying on the unsuspecting and naive investor."

With the same intensity and energy he pursued the gamblers, Sumners attacked the bucket shops. He wrote speeches and articles and in 1906, he drafted an anti-bucket shop bill as a companion to his anti-gambling bill that emerged from the Texas legislature as the Jenkins-Mayfield Bill in 1907. With the adoption of these two bills, Sumners established himself as an influential figure in the Dallas community.[8]

Sumners returned to his law practice in 1907, but did not retire from public life. He continued actively lobbying for agricultural reforms. His work took him to Washington once to lobby for a futures market reform bill, and on a tour of Europe to write articles on the effects of European immigration on the agriculture industry and economy of Texas. As a lobbyist for the Texas cotton industry, Sumners was able to obtain freight rate savings for the farmers of more than a half million dollars.[9]

After the 1910 census, Texas gained two at-large congressional seats. Sumners received enthusiastic encouragement from his friend and ally, Frank Holland, and prominent Dallasites such as Alexander Sanger of the Sanger Brothers Department Store, developer Robert L. Thornton, and Garland publisher John Collum. Running a vigorous campaign across Texas in 1912, his supporters hailed him as "the most patriotic statesman" and praised him for his success in lobbying for agriculture and anti-gambling reforms. His victory was not only a triumph for him personally, but a "sweeping victory" for the national Democratic party.[10]

Sumners traveled by train to Washington for Woodrow Wilson's inauguration, accompanied by fellow freshman Congressman Sam Rayburn of Bonham, Texas. The two became the "bachelor representatives" from Texas, drawing offices next to each other on the fifth floor of the house office building and remaining friends throughout their years in Washington, despite their disagreements on various issues. A noticeable decline in their friendship came after they clashed on Roosevelt's court reorganization plan in 1937.

Sumners wanted to be appointed to the Agriculture Committee, but was assigned to two smaller committees, the Public Buildings and Grounds and the Mileage Committees. In the first session of the Sixty-Third Congress, Sumners introduced his first bill, which concerned making Dallas a port of entry for customs, with the support of Speaker Champ Clark. This bill, the first to be passed by a member of his freshman class, foreshadowed Sumners's effectiveness as a legislator.

With the retirement of six-term incumbent Jack Beall in 1914, Sumners switched his candidacy to the 5th Congressional District of Dallas and surrounding counties. He would represent this district until his retirement in 1946.[11] Positions on the Agriculture and Judiciary committees opened up, and although Sumners retained an interest in agriculture, he opted for the powerful Judiciary Committee. As a member of the Judiciary Committee, Sumners appeared before the Supreme Court four separate times on behalf of the legislative branch. He served as manager of three impeachment hearings against judges George W. English in 1926, Harold Louderback in 1933, and Halsted L. Ritter in 1936.[12] On the Judiciary Committee, Sumners befriended former president and Chief Justice William Howard Taft, who called Sumners the "best lawyer in Congress."

In December 1931, Sumners became chair of the Judiciary Committee, joining several other Texans who also held important positions in Congress. They included John Nance Garner, who was elected Speaker of the House; Sam Rayburn, who headed the Interstate and Foreign Commerce Committee, and Marvin Jones, who headed the Agriculture Committee.

In the early 1930s, Sumners recognized the seriousness of economic conditions. Although he did not agree with many of Franklin Roosevelt's programs, he supported them anyway. He said, "the ability of a people to maintain a parliamentary system of government is . . . dependent upon their ability to recognize when they face a great crisis, and if necessary, to utilize the more efficient but more dangerous powers of arbitrary government in dealing with that crisis." And then, "when that crisis shall have ended, return the Government to parliamentary control." He stated that, "The President is trying to turn us around, to change our direction. . . . We have got to give him some extraordinary power."[13]

As a strict constitutionalist, Sumners disagreed with much of Roosevelt's New Deal legislation, but supported the legislation for the sake of party unity. Roosevelt began to show his dissatisfaction with the Supreme Court when it began overturning the New Deal legislation that Congress had passed.

To ease tensions, Sumners began laying the groundwork for his own court plan. He felt that the Supreme Court was in need of "some new blood," since at that time it was mainly made up of conservatives who disapproved of Roosevelt's New Deal. Early in 1935, Sumners introduced a bill that would have allowed Supreme Court justices to retire at seventy years of age, retaining their status as judges as well as their fixed salaries. Sumners hoped that at least one or two justices would take advantage of the retirement possibilities and that the bill would pass in the House before the White House made any drastic moves.

The drastic move that Sumners hoped to avoid arrived on February 5, 1937. The leaders of Congress were summoned to the White House that morning unaware of the plan that would give the president authority to appoint an additional justice to the Supreme Court for each justice who did not retire six months after reaching the age of seventy.

On the way back to the Capitol, Sumners made an immediate decision. He has been quoted to have said to his colleagues, "Boys, this is where I cash in." This meant that he would make "an irreparable break with the demanding President." He was "willing to sacrifice his political future for principle." There had been rumors circulating about his candidacy for a Supreme Court appointment. Immediately

Sam Rayburn is in the center; Hatton Sumners is to Rayburn's far right; Marvin Jones is to Rayburn's far left. Jones was chair
of the Agriculture Committee, for a brief time Rayburn's brother-in-law, and a federal judge.
Photograph in the collection of the Dallas Historical Society. Used by permission.

From left: Rep. Hatton Sumners; Rep. Albert Thomas; unidentified; Capt. J.W. Flanagan; Rep. Sam Rayburn; Vice. Pres. Garner;
unidentified; Sen. Morris Sheppard; Sen. Tom Connally. May 5, 1937.
Photograph from the collection of the Library of Congress.

45

House leaders study president's message. Washington, DC. President Roosevelt's sensational message to Congress, demanding overhauling of the Judiciary, struck congressional leaders like a bolt from a clear sky. Copies of the speech were at a premium on Capitol Hill. Here we see Rep. Hatton W. Sumners of Texas, chairman of the House Judiciary Committee, and Speaker William B. Bankhead, as they went into a huddle with the message. Speaker Bankhead said the message involved a "sound principle" for judicial reform.
Rep. Sumners refused to comment. February 5, 1937.
Photograph from the collection of the Library of Congress.

46

after the announcement of Roosevelt's plan, Sumners's name appeared in newspaper lists of possible appointees, but it was soon dropped when he did not cooperate.

Sumners' plan to defeat the court-packing bill was simple. He would do nothing. By refusing to take up the bill in the Judiciary Committee, Sumners had "time to stir up opposition." His refusal forced the administration to bring the bill up in the Senate, where it would be more difficult to pass. In the Senate Judiciary Committee, the members voted to send the bill to the Senate with an unfavorable recommendation. The bill was effectively killed. As one writer notes, had the House Judiciary Committee reported on the bill, it would have been easily passed in the House.[14] Therefore, Sumners's opposition to the bill almost ensured its defeat.

When Sumners retired in 1946, he stated that he was not retiring from "active service," but was hopeful that as a "private citizen" he could "bring about a better understanding and better cooperation between the people and their representatives."[15] He returned to Dallas and established himself on the campus of Southern Methodist University, becoming director of Research in Law and Government at the Southwestern Legal Center. In 1949, he established the Hatton W. Sumners Foundation for the Study and Teaching of the Science of Self-Government. His foundation continues to award academic scholarships.

Today Sumners is remembered as "the man who killed the court bill" and as a modest man despite a long list of credentials that spanned seventeen consecutive terms in the House of Representatives. He remained a bachelor for life, caring for his mother and father as long as they lived. Sumners died in Dallas, six weeks before his eighty-seventh birthday on April 19, 1962, and is buried next to his parents in Garland Cemetery.

Senator Tom Connally working at his desk. Photograph from the collection of the Library of Congress.

7

Thomas Connally

US Representative 1917-1929;
US Senator 1929-1953

IF THE NAME Tom Connally is mentioned today, it is likely he will be confused with famed Texas Governor John Connally who was wounded in Dallas when President Kennedy was assassinated. There is no relationship between Tom and John Connally, and Tom Connally's political career was both longer and more significant than John's. Tom was an advocate of the League of Nations, the North Atlantic Treaty Organization, and the United Nations. Although it may seem unlikely that one of the most important advocates for international organizations and for a major role for the United States in the world would be from the tiny town of Marlin in Central Texas, Connally was one of the leading internationalists in the Senate in a time when isolationism was a common political perspective.

Born in 1877, Connally was a volunteer in the Spanish-American War, although he did not see combat. He became a lawyer and was elected to the Texas House of Representatives in 1900 and reelected in 1902. During his two terms, he was an opponent of monopolies and of Senator Joe Bailey, arguably the most powerful figure in Texas politics in that era. He then served as a prosecuting attorney and in 1916 was elected to the US House of Representatives. Connally was assigned to the House Foreign Affairs Committee, where he proved to be a strong supporter of President Woodrow Wilson's war policies and plans for peace after World War I, most notably the League of Nations.[1] Connally joined the army in World War I but, like his service in the Spanish-American War, he did not see combat.[2]

In the 1920s, he was a critic of the corruption of the Harding administration, an opponent of military intervention in the Caribbean and in Central America, an

advocate of non-military solutions to difficulties with Mexico, and a strong supporter of weapons reduction and disarmament.[3]

In 1928, although he had considerable seniority in the House of Representatives and after determining that other key political figures such as John Nance
Garner and Sam Rayburn did not want to seek the post, Connally ran for the US
Senate against the Ku Klux Klan-backed incumbent Earle Mayfield. Mayfield was
elected to the Senate in 1922, which Connally claimed was the time of peak support for the Klan in Texas. In 1924, however, the Klan candidate lost the race for
governor, and in 1926 Dan Moody, who had even investigated the Klan, was elected
governor. Connally correctly concluded that Mayfield was beatable in 1928 and
attacked him as the Klan candidate as well as accusing him of corruption.[4]

Unlike many Texas Democrats who backed Herbert Hoover over Al Smith—a
New York machine politician who was Catholic and opposed to Prohibition—
Connally remained loyal to the Democratic Party and even campaigned for Smith.
Herbert Hoover was elected president and, shortly thereafter, the Great Depression
began. Connally believed Hoover was inept as president and was a strong critic of
Hoover's policies. In 1932, Connally was a strong supporter of fellow Texan and
Speaker of the US House of Representatives John Nance Garner for the presiden-
cy, although Connally admitted in his autobiography that he did not believe that
Garner had much chance to get the nomination.[5] In the end, Connally, along with
Sam Rayburn, worked to put together the 1932 Democratic ticket of Franklin
Roosevelt for president and John Garner for vice president.[6]

With the election of Franklin Roosevelt in 1932, Connally became a supporter
of Roosevelt's first term policies with the major exception of the National
Industrial Recovery Act, which Connally opposed. That act allowed agreements
between business and labor that established codes of fair competition that were
enforceable by the national government. Connally insisted that the act was an
unconstitutional delegation of legislative authority to the president, and he argued,
"The only thing on your side is that the times are so out of joint and the country
is so out of shape that many congressmen are grasping at anything that seems to
offer a hope for stopping the depression."[7] Connally claimed his opposition to this
legislation did not earn him enmity from Roosevelt since Roosevelt did not really
need his vote—the act passed by an overwhelming majority.[8] (In a unanimous opinion, the Supreme Court soon declared the legislation unconstitutional, in part
because the court believed it delegated legislative authority to the president.)[9]

Connally was faced with the collapse of the oil industry brought about by the
discovery of the huge East Texas oil field and, at Roosevelt's suggestion, in an effort

Senator Tom Connally gesturing as he delivers a speech in 1938. Photograph from the collection of the Library of Congress.

to control production of oil and thus increase oil prices, Connally proposed an amendment to the National Industrial Recovery Act. The amendment provided that the federal government would prohibit the shipment of oil in interstate commerce that was produced in defiance of state laws. Given the massive production of oil in East Texas at the time, the amendment was primarily aimed at providing teeth to the production quotas on oil that had been imposed by the Texas Railroad Commission. The amendment rapidly quadrupled the price of oil, but the entire Act was found unconstitutional by the Supreme Court as a delegation of legislative authority to the president.[10] Connally, however, was able to correct the constitutional flaws in the law and soon secured passage of legislation known as the Connally Hot Oil Act, which achieved the objective of enforcing production quotas on oil and increasing oil prices.[11]

In Roosevelt's second term, the relationship between the president and Connally deteriorated when Connally opposed Roosevelt's effort to increase the size of the Supreme Court. Roosevelt was embittered by this defeat, which led to his effort in 1938 to defeat a number of conservative Democrats who had opposed the 1937 court-packing plan (and other New Deal legislation).[12] Connally was not up for re-election in 1938, but wrote, "The President tried to revenge himself against any of us who had opposed him."[13] Connally then explained how Roosevelt sought to gain his revenge against him. Connally had recommended a Houston lawyer, Walton D. Taylor, for a federal judgeship. Roosevelt was traveling by train through Texas, and Connally was asked to join the train in Amarillo. In Wichita Falls, Connally was asked to join Roosevelt on the back platform of the train. Then, wrote Connally,

When I reached the back platform, Roosevelt asked that Allred (Jimmy Allred, a former governor of Texas and a resident of Wichita Falls) to come out, too. And after Allred joined us, he announced to the crowd with a big flourish and in a sarcastic tone of voice that he was appointing Allred to the court vacancy. Evidently he intended to humiliate me publicly, because the crowd before the train knew I had recommended Taylor.

I stood on the back platform throughout it all, blank-faced and stiff as a poker. Roosevelt was showing me I wasn't being consulted in the matter.[14]

For a year after that incident, Connally had no contact with Roosevelt. However, the international situation was then deteriorating, and Connally was a strong supporter of Roosevelt's international policies.[15] He was the leader in repeal of the embargo on arms sales in 1939 and a top supporter of the Lend-Lease Act in 1941. Connally became chair of the Senate Foreign Relations Committee in 1941. He served as chair from 1941-1947 and from 1949-1953. In the interim period, the Republicans controlled the Senate and Connally was the ranking Democratic member of the committee. During these years, he helped create the United Nations, NATO, and a bipartisan approach to foreign policy.[16]

His pro-administration internationalist views were not reflected in his views on domestic policy, where he was notably conservative. Unlike his Texas colleague in the Senate, W. Lee O'Daniel, Connally was a loyal Democrat. Nevertheless, he and O'Daniel supported the Republican-Southern Democratic conservative coalition more than any other pair of senators from the South.[17] Yet he and O'Daniel, in spite of their conservative domestic policy views, could not stand one another. It was said that everyone could feel the tension when the two men were in the same room.[18] He, like almost all Southern members of Congress in that era, was opposed to civil rights, and it was Connally who led a major filibuster against the repeal of the poll tax, which required a payment of a tax in order to vote.[19]

Connally's heyday was in the 1930s and 1940s and he was one of the great Senate showmen.[20] He was tall, heavy, handsome, and had wavy white hair. Connally favored clothing in a style that was common early in the twentieth century—a long suit coat known as a Prince Albert and a string bowtie. He looked the part of a stereotypical Southern senator. But it was said of Connally that he was "the only man in the United States Senate who could wear a Roman toga and not look like a fat man in a nightgown."[21]

One of Connally's great strengths was his oratorical skill—something that had benefited him from his earliest days in politics.[22] He seemed to have a story to illustrate every point, and he could be vicious and bitterly sarcastic in his comments. Yet, the speaking style is archaic today. He was fond of telling stories that often portrayed black people in a negative way,[23] and his homespun tales were not the stuff of typical diplomatic conversation. He, for example, told Vyacheslav Molotov, the Soviet Union's People's Commissar for Foreign Affairs, that Molotov reminded him of "A stubborn East Texas lawyer I knew. This lawyer was at a meeting where he objected to every proposal made. Finally, he said, 'I'm going home now. It's time for supper. And when I get home, if supper isn't ready, I'm going to raise hell. And if it is ready, I ain't going to eat a damn bite!'" Connally relates that Molotov made no reply to him—perhaps because such a tale is so removed from usual diplomatic communications.[24]

Connally's party loyalty was increasingly distasteful to Texans, however, who were unhappy with the trajectory of the national Democratic Party. Connally claimed that in April 1952, he returned to Texas and consulted with friends who told him of the enormous anti-Truman feeling in the state. He claimed that he realized his opponents would attack the Truman administration and oppose him by tying him to Truman. At the time, Texans were concerned about the tidelands, the lands off the Texas coast that were believed to be oil rich. Texas claimed that land, though the Truman administration opposed the claim. In addition, Connally was aware that those who were anti-Truman were collecting large sums of money to oppose him. The result, Connally wrote, was that "I was convinced that if I ran again and made a vigorous campaign, the loyalty of my friends and my political record would insure my re-nomination. However, I concluded that re-nomination would not be worth what a statewide campaign would cost me and my friends in money, toil and in the tax it would impose on my strength and health. . . . So while I was in Texas, I decided not to run again."[25]

There was, however, more to Connally's decision than he related. George Norris Green, one of the leading historians of this period in Texas, wrote that by this point, "Connally was such an ancient blatherskite that his retirement was probably merciful for the state and the Senate."[26] Green wrote that Connally's friends actually told him that he could not beat Price Daniel, then the Attorney General of Texas, who had successfully linked Connally with the unpopular Truman administration. Additionally, Connally had not kept up with his political supporters in Texas. When Connally sent a campaign mailing to his supporters, a large percentage of the letters were returned marked "addressee deceased" or "addressee moved—no forwarding address." Additionally, Connally lost the support of the oil industry in Texas—at that time, the major source of wealth in the state. Although he had saved the Texas oil industry from massive price declines during the Depression with the Connally Hot Oil Act, he had lost their support because of the Truman administration's position on the tidelands and also because Connally was seen by the Texas oil industry as preoccupied with issues such as writing the United Nations charter instead of promoting their interests. Additionally, Connally's staff had declined in effectiveness to the point that it did not know that a major bill pushed by Connally which affected the oil industry was being investigated by the Justice Department.[27]

Connally retired from the Senate in 1953, published his memoirs in 1954, and died in 1963. His congressional career began with Woodrow Wilson and the Declaration of War against Germany in 1917 and ended with Dwight Eisenhower and the Cold War in 1953. During many of those years—and especially in the

*Senator Tom Connally tries out his "shooting irons" for news cameramen in Washington, DC, on June 14, 1938,
just before a congressional recess. He was anticipating a hunting trip back home in Texas.
Photograph from the collection of the Library of Congress.*

1930s and 1940s—he was one of the major figures to influence the course of American foreign policy. Throughout his lengthy career he retained a Woodrow Wilson type of belief in the importance of American involvement in the world and in American involvement in international organizations as a way of securing world peace.

Wright Patman poses with his portrait that now hangs in the US Capitol.
From the collection at the Lyndon B. Johnson Library, Austin, Texas.

8

Wright Patman

US Representative 1929-1977

J IM WRIGHT, speaking at Wright Patman's funeral, said, "Few if any have served the humblest of their fellow creatures so untiringly. Few have given of themselves so unsparingly. Few have dreamed the impossible dream so determinedly, resisted invincible foes so joyously, handled life's disappointments so gracefully, and preserved their basic ideals so uncompromisingly throughout a lifetime."[1] Wright Patman was first elected to the US House of Representatives in 1928 and served in the office until his death in 1976. During his final two terms in Congress, he was its most senior member. Prior to his election to the House, Patman served as assistant county attorney in Cass County, Texas, 1916-1917; served two terms in the Texas House of Representatives, 1921-1924; and served as district attorney in far northeast Texas, 1924-1928. While he was a state representative he shared a desk with Sam Johnson, the father of future president Lyndon Baines Johnson, and it was there that he first developed a friendship with LBJ, then only a boy. Patman made a considerable reputation as an anti-Klan political leader while he was in the state legislature and was a strict enforcer of Prohibition and prostitution laws when he was a district attorney.[2]

In his 1928 campaign for the US House of Representatives, Patman defeated Congressman Eugene Black in the Democratic primary. For most of his congressional career, he faced almost non-existent Republican opposition and usually only minimal opposition in the Democratic primary. In his last primary election in 1974, he won by only a little more than 54 percent of the vote. In most of his other primary elections, he was unopposed, and when challenged, won by well over 60 percent of the vote.[3] Patman was known for his deep concern for his constituents and personal constituent service. He also brought numerous federal projects to his district to benefit the local economy. Examples of such benefits included flood control along the Sulphur River, the Red River Army Depot, and the Lone Star Steel facility, which came about because of a national security measure that he sponsored to spread the production of steel out of New England.[4]

Sam Rayburn was one of Patman's closest friends in politics; his district was immediately to Patman's west. Their districts were similar in constituent makeup—largely rural, comprised of small towns and small farmers.

Sam Rayburn and Lyndon Johnson loved to tell this story that illustrated Patman's relationship to his constituents. They claimed that a young, Harvard-educated lawyer had once run against Patman and, of course, had been defeated. Later the young lawyer concluded that his educational credentials could be used to defeat an incumbent district attorney who was largely self-educated. In a debate between the young lawyer and the district attorney, the lawyer rattled off his Harvard credentials and then the incumbent district attorney replied, "Everything this man has said is true. I have no education. I never had the chance to get any. All the little law I know I learned by lamp light in an old lawyer's office here. Perhaps I haven't any business being here. I do not have much sense, but I have always had sense enough never to run against Wright Patman."[5]

Patman wanted to become a US senator and made a serious attempt in the special election of 1941, in which conservative W. Lee O'Daniel ultimately won the election. Among New Deal Democrats, however, Lyndon Johnson had greater financial support than Patman, greater statewide visibility, and the support of the Roosevelt administration, and so Patman had to abandon his senatorial goals in favor of Johnson. Nevertheless, dropping out of the 1941 campaign was a difficult choice for Patman. He had been a strong supporter of the New Deal and had eight years seniority in the House over Lyndon Johnson. Even though it was clear that with Patman and Johnson both in the race, the New Deal vote would be split and neither would have a chance to win, it took Patman days to decide to stand aside.[6] Patman, however, remained a strong supporter of the Roosevelt administration and remained close to Lyndon Johnson.

Patman has been described as a populist. He was sympathetic to the small farmer and small businessperson and critical of big banks and the Federal Reserve. He was hostile to chain stores, which he saw as detrimental to small businesses. He was a strong supporter of low interest rates and an advocate of credit unions. And he had a deep distrust of big business and government bailouts of business. Of course, as a Texas Democrat in his era, he was a segregationist. It would have been politically impossible for Patman to have been a strong supporter of civil rights from a rural Texas district during most of the years that he served in Congress. And his populism may have been overestimated in that many of his policies, such as his support for small banks and opposition to chain stores, actually benefited small town elites. His politics were a mix of 1890s Texas populism and the New Deal liberalism that continued into Lyndon Johnson's Great Society years.[7]

Patman's cherubic physical appearance belied his strong commitment to his political beliefs and his use of harsh rhetoric in opposing those with whom he disagreed. As Patman grew older, some claimed that he tried to make everything a matter of good vs. evil,[8] although he also demonstrated that perspective early in his political career. Consider this quote from Rufus Rorem as an example. Rorem was one of the founders of modern pre-paid health insurance. In 1932, he was a consultant for the American Hospital Association and was examining the question of whether veterans should be cared for in existing hospitals or whether new hospitals should be built for them. Rorem said:

> I got in to see Congressman Wright Patman. . . . I told him what I was doing there.
>
> He said: "What side are you on?"
>
> "I am not on any side. I have come to find out whether in the public interest it is better to use the voluntary and local government hospitals or to have new ones built."
>
> "I know. Which side? Do you want us to build them, or don't you?"
>
> I said, "I am trying to find out which."

The conversation never passed that stage. Patman just couldn't believe anybody would come to see him who didn't either want to start something or stop something.[9]

Patman was a true believer in his economic reforms, and his strong economic beliefs sometimes clouded his judgment and led him to make questionable political alliances with such figures as the notorious anti-Semite Father Charles E. Coughlin.[10] He also succumbed to ethical lapses by accepting speaking fees from unsavory lobbyists.[11]

When Patman first went to Congress, he wanted to be an economic reformer and sought appointment to the Banking and Currency Committee, which he saw as an ideal platform for his economic ideas. But, because of the seniority system preva-

*Representative Wright Patman, Texas, shown here with Robert L. Doughton, chairman of the House Ways and Means Committee,
told the committee of his bill, H. R. 105, to provide $30 a month to eligible veterans over sixty-five, from federal funds, 2-3-39.
Photograph from the collection of the Library of Congress.*

lent in Congress at the time, it was not until 1937 that he was able to gain assignment to this committee. He was not able to become chair of the committee until 1963, because of the lengthy service of Brent Spence, his predecessor. Spence served as chair of Banking and Currency from 1943-1963 except for the four years when the Republicans controlled the House. Patman considered it an injustice that he had not been put on the Banking and Currency Committee earlier in his career. He calculated that if he had not been held back from the committee for several years by conservatives who resented his defeat of Eugene Black and feared his economic radicalism, he would have been chair of Banking and Currency as early as 1943.[12] Of course, the long tenure of Brent Spence as chair of the committee was a sore spot for Patman. On one occasion, it was claimed that Patman asked Spence, "Mr. Chairman, how are you feeling?" Spence replied, "Wright, you have an undue interest in the state of my health."[13]

At the time of Wright Patman's congressional service, committee chairs were all-powerful, and it was common for them to rule their committees in an autocratic manner. Patman was no exception. Bill Archer, a Houston Republican, served on the Patman committee before moving to the Ways and Means Committee, and remembered him as a complete autocrat who had no interest in Republican input in committee business.[14] Patman exercised tight control over his committee and denied junior members use of staff. He made little use of subcommittees, thus keeping significant bills under his control. There were complaints that he spent too much time studying bills and not enough time explaining them to other members of the committee. When junior members of the committee complained that they were ignored, Patman explained that for years he had been unable to get a seat on Banking and Currency and, when he finally did, he did not even get a chair at the table, but had to stand near the wall.[15]

For all his flaws, it was Wright Patman who first realized that the Watergate break-in was far more than simply a burglary, and he attempted to use the Banking and Currency Committee to investigate the assorted financial and political scandals related to it. Ultimately his efforts failed, however, in large part because he was unable to build a political coalition on the committee to maintain support for the investigation. [16]

Patman's go-it-alone style and his dictatorial approach to running the Banking and Currency Committee ultimately cost him the chairmanship in 1975. In the post-Watergate era, Democrats rebelled against the hard-and-fast rules of seniority that had governed the structure of the House, and challenged the leadership of several committee chairs—removing Patman, fellow Texan Bob Poage from Agriculture, and Edward Hébert of Louisiana from Armed Services.

Loss of the chairmanship of Banking and Currency broke Wright Patman. While publicly he appeared to accept his defeat, in fact his health rapidly declined, and he announced that he would not run for reelection in 1976. His death soon followed.

Patman can be seen as an advocate for rural America—a warrior against modern economic life. He was an economic reformer who fought for credit unions, small banks, small businesses, and low interest rates. He was the arch-enemy of the Federal Reserve, high interest rates, large banks, and chain store businesses. He was a close friend of Lyndon Johnson and Sam Rayburn, politicians who were the ultimate insiders within Congress. As a major committee chair, Patman was an insider whose real audience was not Congress, but small town and rural America. He maintained a consistent liberal-populist philosophy throughout his career and was willing to use extreme public rhetoric to accomplish his goals. In many ways, he succeeded in aiding his small town and rural American world, but he ultimately failed in fighting the evils, as he saw them, in big banking, big business, and the Federal Reserve. And his failure to adapt to changes in America reflected his failure to adapt to changes in Congress. He seemed unable to understand that the days of the autocratic committee chair were gone, and his unresponsiveness to changes within the House led to his loss of control over his committee and ultimately to his death.

9

Martin Dies Jr.

US Representative 1931-1945, 1953-1959

JOHN CONNALLY, a masterful politician and former Texas governor, described Martin Dies as ". . . a reactionary, but one of the best stump speakers I ever heard. . . . "[1] Dies was a colorful figure who began his congressional career as a New Dealer, broke with Roosevelt, became a leader among anti-communists, and ultimately proved such an embarrassment that even the notorious House Committee on Un-American Activities considered Dies such an extremist that it did not want him as a member. Dies' issue was anti-communism, and he promoted it with fanatical zeal and great attention for maximizing publicity for his efforts.

Born in 1900, Dies was the son of a congressman by the same name who served the 2nd Congressional District from 1909-1919. Martin Dies Jr. was elected to the House from that same district in 1930. Due to political opposition, he did not seek reelection in 1944, although he ran in the special senatorial election in 1941 to fill the vacant seat caused by the death of Morris Sheppard. In 1952, he was elected to the US House of Representatives as a congressman-at-large—his district was the entire state of Texas. Dies did not seek reelection in 1958 since the congressman-at-large seats were eliminated through the creation of individual congressional districts. Dies ran again unsuccessfully for the US Senate in the 1957 special election, but was defeated by Ralph Yarbrough.[2]

When Dies was first elected to the House of Representatives in 1930, he was only thirty years old, the youngest congressman serving at that time. He began his service during the Great Depression, and his district had suffered greatly from the economic calamity. Dies was a devoted New Dealer and was quickly advancing in the committee hierarchy in the House. Dies wrote:

Martin Dies Jr., a bombastic public speaker, making a point during a speech. Photograph from the Sam Houston Regional Library and Research Center, Liberty, Texas. Used by permission.

Until 1937, the President and I were the closest of friends. He had given instructions that I was to be admitted to his office by the side door. When he visited Houston I was the only Texas Congressman invited to inspect the ship channel with him. Democratic leaders assigned me to the Committee on Rules, the most powerful committee in the House. This was a coveted assignment, for which others had stronger claims.[3]

Dies thought the New Deal programs should be temporary, however, and that the New Deal was too socialistic. He claimed that two incidents in 1937 led to his break with Franklin Roosevelt and the New Deal: the court-packing plan, Roosevelt's effort to increase the size of the Supreme Court to insure a pro-New Deal majority, and Roosevelt's failure to condemn the sit-down strikes where workers struck factories by occupying the buildings. In 1938, Dies became chair of a Special Committee on Un-American Activities. The goal of the committee was to

Martin Dies Jr., third from left, with his House Un-American Activities Committee investigators. Photograph from the Sam Houston Regional Library and Research Center, Liberty, Texas. Used by permission.

undertake a seven-month investigation of communism, fascism, and nazism. However, he continued as chair of the committee until he left Congress in 1945, and soon the focus of the committee was on communism and the Soviet threat. Within one year of its creation, President Roosevelt was denouncing the Special Committee on Un-American Activities as "flagrantly unfair and un-American."[4] As chair of the committee, Dies proved to be a publicity hound and he soon lost the friendship of Speaker Rayburn as well. Dies wrote of his relationship with Rayburn:

> Up until 1938, we were close friends. He had served in Congress with my father, and when he made his first, and unsuccessful, try for floor leadership, he wired members of the Texas delegation to ask them to come to Washington to help him. I was the only member who made the trip. . . . Rayburn came to dislike me so intensely that when I returned to Washington

in 1953, he would hardly speak to me. . . . I told Rayburn that regardless of political consequences I could not change my convictions. He never ceased to maneuver behind the scenes to destroy the Committee, and to hamper it in every conceivable way.[5]

Writing about the anti-communist hysteria, Don Carleton suggested that Dies "pioneered the techniques that would later be adopted by Joe McCarthy."[6] Under Dies, the committee began compiling lists of suspected subversives, and Dies was largely responsible for creating the image of the federal government as filled with communists and their supporters.[7] Illustrative of this image, Dies wrote:

> Marxists of every hue from the deepest red to palest pink gathered along the Potomac early in the New Deal, and soon began to flourish. Communists, Socialists, Technocrats, Townsendites, Liberals—of all shades from sincere idealists to rabid crack-pots—united in support of Marxist strategy. There developed a concerted campaign of undermining and sabotaging our American political and economic system.[8]

Dies even claimed there was a communist cell at The University of Texas—backing off the charge when J. R. Parten, the chair of the Board of Regents, demanded that Dies provide his information to the regents.[9]

In 1941, with the death of Morris Sheppard, Dies entered the race for the US Senate. W. Lee O'Daniel won that race with his strongest opponent being Lyndon Johnson. Dies saw Johnson as the chosen Roosevelt candidate in the race, because "since his election to the House of Representatives, [Johnson] had assiduously cultivated the New Dealers, and had become one of their favorite errand boys."[10] On the other hand, Dies believed Roosevelt was determined to keep him and O'Daniel out of the Senate.[11] Yet, during the race, Dies tried to present himself as pro-Roosevelt. Although he had alienated the administration because of his allegations of communist infiltration of government agencies, he was a strong supporter of Roosevelt's defense policies. He argued that Roosevelt needed him in the Senate and presented the other major candidates as "yes-man" (Johnson); "green man" (the popular but inexperienced candidate, Gerald Mann); or "showman" (W. Lee O'Daniel).[12]

Dies claimed that he lost because his "mistake was in not recognizing the difference between my district with its fourteen counties, and a state of 254 counties. In a limited area, an honest man can win with an honest campaign. In a large area,

Cartoon about Dies's extreme anti-Communist leanings. It depicts Dies in a nest with Nazis and other far right extremists. Cartoon by Gropper appeared in the Communist Party's Sunday Worker. *Used by permission.*

he has to depend on radio, television, newspapers, public relations men, etc., and this costs enormous sums of money."[13]

Dies claimed that by 1943, the administration was actively working against him in his district. Large government contracts were being awarded in the Gulf part of his district, and with those contracts large numbers of out-of-state workers were being hired who were beholden to the Roosevelt administration. He then claimed the administration harassed him with an IRS investigation. And, claimed Dies, influential people in the district were told that the district would fare better with federal funds if they had a congressman with a more favorable attitude toward the administration. Local labor leaders also turned against him. Then, claimed Dies, he had a health scare—a possible malignancy. That was enough for him. He announced his retirement.[14] The fact of the matter was that Dies knew he could not win reelection.[15] His replacement was J. M. Combs, an administration supporter who was immediately rewarded with a place on the Ways and Means Committee.[16]

Dies considered running for the Senate again in 1948, but decided against it. Interestingly, he claimed he withdrew from the race because he could not persuade Attorney General Price Daniel to increase the campaign spending limit from $10,000 to $60,000, and claimed that the spending limit was absurdly low and was ignored by most candidates. He claimed that political office in Texas was "sold to the highest bidder on public auction. . . ."[17] During this period in his life, he became a popular speaker at organizations throughout Texas, but especially in Dallas and Houston, where he continued to stress the communist threat.[18] He also practiced law and represented the "Marshall Housewives"—a group of women from Marshall, Texas, who unsuccessfully went to court to avoid collecting and paying social security on their domestic servants.[19]

Prior to Supreme Court decisions requiring reappointment of congressional districts, it was common for Texas congressional districts to be malapportioned where some districts had far smaller populations than other districts. With the addition of new congressional seats because of population growth, it was possible to avoid any reapportionment by making those seats state-wide offices where congressional candidates ran state-wide (like a US senator) rather than running in a district. Dies received the financial support of reactionary Texas oilmen such as Hugh Roy Cullen of Houston, who shared Dies's extremist views about the imminent communist threat, and he won a state-wide congressional seat in 1952, in large part because he had financial support from ultra-conservatives and state-wide name recognition.[20] Dies returned to Congress, but he was not allowed to return to the House Un-American Activities Committee. As disreputable as the committee had become, Dies was anathema because the committee members believed his antics had damaged the cause of anti-communism.[21]

In 1957, US Senator Price Daniel was elected governor, requiring him to resign his Senate seat. As a result, there was a special election to fill Daniel's unexpired term. Liberal Democrat Ralph Yarborough was a major contender; Dies was the ultra-conservative candidate in the race. Democratic leaders thought Dies was too

Martin Dies Jr. at the pool table. Photograph from the Sam Houston Regional Library and Research Center, Liberty, Texas. Used by permission.

conservative to defeat Yarborough and tried to persuade him to withdraw from the race. Dies, however, stayed in the race and Yarbrough did defeat him.[22]

In 1958, the congressman-at-large position was changed to a district-based election system. Dies was out of office again since he did not seek election from a congressional district. In retirement, he continued his anti-communist crusade by writing numerous articles and books.[23] He died in 1972.

Dies's political career was on track for him to become a major congressional figure. His appointment as a junior congressman to the Rules Committee and his
friendship with Franklin Roosevelt and Speaker Sam Rayburn marked him as an
up-and-coming congressional leader. Dies, however, was sidetracked by the communist issue which became an obsession to him and alienated him from Roosevelt and
Rayburn and from most of his colleagues. He became a political demagogue preying on the fears of many Americans of an internal communist threat. The communist issue did sustain him politically for years, but, as he became more extreme, he
grew quite distant from the levers of real power in the national government.

10

George Mahon

US Representative 1935-1979

ORN NEAR Haynesville, Louisiana, in 1900, George Mahon was to become one of West Texas's most powerful and effective congressmen. In 1908, his father moved the family to Loraine in Mitchell County, Texas. George attended rural schools, then Simmons College in Abilene, and received a law degree from The University of Texas. In 1925, he began practicing law and was elected Mitchell County Attorney in 1926. In 1927, he was appointed district attorney and then elected to that office in 1928 and again in 1930. With congressional reapportionment resulting from the 1930 census, a new congressional district, the nineteenth, was created. He won election from that district in 1934 and held that seat until his retirement from the US House of Representatives in 1979. At the time of his retirement, he was chairman of the powerful House Appropriations Committee and was the longest serving sitting member of Congress.[1]

As a young congressman, Mahon naturally wanted assignment to a powerful committee, but was unable initially to gain a top committee. Instead, his early committees were the Census, Civil Service, Election, and Insular Affairs. When a vacancy occurred on the Appropriations Committee, Mahon tried for an appointment to it, but Sam Rayburn told him that the position had been promised to another representative and that if Mahon agreed to wait, he would get the next available seat. Mahon accepted Rayburn's decision, and Rayburn kept his promise. Mahon was appointed to the prized Appropriations Committee in 1939. In 1940, he was appointed to the War Department Appropriations Subcommittee (later called the Department of Defense Subcommittee on Appropriations). In 1949, Mahon became chair of this subcommittee, one of the most important because it was responsible for the appropriation of funds for defense. This position would

*George Mahon delivers a backyard speech. Photograph from the Southwest Collection Library,
Texas Tech University, Lubbock, Texas. Used by permission.*

Representative George Mahon (seated), chair of the Appropriations Committee with Representative Wilbur Mills,
chair of the Ways and Means Committee. Mr. Tax and Mr. Spend.
From the collection at the Lyndon B. Johnson Library, Austin, Texas.

become an important base of power for Mahon, given the enormous sums with which the subcommittee dealt. When Mahon succeeded Clarence Cannon of Missouri as chair of the entire Appropriations Committee in 1964, Mahon retained his position on the subcommittee.[2]

Mahon remained a Democrat throughout his political career, although he was a fiscally conservative Democrat who maintained close friendships with Republicans such as Dwight Eisenhower, Richard Nixon, and Gerald Ford. He was known as a hard worker in Congress, a man of great integrity, a congressman with an exceptionally strong knowledge of defense issues, and as a quiet and low-key man with enormous power. He never lost the common touch or his close ties with his roots in the farm land of West Texas.[3]

That quiet conservatism was seen early in his career when Mahon visited with Dillon Myer about the possibility of getting a dam built in his district. Myer told him that he thought it was impossible because a dam had previously been built near-by in a neighboring congressional district and that, given the limits on funding, it was unlikely the federal government would be building new dams in the near future. Then Myer asked the youthful congressman if he thought that such a dam would be a good expenditure of funds even if funds were available. Surprisingly, Mahon responded with complete candor that he did not think it would be a good expenditure of funds and that he was only asking because his constituents wanted the dam. Myer considered Mahon to be a man of such good judgment and decency that over the years he often solicited Mahon's advice—including advice on how to deal with the political tirades of Martin Dies Jr. Mahon, by the way, told Myer just to go ahead with his work and ignore Dies.[4]

Mahon's biographer suggests that Speaker Rayburn initially saw Mahon as a potential leader of the House of Representatives. However, Mahon was too conservative for that role and was not enough of a party loyalist to lead the Democratic Party in the House.[5] It is likely that the conservatism of his West Texas district also prevented him from being a strong national Democrat. Still, as a member of the Appropriations Committee, Mahon was in an ideal position since that was a post involving the expenditure of funds where his inherent conservatism was important.

Mahon was largely an unknown figure to the public. Wanda Evans, his biographer, wrote that if one asked any ten people who George Mahon was, none of the ten would know.[6] Yet, Mahon was responsible for billions of dollars in appropriations. When he was seventy-seven years old, the dean of Congress, chairman of the largest standing committee in the House, confidant of several presidents, and a con-

George Mahon, standing with Admiral Frederick Warder, welcomes the nuclear submarine Seawolf *in 1958. Photograph from the Southwest Collection Library, Texas Tech University, Lubbock, Texas. Used by permission.*

gressman during the administrations of eight different presidents, Mahon remained "a mixture of sophistication and wide-eyed, country boy wonder."[7] Mahon, who enjoyed poetry and song and was a master of defense spending, remained in love with the West Texas soil and modest about his own accomplishments, pointing out Barbara Jordan to a constituent and remarking, "She's the star of the House."[8]

Early in his career, Mahon played a major role in World War II. As a member of the War Department Appropriations Subcommittee, he was involved in the secret appropriations that led to the development of the atomic bomb. It was a time of intensely hard work for Mahon and his fellow subcommittee members. Since 1942 they had been funding the Manhattan Project in secret, based on limited information provided by General George Marshall and Secretary of War Henry Stimson. The political risk, of course, was that this huge sum was being thrown away. But that expenditure produced the atomic bomb and the attacks on Japan that soon led to the war's end.[9]

Once Mahon became chair of the subcommittee, he chafed under the chairmanship of Clarence Cannon of Missouri, a former parliamentarian of the House of Representatives, a very difficult personality, and an autocratic committee chair. In a 1959 interview with political scientist Richard Fenno, Mahon stated that he had no control over hiring his subcommittee staff, that Cannon did it, and that the first Mahon would know about the new staff members "was when I was introduced to them in the subcommittee hearing." Mahon added, "Mr. Cannon works in unusual ways." Nevertheless, Mahon noted that when he first went to Congress and was on the minor committees, "I realized I wasn't doing much to shape the destinies of the nation." Indeed, he was not really doing "any work" and was "disgusted." Being on appropriations, however, provided him "an inner feeling of satisfaction." He thought that it was a committee where the members worked hard.[10]

Mahon was never 100 percent in support of Franklin Roosevelt and the New Deal, although he was sympathetic to Roosevelt's efforts to relieve the suffering of the Great Depression. He was a strong supporter of Roosevelt's war effort, but had it not been for the war on the horizon in 1940 and full-scale hostilities in 1944, he would have opposed a third and fourth term for Roosevelt. In 1963, Mahon was actually riding in the presidential motorcade in Dallas when John Kennedy was assassinated. He had been a friend of Lyndon Johnson for over two decades, but he opposed parts of Johnson's Great Society, especially aid to Appalachia, federal aid to education, and Medicare. He was opposed to relaxed immigration laws and some civil rights legislation. He thought Johnson's appropriations requests too high, though Republicans wanted to cut the appropriations even more than Mahon.[11] He worried about federal spending. Indeed, Congressman Jim Wright claimed that Mahon would have been "horrified" by federal spending in the 1980s and onward.[12]

There were claims that Mahon was so low-key that he lost too many battles with congressmen with competing agendas. Congressman Wilbur Mills of Arkansas was chairman of the Ways and Means Committee, the tax-writing committee of the House, during many of the years when Mahon was chairman of Appropriations. Prior to a breakdown brought on by alcoholism, Mills was an exceptionally able committee chair who was considered by some to be a contender for the speakership and who had presidential ambitions in the early 1970s. When President Nixon helped maneuver his thirty-billion-dollar revenue sharing bill into Mills' committee instead of the more conservative Appropriations Committee, Mahon objected, but it was too late and he could not defeat Mills, who was supported by Nixon and by the city mayors who stood to gain from revenue sharing.[13] Still, Mahon won significant victories as well, such as his fight with Congressman Otto Passman of Louisiana who was opposed to foreign aid. Mahon believed that President Johnson should have been supported on that issue and was able to defeat Passman both in committee and on the floor of the House.[14] Yet there was a belief among some that Mahon was not aggressive enough. Congressman Jamie Whitten of Mississippi described Mahon in this way:

> He lets you get by with more than most, but if he gets his dander up and wants to fight, he'll win because he has made fewer people angry than you have. Mahon saves himself for the main event and doesn't squall over the little things. He's slow to act and slow to come to the point, but it's because he's a very fair-minded person.[15]

There was also some criticism in his district that Mahon did not bring a lot of federal money back to the district. Mahon was aware of the criticism and noted that the "... area is not conducive to a lot of grants. There are no rivers to dam, floods to control or harbors to develop."[16] Mahon did, in fact, bring to his district such major projects as Webb Air Force Base in Big Spring and Reese Air Force Base in Lubbock. Interstate 27 from Lubbock to Amarillo was still another major project that was largely accomplished through Mahon's efforts.[17]

When the easy-going Mahon was provoked, his reaction could be strong. In 1975, Secretary of Defense James Schlesinger publicly criticized the Appropriations

Committee and Mahon for cuts in the defense budget. Claimed Schlesinger, the cuts ". . . will have harmful effects upon the defense posture of the United States."[18] Mahon responded with full force and the cuts in the defense budget remained.[19] Not long after that conflict between Mahon and Schlesinger, Schlesinger was out of his job as Defense Secretary. It was not due to vindictiveness on Mahon's part, however. Shortly before Schlesinger's firing, Mahon had golfed with President Ford but made no mention of the conflict with Schlesinger. Ford was nevertheless troubled by Schlesinger's personality and believed that Schlesinger could not deal with Congress.[20] The conflict with Mahon, no doubt, added fuel to Ford's misgivings.

Mahon's low-key personality was enormously beneficial to him in the 1975 Democratic Caucus. There was a revolt against the seniority system that for decades had governed the way members of Congress rose to committee chairmanships. Three chairs were deposed in the caucus—Wright Patman of Texas, who was chair of Banking and Currency; Bob Poage of Texas, who was chair of Agriculture; and F. Edward Hébert of Louisiana, who was the chair of Armed Services. All three of those chairmen were elderly, Southern, and autocratic in behavior. Mahon was also elderly and Southern, but not autocratic, and that probably saved his chairmanship. Still, it was clear that the seniority system was no longer the absolute rule for determining committee leadership. Mahon and the other chairs had to feel threatened by this action of the caucus. Then, in 1976, a Republican opponent, Jim Reese, challenged Mahon, and Mahon only received 54.6 percent of the vote.[21] For many congressmen, of course, such a margin of victory would be huge, but for Mahon it signaled that the Republican Party was growing dramatically in his district, and he was now facing a serious threat to his reelections back home as well as to his security as a committee chair in Washington. He had not faced any opposition to reelection in 1936-1944, 1952-1958, or 1966-1974.[22] Mahon was seventy-eight years old in 1978, and he chose not to seek reelection. He was to live another seven years and died in 1985.

George Mahon was one of the last of the old-time committee chairs from Texas. His life was the House of Representatives—Congressman Charles Wilson, had immense respect for Mahon and thought all of Mahon's friends were members of Congress.[23] Mahon served forty-four years in Congress, and in many of those years he had no opposition (or insignificant opposition) back home. He gained a seat on a major congressional committee and worked diligently on the committee. The years went by and seniority first made him a subcommittee chair and then a committee chair. Unlike many of the old committee chairs, he was not an autocrat, but he wielded enormous power which brought considerable benefits to his Texas district.

Members of Congress are sometimes classified into two groups—"showhorses" and "workhorses." People like Martin Dies or W. Lee O'Daniel were among the Texas "showhorses." They were interested in publicity and they were very visible political actors. Mahon, on the other hand, was a classic "workhorse." He was not widely known outside Washington, but for decades he worked and had major impact on the public policy of the nation.

George
Mahon

Senator Lyndon Baines Johnson in 1955. Photograph by Thomas J. O'Halloran.
Photograph from the collection of the Library of Congress.

II

Lyndon Baines Johnson

US Representative 1937-1949;
US Senator 1949-1961 (Majority Leader 1953-1961);
President US Senate 1961-1963
US President 1963-1969

IN MANY WAYS, Lyndon Johnson is the largest figure in Texas political history. Maybe it was the legacy of political involvement he inherited from his father, or his cutting his political teeth under the tutelage of Richard Kleberg of the famous King Ranch family. Maybe it was that he caught the eye of President Franklin Roosevelt as a talented young "New Dealer" before becoming a close protégé of his surrogate father, Speaker Sam Rayburn. Or perhaps it was his being a prototypical Texan in his pathway to power as a young and dynamic Senate majority leader with his legendary arm-twisting—what became known as the famous "Johnson Treatment." Or his love of the LBJ ranch along the Pedernales River, his deep Texas accent, or his larger-than-life persona. But one thing is clear: there was only one LBJ.

Johnson is perhaps best known for his succession to the presidency and for the more than five tumultuous years in office, but the focus of this essay is on his career before the presidency, his representation of Texas in the House of Representatives and in the Senate. His career in Congress, even without the presidency, was full of great accomplishments. Of all the presidents, Johnson stands out as having had the greatest congressional career.

He began life on August 27, 1908, in Stonewall, Texas. His parents, Sam Ealy and Rebekah Baines Johnson, had a family of five children. Johnson was the older of the two boys. After graduating from high school in Johnson City and a brief adventure in California, Johnson attended Southwest Texas State Teachers' College, receiving his degree in 1930. He taught for one year in a poor, largely Hispanic school in Cotulla, Texas, where "the wretched condition of his students struck a sympathetic chord in Lyndon."[1]

Johnson's father had served five terms in the Texas legislature, where he had been an anti-Joe Bailey member and had been close friends with Sam Rayburn. Following his father's career, Johnson began working in politics, and was recommended for the staff of Richard Kleberg. He went to Washington in late 1931, all of his possessions in a cardboard suitcase. There he soon found a home for his ambition—he very quickly became the leader of an organization of aides called "Little Congress."[2] Johnson remained in Kleberg's office, making connections with powerful officials, until he had a falling out with Kleberg and sought other opportunities.[3] While working for Kleberg, on November 17, 1934, Johnson married Claudia Alta "Lady Bird" Taylor after a whirlwind romance. The couple would form a strong personal and political alliance and have two daughters—Linda and Luci.

With the creation of the New Deal Programs, Johnson took the opportunity, apparently on the recommendation of Sam Rayburn, to become Texas director of the National Youth Administration in 1935. There, he turned his considerable energy to running a strong program, and made a name for himself by his inclusive approach to African American youth, earning the respect of Mary McLeod Bethune, director of the Office of Negro Affairs of the NYA.[4]

Johnson left the NYA to run for Congress when James Buchanan, the incumbent in his district, died in 1937. Although the election was contested, he won, and so began his trajectory toward national prominence. Johnson was a committed New Dealer, working with Vice President John Nance Garner and House Majority Leader Sam Rayburn on projects such as rural electrification. He began developing a relationship with Texas business leaders as well, and they would provide LBJ (as his nickname had become) with future financial backing. His six terms in the House gained him a reputation as an energetic politician with a bright political future.

Johnson soon chafed at the seniority structure in the House of Representatives. In his only unsuccessful campaign, he ran for the open US Senate seat when Morris Sheppard died, but lost the Democratic primary to Governor W. Lee O'Daniel in 1941. Still, the election gave LBJ the statewide exposure that he would use to his advantage seven years later. Meanwhile, the winds of World War II led to Johnson's next adventure. With the outbreak of war, and Johnson still in the House, he was commissioned in the Naval Reserves. He was sent to the Southwest Pacific and there received a Silver Star for his service when his airplane came under fire. Critics charged that the award was politically motivated.[5] Franklin Roosevelt called all members of Congress back to Washington soon thereafter, and LBJ went back to his congressional duties. Johnson applied his military experiences to his service on the House Armed Services Committee.

By 1948, LBJ was chomping at the bit for a larger stage than his House seat, and he declared for the US Senate seat open in that year. The campaign for the Senate in 1948 is perhaps the most storied campaign in US history. In that year, Johnson ran against former governor Coke Stevenson. The runoff primary between the two was exceedingly close, and Johnson won by a mere eighty-seven votes, earning the nickname "Landslide Lyndon." The circumstances of votes for Johnson that came late from Jim Wells County under the influence of the political boss George Parr led to charges and countercharges about corruption during the campaign. If Johnson had not "stolen" the vote, Stevenson would have won by just as artificial a majority.[6] But LBJ's victory held, and he went to the Senate.

Of all political bodies, Johnson's personality and style probably fit best in the Senate. He quickly felt at home, and moved up the ranks of influential senators, in part by cultivating older members, the ones he called the "whales" of the Senate as opposed to the "minnows." Perhaps the biggest Senate "whale" was Richard Russell of Georgia. By 1951, with Russell's sponsorship, Johnson became the Democratic whip.[7] After the election of 1952, he became the party floor leader, and when the Democrats took control of the Senate following the 1954 elections, LBJ, still in his first term and at the tender age of forty-six (in the tradition— and seniority–oriented Senate) became majority leader. How had this rise to power occurred so quickly? Russell thought "Johnson displayed a remarkable ability to twist arms, cajole, and compromise the positions of both sides so that they could work reasonably well together on most major issues."[8]

As a senator, Johnson was noted for three major accomplishments—helping manage the Joe McCarthy problem, helping pass the Civil Rights Act of 1957, and helping secure the United States' place in the competition for dominance in space. An early tricky problem for Johnson was how to deal with Joe McCarthy. McCarthy's extreme communist baiting tactics had won him a strong following nationwide, and though he had clearly spun out of control on the issue, no politician wanted to be seen as weak on communism. After the Army-McCarthy hearings in 1954 had exposed McCarthy's excesses, the problem was how to punish him without causing undue conflict within the Senate.[9] Johnson implored the Democrats not to invoke partisanship in their statements about Republican McCarthy, and, as a result, McCarthy was censured on December 2, 1954, in a "conscience" vote rather than a party line vote. The ability to accomplish this without partisan wrangling served Johnson well as he moved forward with his other political agendas.[10]

In 1957, the issue of civil rights, the most divisive issue within the Democratic Party and indeed, for the nation, came to a head. Of course, the Democrats were split between Southern segregationists and Northern members who favored civil rights. President Dwight Eisenhower sent a civil rights bill to Congress in 1956, and Speaker Sam Rayburn ushered it through the House, his major challenge being getting the bill out of the Rules Committee. In the Senate, Johnson sent the bill to the judiciary committee where it languished. Johnson knew that action was needed, but in order to enjoy success, he would have to include a provision that would make it less objectionable to Southerners. He included a "jury trial" amendment in the bill, assuring that no one could be cited for contempt of court for denying the right to vote without a jury of his peers convicting him. This placated some members, even though it probably had little real impact. This added to the bill, LBJ went to work as only he could. In the words of his advisor George Reedy, Johnson's energy and persuasiveness was decisive. "Virtually single-handed, he kept a large body of very strong-minded and willful men concentrating on a purpose which most of them thought could not be achieved."[11] With the passage of the 1957 Civil Rights Act, there were conflicting interpretations. On the one hand, Johnson had successfully watered down the bill so that it had little real impact. But LBJ understood that it was the passage itself that was important, for it would set into motion an unstoppable movement to ultimately achieve civil rights.[12]

The launching of Sputnik in the fall of 1957 set off panic among the American public. Johnson was a leader in coordinating the congressional response. He began a long commitment to the American space program and nurtured the passage of the National Aeronautics and Space Act of 1958.[13] Of course, this also gave him the opportunity to make certain that the National Aeronautics and Space Administration would locate its headquarters in Houston, Texas, a bit of patronage that would help Johnson with his constituents back home.

Johnson's run as Senate majority leader placed him on a trajectory for presidential aspirations. In 1955, a heart attack set him back, and heart problems would ultimately cause his death on January 22, 1973. By 1960, he joined a contest for the

Lyndon Johnson being sworn in as president by Judge Sarah Hughes on Air Force I upon the death of President John Kennedy.
Lady Bird Johnson is at his right, Jackie Kennedy is at his left, and Jack Brooks is behind Mrs. Kennedy.
From the collection at the Lyndon B. Johnson Library, Austin, Texas.

Democratic nomination for president, a campaign he ultimately lost to his junior colleague in the Senate, John F. Kennedy. But Kennedy knew he needed to balance his ticket with a Southerner and asked Johnson to run as his vice-presidential running mate, a position that LBJ reluctantly accepted. Their narrow victory in the

86

1960 election gave Johnson a new Senate title: President of the Senate. That position, of course, was largely symbolic, though Johnson tried to retain some of his Texas patronage influence, setting off a struggle with his Texas Senate colleague Ralph Yarborough. In general, Johnson found the vice presidency stifling, but he would soon be thrust into a leading role with the assassination of Kennedy on November 22, 1963, in Dallas.

Johnson's presidency was eventful, with seminal legislative and foreign policy drama. In 1964, invoking the memory of Kennedy as a persuasive technique, Johnson ushered in the historic 1964 Civil Rights Act. In November 1964, he won a landslide victory for a full term over Senator Barry Goldwater of Arizona. Johnson's legislative accomplishments in 1965 and 1966 came in the form of his "Great Society" programs. Those programs created a war on poverty, urban renewal, and an increased federal role in education, among other things. Though the programs met with mixed success, they clearly expanded the role of the federal government far beyond what it had been before. But Johnson's presidency lost its momentum and confronted its greatest difficulty in the war in Vietnam, a conflict that cost Johnson his popularity and led him not to seek reelection in 1968.

Johnson has been the subject of a huge body of academic literature. He was an enormously compelling personality with a larger-than-life reputation. He served during momentous times in the United States, and was in the thick of the major decisions that shaped them, throughout his long political career. His greatest accomplishments were in the legislative realm—as a member of both chambers, as a powerful majority leader and vice president, and as the "chief legislator" during his years in the White House.

Opposite: *Senator Ralph Yarborough and Lyndon Johnson, arch-rivals in Texas politics, shaking hands. From the collection at the Lyndon B. Johnson Library, Austin, Texas.*

Bob Poage in a jovial mood during a panel discussion.
From the Poage Library, Baylor University, Waco, Texas.

12

Bob Poage

US Representative 1937-1978

JUST AT THE END of the nineteenth century, on December 28, 1899, William Robert "Bob" Poage was born in the house his father built in Waco, Texas. Through his forty-two year tenure representing Texas' 11th US House District, fourteen of them as chair of the Agriculture Committee, Poage would become a leading light in farm and ranch policy. In fact, Poage's lengthy congressional service to agriculture and to rural Americans earned him the nickname "Mr. Agriculture." Poage campaigned as the farmer's friend and remained "a loyal son of Central Texas," who, to use his words, "always wanted to be in Congress."[1]

Descended from Scottish-Irish immigrants, Poage's family came from Virginia to Texas in 1862. Married in 1898, Poage's parents, Bill Poage and Helen Conger Poage, were farmers and members of the Universalist Church and Democratic Party. After Poage turned two, he and his family moved to Throckmorton County, where he spent much of his early youth.[2]

The Poage family was well above the average economic level of Throckmorton County as they owned a one-fourth interest of the Leven Ranch, where the family lived until 1912. Poage wrote that his "rural boyhood" was the "greatest stroke of good fortune" he ever experienced.

Poage's parents influenced him profoundly. While his father implanted conservative values in his son, disliking "dead beats" and never asking someone to do work that he would not do himself, his mother taught him the value of saving. This emphasis on saving became a lifelong habit; during the years he presided as chairman of the Agriculture Committee, Poage returned a total of $363,494.26 designated for use by his committee.[3] Poage also inherited an interest in politics from his father, who served on the Waco city council and as mayor pro tempore before spending the last four years of his life in the Texas legislature.

In July of 1913, Poage's father moved the family to Waco, and there Bob Poage graduated from high school. Poage served in the Navy during the First World War, then attended three universities before graduating from Baylor. After working a couple of years, he attended law school at Baylor, earning his law degree in 1924.[4]

In 1923, Poage, still a student at Baylor, ran as a Democrat for a position in the Texas House of Representatives. Commenting on the race, Poage wrote, "There were no issues and frankly I don't know why people voted for me except that some remembered my father who had held the place a few years earlier." Poage won easily.

Poage served in the Texas House for four years, then ran for the state Senate and lost that bid to his friend, Edgar Witt. Having been admitted to the Texas bar in 1924, Poage practiced law until Witt became lieutenant governor in 1931, and this time, Poage's bid was successful.[5] In the Texas Senate, Poage served on the Agriculture Committee and wrote the bill that became Texas' motor vehicle licensing law.[6]

In 1934, Poage ran unsuccessfully in the Democratic primary for the United States House against the incumbent, Congressman Oliver Cross. Poage felt that Cross was ungracious in accepting his call of congratulations and vowed to repeat the contest two years later. As a loyal Democrat, though, he voted for Cross in the general election.[7] Cross retired in 1936, and Poage ran successfully in that year.

Poage represented an agricultural district and owned farmland all his life. He wrote Representative Sam Rayburn, then the most influential member of the Texas delegation, to ask for a seat on either the Agriculture or Interstate and Foreign Commerce committee. Initially, Poage received less influential assignments on the War Claims Committee, the Naturalization Committee, the Census Committee, the District of Columbia Committee, and the Flood Control Committee, none of which satisfied him. In his third term, Rayburn, now Speaker, placed Poage on the Agriculture Committee, and this became the focal point of Poage's career.[8] By 1953, Poage had built enough seniority to become vice chair, and in 1967, after Chairman Harold D. Cooley failed to win reelection, Poage became chair. He now oversaw a seven-billion-dollar agriculture budget.

Poage's leadership left a lasting mark on the United States—especially rural America. Poage was a congressman's congressman, serious of purpose and prolific in his advocacy of the interests of rural America. Among his accomplishments: the Rural Telephone Act of 1949, bringing telephone service to much of rural

Early Bob Poage campaign poster. From the Poage Library, Baylor University, Waco, Texas.

America; helping support rural electrification to extend service to ranches and farms; the Watershed Protection and Flood Prevention Act, a bill to provide for upstream flood prevention; the Humane Methods of Slaughter Act, insuring the humane slaughter of livestock; a soil conservation bill to protect farm and ranch operators against loss of acreage allotments; and the Poage-Aiken Act. Poage regarded this act, which provided government loans and grants for wastewater disposal systems and helped supply clean water to rural America, as his greatest contribution. He considered the Poage-Aiken Act—along with the rural electrification and the Rural Telephone Act—as three "revolutionary improvements" to rural life.[9]

Later in his career, Poage continued to sponsor influential legislation. In the early 1970s, Poage sponsored the School Milk Act (1970); the Farm Credit Act (1971); the Rural Telephone Bank Act (1971); the Sugar Act (1971); the Emergency Loan Act (1974); and the Commodity Exchange Authority Act (1974). These pieces of legislation accomplished everything from the distribution of milk to students to the creation of an independent regulatory commission for futures trading.

Poage's 11th District contained two good-sized cities, Waco and Temple, and traditionally voted for the Democratic ticket during those one-party Texas days, though in 1972 the district overwhelmingly supported Richard Nixon over the anti-Vietnam War candidate George McGovern. The district was conservative, and resonated well with Poage's political philosophy. As a result, he faced very little Democratic opposition of any kind during his career, and even less from Republicans. In 1976, after running an intense campaign, and even receiving a presidential endorsement from Gerald Ford, Jack Burgess, the most serious Republican contender Poage would ever face during his career, mustered only 43 percent of the vote. To emphasize how entrenched Poage's seat in the House was, Poage, in his autobiography, wrote: "My recollection is that since I was elected in 1936, I never lost but one county. That was Mills County when it was first brought into the Eleventh District."[10]

Despite having the luxury of a secure congressional seat, Poage never forgot who elected him. Since Poage's greatest disappointment was having no children, Poage and his wife treated their district almost as if it were family.[11] Lyndon Johnson credited Poage with inventing the eighteen-hour workday in Washington, and, indeed, he worked unrelentingly for his district.

Poage's square-jawed face often bore a pleasant smile and the many people who knew Poage describe him as gentle and kind. In addition, he was typically a gregarious and friendly person. In his campaign for the Texas Senate, Poage learned that his opponent, Edgar Witt, could not drive an automobile. Poage then offered to take his opponent with him in his car, and they campaigned together—against each other. When asked why Poage would chauffeur his opponent, Poage commented, "We were friends." His friendliness went hand in hand with his reputation for personal integrity and honesty. Poage's nephew, Scott T. Poage, noted that after his uncle's last campaign in 1978, he returned campaign contributions even though, under the laws of that time, he could have legally kept the money. [12]

Still another personal characteristic that helped Poage during his political career was his encyclopedic memory and thoroughness in preparation. Poage's former staff worker and congressional successor, Representative Marvin Leath, described Poage as having "an enormous knowledge of history and geography. He could take a Texas map and draw every railroad and every river."[13] Poage's knowledge of both national and international agriculture became legendary, and he was "a seldom-disputed authority in debates on farm problems." This substantive expertise, along with a comprehensive knowledge of the committee process, was the source of his powerful leadership. Former Speaker of the House Jim Wright emphasizes this point:

> After the beginning of the Eighty-Seventh Congress a new member asked my opinion on a particular agricultural matter. I suggested, "If you're interested in this thing, why don't you talk with Bob Poage? He knows more about it than any of the rest of us." He shook his head. "Thanks . . . I really don't want to know *that* much about it."[14]

Poage set high standards for himself and expected the same level of work from others. He could, however, be ill-tempered and undiplomatic. One farm lobbyist remembered that during debates and negotiations, Poage would sometimes "shoot off at the mouth," causing him to "lose more votes by one speech than anyone else can collect in a week's work." And his criticism of others could be harsh, as when he once made Missouri representative Leonor K. Sullivan cry during a hearing.[15]

Poage remained loyal to his Democratic Party, even as it became increasingly more liberal than he was. When conservative Democrats such as Allan Shivers endorsed Dwight Eisenhower in 1952 and 1956, Poage supported Democrat Adlai Stevenson.

Yet, at the same time, Poage remained a conservative on many issues. He opposed a minimum wage in 1959, calling it "illegal, impractical, and immoral."[16] He opposed the Equal Rights Amendment, one of only six Democrats to take that stand. He voted against the Twenty-Sixth Amendment giving eighteen-year-olds the right to vote, and co-sponsored an amendment to the Constitution that would guarantee the right to pray in a public building. And he consistently was rated as a conservative by the liberal Americans for Democratic Action.

He brought his conservatism to the Agriculture Committee as well, opposing food stamp legislation in his committee. Poage reasoned that the legislation would support people who did not want to work: "Jobs were available in a community but were rejected by able-bodied men . . . families on food relief often had TV sets and nice autos."

In 1975, the Democratic Caucus, by a meager three-vote majority out of 285 votes cast, voted to remove Poage as committee chair. This post-Watergate Congress wanted to impose its will to make the House more democratic and its leadership younger, and rejected the time-honored tradition of seniority and the traditional strong-armed chairs. As a show of support, Agriculture Committee members unanimously voted to restore Poage to his former position of vice chairman. Poage reacted with gentle grace, declaring his support for Tom Foley, his successor as chair and reflecting that "I think a majority of this caucus should be represented as it sees best" while noting ruefully that he "cherished an ambition to complete [his] service as Chairman of the Agriculture Committee."[17] His good grace in accepting the decision of the caucus gained him respect from many who had opposed him, and he was able to push through influential legislation such as the Food and Agriculture Act of 1977.

Poage relished opportunities to travel around the world. He was so well known for this that when Lyndon Johnson heard Poage was visiting somewhere he had never been, Johnson commented, "Be sure Bob has the American flag with him, so he can plant it when he gets there. Because if Poage hasn't been there before, it's undiscovered territory."

In 1977, Poage, having devoted more than a half-century of his life to Central Texas, announced that he would not run for reelection and would retire from Congress. He dedicated the remainder of his life to writing his autobiography, *My First 85 Years,* and raising money for the W. R. Poage Legislative Library. On December 10, 1986, Poage was seriously injured in an auto accident, and he died after a failed coronary bypass surgery on January 3, 1987. Poage left $100,000 to establish a wildflower reserve, a gift befitting a life committed to the land and agricultural beauty.

13

W. Lee O'Daniel

US Senator 1941-1949

W. Lee O'Daniel was one of the great characters in Texas politics. This radio broadcaster, entertainer, and flour salesman served as governor and senator from Texas. He was first elected governor in 1938 and reelected in 1940. O'Daniel then resigned from the governor's office in 1941 when he was elected to fill a vacancy caused by the death of Senator Morris Sheppard. He was reelected in 1942 and served until 1949, but wasn't a candidate for reelection in 1948. O'Daniel's appearance on the political scene marked the beginning of the successful use of mass media in political campaigning, and his use of radio appealed to a heavily rural and small town constituency that was suffering through the Great Depression. As a policy-maker, he was largely a failure. Indeed, he had virtually no credibility within the US Senate. For example, O'Daniel attacked as communistic such legislation as rural electrification, housing for veterans, the Tennessee Valley Authority, and the Wagner Labor Relations Act. He had criticized members of Congress who "run around the world trying to attend to everybody else's business while the Communists and Communistic spies are infesting this Government."[1] O'Daniel was elected as a Democrat, but he had no real party ties and considered the leaders of both parties to be "like two peas in a pod."[2]

Born in 1890 in Malta, Ohio, he lived in Kansas and moved to Fort Worth in 1925. O'Daniel held a variety of positions, once operating a restaurant, then becoming a stenographer for a milling company, then a partner in the milling company, which went bankrupt. With his move to Fort Worth, he worked for J. Perry

95

W. Lee O'Daniel on the radio—a master at his art.
Photo in collection of the Dolph Briscoe Center for American History, Austin, Texas. Used by permission.

W. Lee O'Daniel and the Hillbilly Boys in 1936—prior to the O'Daniel political career.
Photograph from the Texas State Library and Archives Commission. Used by permission.

Burrus of the Burrus Mill and Elevator Company, which made Light Crust Flour. Showing incredible talent as a salesman, O'Daniel became president and general manager of the mill.[3]

In 1931, Light Crust Flour began sponsoring a radio show featuring music from a band called the Light Crust Doughboys. It quickly became a popular program, and when O'Daniel substituted for the regular announcer, it became clear he had incredible radio appeal. Though he did not play an instrument, he wrote many of the songs and poetry performed by the band. The show began on a small local station, quickly moved to a much larger station, and then to a network that broadcast the show from Dallas, San Antonio, and Houston. In 1935, O'Daniel started his own company selling Hillbilly Flour with a new band, the Hillbilly Boys.[4]

The bands sang about flour, about Texas, about cowboys, about current events, and, especially popular, the bands sang about motherhood. O'Daniel started delivering short speeches urging country people to stick together, go to church, and avoid sin. By 1935, he became "Pappy" O'Daniel, and the show would open with a woman's request to him to "Please pass the biscuits, Pappy." With less music and more O'Daniel, the show became even more popular, and by 1938 it had more listeners than any daily show in the history of Texas radio. It was pure cornpone, and Texans—still in a very rural state—loved it.[5]

O'Daniel was a natural actor. He could turn on laughter and tears in an instant. His voice was so friendly and so sincere that he convinced viewers that he was a poor country boy like them—although he was actually a successful businessman—and that he shared their fundamentalist Protestant faith—even though he rarely attended church.[6]

His hold on his listeners was remarkable. When he urged them to adopt orphans, every orphan's home in Texas was overwhelmed with demand.[7] Then, he asked his listeners if he should run for governor. He had been asked, he said, by a blind man, and he sought the advice of his listeners. He claimed that he received 54,449 letters. Of those, 54,446 urged him to run and the other three told him that he was too good for the office.[8] He was not even eligible to vote in the election because he had not paid his poll tax. But this politically inexperienced candidate attracted huge crowds wherever he went.

Campaigning from a red circus wagon with the musical accompaniment of the Hillbilly Boys, his platform was the Ten Commandments and the Golden Rule.[9] His campaign slogan was "Less Johnson Grass and Politicians, More Smokestacks and Businessmen." He won the 1938 governor's race without a runoff with 30,000 more votes than the other eleven candidates combined.[10]

W. Lee O'Daniel campaigning for the US Senate. Photograph from the Texas State Library and Archives Commission. Used by permission.

As governor, he supported a sales tax by another name—though he had opposed the sales tax in the campaign—and low taxes on oil, natural gas, and sulphur. He also wanted to make these low rates part of the Texas Constitution. He had backed an old-age pension as a candidate, claiming that the Fourth Commandment—Honor thy father and thy mother—meant "old-age pensions as plain as day," but he refused to commit to funding the pension, thus killing the pension proposal.[11]

He offered little real leadership to the Depression-ridden state government. Nor did he have a good relationship with the Texas legislature. He vetoed bills that he did not understand, and the legislature overturned twelve of his fifty-seven vetoes of legislation in his first term in office.[12] However, he continued his contact with the voters of Texas through regular broadcasts from the governor's mansion. In one broadcast, with Texans suffering from the Depression, he said, "Don't let anybody worry about Texas. . . . The rest of the world may be in a mess, but Texas is OK."[13] When he ran for reelection, he attacked communists and nazis who, he claimed, had infiltrated the state, as well as communist labor union racketeers in the state's labor unions. He campaigned in a white bus with a dome of the capitol on the roof and he got a greater percentage of the vote for governor in 1940 than he did in 1938.[14]

Shortly after beginning his second term, US Senator Morris Sheppard died. O'Daniel called a special election and in the interim appointed eighty-seven-year-old Andrew Jackson Houston as interim senator. Houston was in his dotage, the son of General Sam Houston, and he would pose no threat to O'Daniel in the special election. Indeed, Andrew Jackson Houston died in office after attending one committee meeting.[15]

Along with twenty-six other candidates, O'Daniel ran for the Senate in the 1941 special election. Several of his opponents were major political forces such as Lyndon Baines Johnson, Martin Dies, and Texas Attorney General Gerald Mann. Again, O'Daniel brought out the Hillbilly Boys and escalated his rhetoric against his opponents. His opponents, according to O'Daniel, were "the howlings of two or three wise-cracking political proselytizers polluting the place performing a personality piracy plot for the purpose of plucking personal publicity by the papers printing their prattle."[16]

Lyndon Johnson, campaigning on a pro-Roosevelt platform, was O'Daniel's greatest threat, and in the immediate aftermath of the election, it appeared that Johnson had won. But the remaining votes and "corrected" votes sent in by some counties gave O'Daniel the election by 1,311 votes. It was claimed by a Johnson aide that O'Daniel wound up stealing more votes than Johnson did. It does appear that considerable vote fraud occurred where O'Daniel's enemies wanted him out of the governor's chair and believed he was less a threat to them in the Senate. O'Daniel had promised old age pensions; the stickler had always been the funding of the pensions. If this mainstay promise of O'Daniel's were ever to materialize, it would have to be funded, most likely by natural resources taxes. That possibility, coupled with O'Daniel's unpredictability, encouraged the oil, gas, and sulphur lobbyists to assist him in getting to Washington. Additionally, if O'Daniel had one principle, it was

Governor W. Lee O'Daniel and his appointee to the late Senator Morris Sheppard's seat, Andrew Jackson Houston, the surviving son of Texas founder Sam Houston. Houston's advanced age and death not long after his appointment guaranteed that O'Daniel would not face an incumbent senator when he ran for the position.
Photograph from the Texas State Library and Archives Commission. Used by permission.

that he was opposed to alcohol. O'Daniel's prohibitionist views encouraged liquor interests in the state to help move him into the Senate, where he would be less of a threat to them. And, even more importantly for Texas liquor interests, a strong opponent of Prohibition, Lieutenant Governor Coke Stevenson, would replace O'Daniel as governor.[17]

O'Daniel's victory, however, was in a special election. He would have to run again in 1942, and Lyndon Johnson was ready to mount another challenge against him. A race against O'Daniel in 1942 would force Johnson to give up his House

Clifford Berryman cartoon in which Senator Tom Connally warns newly elected Senator W. Lee O'Daniel
against trying to organize a hillbilly band in the US Senate.
Clifford Berryman cartoon in the collection of the National Archives. Used by permission.
This is the original cartoon that Berryman sent to Connally.
Note the dedication in lower right corner.

W. Lee O'Daniel's song, "Beautiful Texas." Photograph from the Texas State Library and Archives Commission. Used by permission.

seat and as an incumbent senator, O'Daniel would be harder to beat than in 1941. Additionally, the attack on Pearl Harbor changed Johnson's plans. Johnson had pledged to serve in the military, and he kept that pledge. O'Daniel was safe from Johnson, but he still faced a major challenge from New Dealer and former governor James Allred.[18]

His career as a senator was disastrous, and he chose not to run for reelection in 1948. A 1947 Beldon Poll found that in a race between Johnson and O'Daniel, 64 percent would vote for Johnson. O'Daniel's isolationism and his attacks on unions and federal officials, claiming they were setting up a communist dictatorship, had alienated many of his fellow senators. In addition, his highly profitable business dealings had ruined his reputation as a common man.[19] It was claimed that no proposal O'Daniel made in the Senate got more than two or three votes. He voted Republican more than 80 percent of the time and backed the Texas Regulars (a conservative splinter group from the Democratic Party) in the vain hope that he could deny Franklin Roosevelt another term. One public opinion poll gave O'Daniel only a 7 percent approval rating.[20] O'Daniel was ridiculed in private and pelted with eggs and rotten tomatoes in public, though he still had appeal among the poor, ignorant, and devout in Texas.[21] However, O'Daniel claimed that the real reason that he did not run again is that he believed he could no longer save America from communists.[22]

After leaving the Senate, he became a rancher, invested in Dallas real estate, and established the W. Lee O'Daniel Life Insurance Company. He sought the governorship again in 1956 and in 1958, but by then Texas had grown beyond W. Lee O'Daniel. He did not make the runoff in the Democratic primary. His issue in these campaigns was *Brown v. Board of Education*, the Supreme Court decision that banned segregation in public education. To O'Daniel, the Supreme Court was communist inspired and the decision would lead to blood running in the streets. O'Daniel died in 1969.[23]

Ineffective as an elected official, O'Daniel was a masterful campaigner. He, more than any other Texas politician, turned politics into entertainment through his campaigns and his use of radio. His legacy lives on in the popular 2000 feature movie *O Brother, Where Art Thou?* That movie, a parody of *The Odyssey* set in the southern United States in the 1930s, featured a fictitious political figure named Pappy O'Daniel modeled on the original. It may be truly said that the fictitious character was not as entertaining as the real "made for movies" character who once represented Texas in the US Senate.

14

Lloyd Bentsen

US Representative 1947-1955;
US Senator 1971-1993

LOYD MILLARD BENTSEN JR. led a life marked by numerous personal achievements. He chaired important senate committees and, by the end of his tenure, was generally recognized as the most knowledgeable man in either house in trade and tax policies. He ran as a vice presidential candidate of his party in 1988. After his service in the Senate, President Bill Clinton appointed him Treasury Secretary, a position in which Bentsen showed leadership during the early 1990s. Following his retirement from public service in 1994, Bentsen returned to private life, but embraced his role as an elder statesman. Former Texas Governor Ann Richards described Bentsen as "an outstanding Treasury secretary, but as far as Texans are concerned, he's always going to be the Gentleman from Texas, a tremendously effective and efficient senator whose ability to get the job done was literally legendary."[1]

Bentsen's rise to national prominence began in an unlikely location, the tiny town of Mission, Texas. Born February 11, 1921, Bentsen grew up in an impoverished region—the semiarid brush and mesquite country of the Rio Grande Valley. His parents, Lloyd and Edna Ruth "Dolly" Bentsen, emphasized the importance of family and place. Lloyd Sr., the son of Danish immigrants, had the strong work ethic to make his way as a citrus farmer in the harsh climate of the valley. Shortly after World War I, Lloyd Sr. and his brother, Elmer, opened a land-clearing operation that grew into a successful farming and ranching enterprise sprawling across South Texas. A family fortune was slowly amassed as the Bentsens gained control-

Senator Lloyd Bentsen makes a point during a speech. Photo from Jimmy Carter Library, Atlanta, Georgia. Used by permission.

ling interest in eight South Texas banks.[2] Bentsen family business dealings at this time would later become a source of controversy for Lloyd Jr. after several lawsuits alleged that Bentsen's father and uncle had sold overvalued property to unsuspecting buyers as part of their "immigrant land business." Though these legal actions were for the most part settled out of court during the early 1950s, and Bentsen himself had not been involved in the transactions, his entry into political life had been largely backed by family money.[3]

Bentsen attended Sharyland High School where Austin attorney and longtime family friend Joe Kilgore remembered Bentsen as "active in whatever transpired," and "a good student, good athlete, well-liked . . . very much like his father: tall, rangy, wiry, athletic, witty." At the age of fifteen, Bentsen graduated from Sharyland and headed to The University of Texas. He excelled academically, earning a law degree from UT before he turned twenty-two (he never received an undergraduate degree). While at the university, Bentsen joined the Sigma Nu fraternity, making lifelong friends that included John B. Connally.[4]

Shortly after his admission to the Texas State Bar in 1942, he married Beryl Ann (B.A.) Longino of Lufkin and then enlisted in the United States Army. He became a B-24 pilot and flew thirty-five missions over southern Italy, Germany, Austria, Czechoslovakia, Hungary, Romania, and Bulgaria from 1944 through the end of World War II. By the age of twenty-three, Bentsen had attained the rank of major and was placed in command of the 449th Bomb Squadron. His service earned the Air Medal and the Distinguished Flying Cross.

In 1945, Bentsen returned to Texas and entered the private practice of law in McAllen. His time as a practicing attorney was short-lived, however, as Bentsen started his career in politics the following year. He was elected county judge for Hidalgo County at the age of twenty-four, serving in that position from 1946 to 1948. When incumbent Congressman Milton West decided not to run for reelection in 1948, Bentsen announced his candidacy for the vacant seat. He faced an imposing battle. In order to win the election, he would have to face whichever candidate was chosen to run against him by South Texas bosses George Parr and Mannie Raymond. Bentsen used this to his advantage through his slogan of "Beat the Machine," in reference to Parr's dominance of the Rio Grande Valley. Bentsen won the election and, at twenty-seven, became the youngest representative in the Eighty-First Congress.[5]

Upon entering the House in 1949, Bentsen closely followed Speaker Sam Rayburn's advice to be patient and stay on the backbench of the legislative process where he could listen and learn. Bentsen's intellect, pragmatism, and loyalty quickly earned him the confidence of many of the more senior members of Congress. He became a regular at Rayburn's "Bureau of Education," where Democratic leaders would meet after-hours to discuss strategies for dealing with the important issues of the day. Bentsen built strong friendships in Congress, enjoying games of five-card stud poker at his home on Friday evenings, sometimes with Rayburn, Senator Lyndon Johnson, Supreme Court Chief Justice Fred Vinson, and others. During his six years in the House, Bentsen became a strong anti-communist determined to "ferret out the Reds" from the departments of state and defense. He also gained a reputation as a conservative spokesman on fiscal and national defense issues, making a speech during the Korean War urging President Harry Truman to issue a nuclear ultimatum to North Korea. In 1949, Bentsen was one of only two Texas congressmen to vote against the poll tax as a requirement for participation in federal elections. Bentsen's tenure in the House would not last long, though. The tedious work involved with the legislative process became boring, and the $12,500 annual salary was not sufficient, Bentsen believed, to support three children. In 1954, Bentsen decided to give up his seat in the House and to enter private business.

After returning to Texas, Bentsen, with substantial start-up capital from his father and Uncle Elmer, moved to Houston and formed the Consolidated American Life Insurance Company (CALICO). Shortly after going into business, Bentsen acquired, via a leveraged buyout, the established firm of Lincoln Liberty Life Insurance Company of Omaha. He expanded and diversified his business interests, amassing a personal fortune estimated to be worth $2.3 million by 1970.[6]

After fifteen years away from Washington, though, Bentsen, encouraged by former President Lyndon B. Johnson and Governor Connally, decided to return to public service. He announced as a candidate against incumbent Democratic Senator Ralph Yarborough. Though he had ample finances to mount a long and arduous campaign, Bentsen faced a daunting task. One poll indicated that he had only 2 percent name recognition across Texas at the outset of the campaign, but Bentsen counteracted that with a blitz of television ads across the state. The ads were geared toward painting a picture of Yarborough as a left-wing liberal who had opposed school prayer and the death penalty. Yarborough retaliated by accusing Bentsen of being an instrument of big oil companies and a war hawk. In the end, Bentsen was victorious with a 53 percent majority. He mended fences within the party from his battle with Yarborough and, again using a television saturation strategy, defeated Houston Congressman George H. W. Bush in the November election.[7]

For the next twenty-three years, Bentsen rose through the ranks of the Senate to

Left to right: Texas Congressman Bob Poage, Speaker Carl Albert of Oklahoma, Senator Lloyd Bentsen, Congressman George Mahon, Congressman Richard White, Congressman Wright Patman. Photo in collection of the Dolph Briscoe Center for American History, Austin, Texas. Used by permission.

become one of the most powerful and influential men in Washington. He befriended Senate Majority Leader Mike Mansfield and Senate Finance Committee Chairman Russell Long, who helped secure Bentsen a seat on the Senate Finance Committee. His quick rise to power drew many comparisons to former President Johnson (and the nickname LBJr.) and mention as a possible presidential candidate 1976.

Bentsen's run in 1976 was a major disappointment. He was unable to overcome name recognition problems or to inspire a large following. His fundraising efforts were hampered by the possible Republican candidacy of his old friend John Connally. After poor showings in the Oklahoma and Arkansas caucuses, Bentsen withdrew from the race in favor of former Georgia Governor Jimmy Carter, who by that time seemed unbeatable for the nomination.[8]

After his aborted run for the presidency, Bentsen continued his rise to influence in the Senate. In due course, Bentsen became chair of the Finance Committee and was known as an effective legislator. He generally voted with other Democrats, voting for civil rights legislation, expanding Medicare and Medicaid programs, for increased funding for prenatal and neonatal care, for laws to limit campaign contributions, and for worker's rights. Additionally, he voted in 1977 to eliminate all prohibitions on the use of federal funds to pay for abortions, and then opposed an attempt to limit federal funding to instances where the mother's life would be endangered by a full-term pregnancy. In 1987, Bentsen voted to uphold a two-year ban on any testing or development of the Strategic Defense Initiative, feeling that the United States should not jeopardize the Anti-Ballistic Missile Treaty.[9]

Bentsen's strongest influence involved taxation and the federal deficit, and he worked during the 1980s to balance the federal budget. This required that he work with the Republican Reagan and Bush administrations and he faced opposition within Congress. In 1987, for example, Bentsen and other Senate tax writers pieced together a $9 billion package of tax increases in accordance with a deficit-reduction agreement that had been prearranged with the White House.[10] In 1990, Bentsen pushed another deficit reduction plan that included $3.4 billion in tax breaks for the oil and gas industry. Bentsen was committed to getting a bill out of conference that could be supported by both Democrats and Republicans, but that would also include tax breaks for oil and gas producers.[11]

In his search for a running mate, 1988 Democratic presidential nominee Michael Dukakis of Massachusetts wanted to balance the ticket ideologically and geographically. Bentsen, with his Texas pedigree and reputation as a moderate conservative, seemed a logical choice. Dukakis remembered that another son of

Lloyd Bentsen in Beaumont, Texas, shaking hands with President Jimmy Carter. Jack Brooks, whose district is being visited, is looking on. Neighboring Texas Congressman Charlie Wilson is standing in the background. Photograph from the Jimmy Carter Library, Atlanta, Georgia. Used by permission.

Massachusetts President John F. Kennedy had successfully selected Texan Lyndon Johnson as his running mate in 1960, and he hoped history would repeat itself.[12] Through a special legal exception, Bentsen ran for vice president and US senator simultaneously. In his vice presidential acceptance speech, Bentsen attacked his Republican opponents, claiming that "America has just passed through the ultimate epoch of illusion: an eight year coma in which slogans were confused with solutions and rhetoric passed for reality. . . . At long last the epoch is drawing to a close." In October of that year, Bentsen squared off against Republican vice presidential nominee Dan Quayle in what has become one of the most famous political debates of American history. After Quayle made a comparison between himself and John F. Kennedy at the same point in their political careers, Bentsen quipped: "Senator, I served with Jack Kennedy. I knew Jack Kennedy. Jack Kennedy was a friend of mine. Senator, you're no Jack Kennedy."[13] Quayle had clearly been outwitted and, even when Dukakis carried only ten states in his general election loss to Bush, Bentsen emerged with an enhanced reputation.

After serving part of another term in the Senate, Bentsen was tapped by President Clinton to serve as Treasury Secretary in 1993, a position he kept for two years. He made a mark in that role, pushing the North American Free Trade Agreement to eliminate tariffs and other barriers to trade among the United States, Canada, and Mexico for a fifteen-year period.[14] Ultimately, Bentsen was instrumental in the passage and implementation of NAFTA, which began in 1994.

Overall, Bentsen received high marks for his service at treasury. In 2001, Federal Reserve Chairman Alan Greenspan credited Bentsen with instilling "fiscal discipline" in the federal government in President Clinton's 1993 economic package. Similarly, Clinton said in 1999 that, "At an age when most of us look to fishing and grandchildren for our next challenges, Lloyd accepted the toughest job I had to offer."[15] Bentsen died May 23, 2006, of complications from a stroke suffered in 1999.[16]

It would be an understatement to say that Lloyd Bentsen served his country with distinction; he used his considerable skill to make the United States a better place for people from every walk of life. He was not typically a colorful politician—one Democrat said in describing him, "there isn't a lot of Elvis in Lloyd Bentsen"—but Bentsen always seemed to get the job done.[17] Bentsen's place in history is firmly secured and he will hold a position among the most highly respected of Texas political leaders.

15

Jack Brooks

US Representative 1953-1995

WHEN REPORTERS described Jack Brooks, they used words like "wily, blunt, gleefully profane and deceptively folksy,"[1] "outspoken,"[2] "crusty,"[3] "tough, prickly,"[4] "gritty,"[5] and "downright ornery."[6] Richard Nixon called Brooks "the executioner."[7] Senator Joe Biden spoke of Brooks's "phenomenal legislative skills."[8] It was claimed that Brooks was the only man that Lyndon Johnson ever feared.[9] Brooks said that although President Johnson was famous for calling people at all hours of the night, "He knew better than to do that to me."[10] Brooks was, first and foremost, a master interrogator who seemed to have the ability to smell a lie coming from a witness's mouth. From the House Government Operations Committee, he ran investigations where, it was claimed, "Federal bureaucrats who sought to outfox Brooks. . . . have emerged from the committee room pale and wobbly on their feet after getting a dose of his treatment."[11] First elected to Congress in 1952, he quickly became a protégé of Speaker Sam Rayburn whom he greatly admired. Brooks said of Rayburn, "I ran investigations and when you run investigations, you need someone to watch your back. Rayburn watched my back."[12] Brooks campaigned for the Democratic ticket in 1952, a time when many Texas Democrats backed Republican Dwight Eisenhower for the presidency, and Rayburn was impressed with Brooks's party loyalty.[13] Partisanship was to become a hallmark of Brooks's career.[14] When younger Democrats in the Texas delegation, for example, sought a closer relationship with Republicans in the delegation, Brooks would have none of it. And, as chairman of the Texas delegation, he prevented an effort to allow Republicans into the delegation's Wednesday lunches which, since Sam Rayburn had banned Republican

Jack Brooks (seated at right) campaigning at a gas station in 1951. Photo in collection of the Dolph Briscoe Center for American History, Austin, Texas. Used by permission.

Congressman Bruce Alger from the lunches, had been traditionally reserved for the Democratic members.[15]

A classic Brooks pose during his congressional investigations was to perch his glasses on the tip of his nose, peer over the top of the glasses, and chomp down on a cigar. He attacked the Air Force for its excessive computer purchases and the State

Department for its effort to replace the silverware in US embassies worldwide. During the Iran-Contra investigation, Brooks called both former State Department official Elliott Abrams and former national security adviser John Poindexter "a lying son of a bitch."[16] Brooks was one of the House managers of the impeachment proceedings against federal judges Alcee Hastings and Walter Nixon. He was also one of the Judiciary Committee members who held hearings on the impeachment of Richard Nixon. Brooks was so proud of his fierce image that when the *Washington Post* published a photograph of Brooks with an unusually angry expression, he proudly displayed the picture to his fellow congressmen.[17]

Brooks was born in 1922, joined the Marines in World War II, and served nearly two years on the Japanese fronts at Guadalcanal, Guam, Okinawa, and in North China. After the war, he served in the Texas House of Representatives from 1946-1950, was admitted to the Texas bar in 1949, and was elected to the US House of Representatives in 1952. He served in the House from January 1953-January 1995. During that time, he served on the Joint Committee on Government Operations, the Committee on Government Operations, the Committee on the Judiciary and, at some point in his career, he served as chair of each of the committees.[18] Had he not been defeated for reelection in 1994, he would have been the Dean of the House— the most senior member of the House of Representatives.

Brooks was known for his efforts to bring government projects to his district. A number of years ago, Brooks wanted to build a dam that was eventually to become the huge Sam Rayburn dam and reservoir in East Texas. When he was told by an Army Corps of Engineers general that the dam would never be built, Brooks sneered and said, "General, long after you're gone, I'm still going to be here and so is that dam."[19] And, of course, Brooks was right. President Carter joked about all the federal expenditures in Brooks's district when he came to Beaumont, Texas, to speak at the dedication of the Jack Brooks Federal Building. Carter stated:

> Twenty-five years ago, when I was leaving the Navy to come home to Plains, Georgia, to be a farmer, a young freshman Congressman was leaving Beaumont to go to Washington. In that quarter of a century, the Ninth District has garnered more Federal projects than ever before: the Intracoastal Canal, the Nation's first strategic storage facility for oil, a whole host of Federal works projects too numerous to name this morning, research grants for your district colleges and universities, and a wide variety of miscellaneous Federal contracts and awards.

I don't recall a single major Federal program in Plains in the last 25 years. One reason I came here was to get Jack Brooks to help me in the future. If he brings down to Beaumont more than you can handle, I want Plains to be the first spillover point for things that you reject.[20]

Driving a reporter around the district, Brooks pointed out some of the federal money he had brought to his district: "St. Elizabeth's Hospital," he said. . . . "Got them the first million they ever got." The big Pontiac glided past a local television station ("Helped them with the F.C.C."); a brief stop at the Gulf Intracoastal Waterway in nearby Port Arthur ("I widened it, deepened it."); a pause at the sea-wall ("Forty, fifty million dollars"). Later he fired up a cigar and cruised past the site of the new federal prison ("2,000 jobs, $150 million") and Lamar University in Beaumont, where a cigar-clutching statue honors the congressman whose labors elevated the school from backwater junior college to four-year university.[21]

In Washington, Brooks essentially molded the Government Operations Committee into a powerful oversight body.[22] Brooks was in the motorcade in Dallas when President Kennedy was assassinated and was aboard *Air Force One*, immediately behind Mrs. Kennedy, when Lyndon Johnson took the presidential oath. Brooks quickly became Johnson's key man on Capitol Hill.[23] Brooks had refused to sign the Southern Manifesto in 1956 that was a declaration of opposition to *Brown v. Board of Education* by almost all Southern senators and congressmen, although he had not been a supporter of many of the early civil rights bills. With Johnson in the White House, however, Brooks was one of the few Southern Democrats who backed the 1964 Civil Rights Act. He then voted for all subsequent civil rights bills and for LBJ's Great Society program. He was also a supporter of the Vietnam War. Brooks was exceptionally close to Lyndon Johnson, and he was never to have that strong and positive relationship with any other president. Brooks had the most negative relationship with Richard Nixon. Brooks investigated Nixon's use of funds for improvements to his homes in San Clemente, California, and in Key Biscayne, Florida. He pushed for an article of impeachment against Nixon for those home improvements and he voted for all five of the articles of impeachment that were adopted by the committee. The Nixon administration supported revenue sharing where federal funds would be provided to local governments. Brooks strongly opposed revenue sharing and made his views about it known in a sarcastic speech to 1,000 county governmental officials. Brooks told them:

Jack Brooks (center left) at a White House meeting between Vice President Nelson Rockefeller and President Gerald Ford (center right). Photograph from the Gerald Ford Library, Ann Arbor, Michigan. Used by permission.

I can understand your dedication to such a program [as revenue sharing]. It is a great treat for a public official to enjoy the pleasures of spending without the pain of raising the money. I don't blame you for enjoying it. I'd dedicate those parks and the street work and that pothole work. I'd pay a couple of cops extra money, a couple of nurses, a couple of firemen. I'd buy a new something-or-other. . . . Don't say one damn word about where the money's coming from. Just tell 'em, I'm trying to help you all.[24]

But, warned Brooks, revenue sharing was a fraud and the American people were demanding a reduction in spending. Amazingly, he received a standing ovation.[25]

In 1976, Jack Brooks and Bob Eckhardt were the only two members of the Texas delegation who did not endorse fellow Texan Jim Wright for majority leader. It may be that the reason was simply that Wright was late getting into the race and Brooks and Eckhardt had already made other commitments. However, it is also the case that any plans Brooks might have had for the leadership would be derailed when a fellow Texan became majority leader.[26] Nevertheless, when Speaker Wright was faced with ethical charges, Brooks was his most outspoken defender.[27]

With Brooks' seniority, his vast power, and his incredible success in gaining governmental projects for his district, it is remarkable that he was defeated in 1994. Although he did not seem like a serious opponent, Steve Stockman, who, during his college years, had been homeless and living out of his station wagon for a time, defeated Brooks.[28] He was little known and ran his campaign out of his home, but he had run against Brooks in 1992 and had limited Brooks to a 53.6 percent majority. That was Brooks's poorest showing in a general election. In 1994, term limits were a popular idea to limit the amount of time a public official could serve in office. Stockman argued that forty-two years in Congress was enough, and that if Brooks had not done his job in that amount of time, he did not deserve another chance.[29] Brooks also came across to many of his constituents as arrogant and, as proof, they pointed to the large bronze statue of Brooks that was at Lamar University.[30] Brooks's loss was also part of the "Republican Revolution" where Republicans were making great strides against incumbent Democrats in many parts of the country. The main explanation for his defeat, however, was probably his support of the 1994 crime bill, which included a ban on assault weapons. Brooks was a long-time opponent of gun control in a district with more gun dealers than New York State. On the one hand, Brooks was arguing that he needed to be reelected because of his power, but he was not powerful enough to keep that ban out of the crime bill. As Stockman explained, Brooks had painted himself into a corner and the National Rifle Association opposed him along with the Christian Coalition, the National Right-to-Life Committee, the Traditional Values Coalition, and the Democrats for Conservative Government. The National Republican Party also smelled blood and put money into the race, among other things accusing Brooks of being soft on pedophiles. Brooks blamed his loss on Rush Limbaugh and other right-wing talk show hosts who attacked him.[31] Brooks received only 45.7 percent of the vote compared to Stockman's 51.9 percent, with minor candidates receiving the remaining votes.

It was a remarkable loss for such a senior, powerful, and effective congressman. Brooks was not inspirational like Barbara Jordan; nor was he like George Mahon, low-key and well-liked. He was a tough, bare-fisted politician who feared no one, and who provided vast benefits to his district while having significant policy impact in Washington as a fierce investigator and committee chair.

Price Daniel at his desk. Photograph from the Texas State Library and Archives Commission. Used by permission.

16

Price Daniel

US Senator 1953-1957

SPEAKER OF THE Texas House of Representatives, attorney general of Texas, US senator, governor of Texas, and justice on the Texas Supreme Court, Daniel held offices in all branches of government. A Democrat, he was not loyal to the party during the Eisenhower era, yet he was able to re-establish a working relationship with party loyalists Speaker Sam Rayburn and Senator Lyndon Johnson to gain control of the state Democratic Party. Daniel had supported segregation of The University of Texas Law School when he was state attorney general and campaigned as a segregationist, yet he rejected the extreme racist poses of many Southern governors of the era, including his predecessor as governor, Allan Shivers. A good part of Daniel's career as governor was occupied with his opposition to the sales tax, yet he allowed a sales tax to be passed without his signature—an action that probably was the major cause of his defeat by John Connally for a third term. His previous service as a US senator was largely because he knew he could not defeat Allan Shivers for the governor's seat, and so becoming a senator was his second choice. Yet, he was popular enough to drive long-time Senator Tom Connally from office.[1] Daniel's major issue for many of his years in office was the tidelands—the issue of control over the submerged land off the Texas coast because of the oil located there. Daniel fought for state versus federal control of these submerged lands, although his efforts alienated him and the state's electorate from the national Democratic Party that supported federal control. Daniel's states' rights philosophy led him to some foolish proposals; the most out-rageous was his effort to reinstitute the Texas Navy to protect the state's claim to the tidelands and his effort to recruit the state's pleasure boat operators as a naval force.[2]

To Senator Lyndon Johnson's amazement, Daniel's goal was to be governor of Texas rather than a US senator, and his service as governor, although mostly remembered today for the initiation of the sales tax, was moderate by Southern standards on racial issues. And, Daniel was no fan of the sales tax—he preferred a tax that was assessed partly on business and partly on sales. He reorganized the Board of Insurance Commissioners, something desperately needed in the wake of insurance scandals during the Shivers administration. He supported an abandoned property act, which would give unclaimed property held by banks and utilities to the state, and he supported the first statewide water plan for Texas.[3] As a senator, hopelessly overshadowed by his colleague, Lyndon Johnson, who was a major force—if not *the* major force—in the US Senate. However, he was successful in achieving his objectives in getting Texas control of the tidelands.

Daniel was born in 1910, worked as a newspaper reporter after graduating from high school, and then attended Baylor University, where he received both an undergraduate degree and a law degree. He was elected to three two-year terms in the Texas House of Representatives, where he served from 1939-1943. He was elected Speaker of the Texas House in 1943.[4] Daniel was later to claim that Speaker Sam Rayburn told him of all his years in office, he had enjoyed being Speaker of the Texas House more than any other thing. Daniel admitted his surprise at Rayburn's remark, but commented that he felt the same way about his service as Speaker.[5] Daniel, in those Texas legislative years, was continually in dispute with Governor W. Lee O'Daniel who wished to impose a sales tax in Texas, while Daniel adamantly opposed the tax.[6]

Leaving the Texas House for the Army in World War II, Daniel was discharged in 1946 and ran for Texas Attorney General. He became the youngest attorney general in the state's history. He soon became enmeshed in one of the most important of the major civil rights cases that was heard by the US Supreme Court prior to *Brown v. Board of Education.* Heman Sweatt sought admission to The University of Texas Law School, which was racially segregated. Daniel was a supporter of segregation and sought funding from the legislature for a separate-but-equal law school for blacks, which he thought would bring the state into constitutional compliance under the separate-but-equal doctrine that upheld segregation in the Supreme Court case of *Plessy v. Ferguson.* Texas State University for Negroes was established, although Sweatt continued to argue that Texas was still denying him equal protection under the laws. The US Supreme Court ruled in favor of Sweatt and held that the Texas State University for Negroes was not equal to The University of Texas Law School. While the decision did not abandon the separate-but-equal doctrine of

Plessy v. Ferguson, after *Sweatt*, at least in higher education, it was difficult to imagine how segregated higher education facilities provided equal protection under the law, and the case heralded the later *Brown* decision which overturned the separate-but-equal doctrine in public education.[7]

Yet, Daniel's efforts to maintain segregation at The University of Texas Law School boosted his popularity with white voters in the state. Daniel also tried to shut down organized gambling in Galveston, then a haven for large-scale illegal gambling. However, it was his involvement in the tidelands dispute that was to make his reputation not just as Texas's attorney general—it was to become the most important issue of his political career.[8]

With the recognition that there were major oil deposits in the submerged lands off the Texas, California, and Louisiana coasts, a major dispute emerged between these states and the federal government about ownership of this land. All three states had sold leases to oil producers between 1939-1948. When, in 1945, President Truman ordered Attorney General Tom Clark to file a test suit against California, Congress passed legislation ceding the submerged lands to the states. Truman vetoed this bill. In 1947, the Supreme Court ruled against California's tidelands claim. However, Texas Attorney General Daniel claimed that Texas, under its annexation agreement, owned the rights to the tidelands. The House passed quitclaim legislation in the aftermath of a new lawsuit filed by the federal government against Louisiana and Texas, but the bill failed in the Senate. In 1950, Sam Rayburn pursued a compromise where the three states would have the rights to two-thirds of the oil and gas within a 10.35-mile limit and one-third from there out to the continental shelf, which was about 125 miles. Daniel was the major opponent of the compromise, leading Rayburn to state, ". . . I realized that he didn't want a settlement—he wanted the issue to run for office on. He wanted to demagogue it. So it couldn't be settled." A four-to-three US Supreme Court decision, *US v. Texas*, seemed to destroy Texas's claim to the tidelands. Again, Congress passed quitclaim legislation ceding ownership of the tidelands to the states, and President Truman vetoed it.[9]

However, this issue proved an ideal stepping-stone for Daniel's move to the US Senate. He entered the 1952 Senate race vowing to continue the fight against the federal government from the US Senate. Behind the scenes, Daniel actually wanted to be governor of Texas and thought the only person who could beat Senator Tom Connally was Governor Allan Shivers. However, Shivers wanted to stay as governor. It was unlikely that Daniel could beat Shivers, and Shivers convinced Daniel that Connally was beatable because Connally had not maintained his political organization.[10] As a result, Daniel entered the Senate race because his access to the governor's seat was blocked.

Many conservative Democrats in Texas were supporting Republican Dwight Eisenhower for President.[11] The Democratic presidential nominee was far more liberal than most Texas Democrats, Eisenhower was a war hero, and conservative Democrats had become increasingly disenchanted with the national Democratic Party and with the Truman administration. Additionally, Eisenhower supported Texas's position on the tidelands issue, contrary to Democratic nominee Adlai Stevenson. Daniel supported Eisenhower, basing his decision on Eisenhower's support for Texas's claims. In 1953, Daniel succeeded in accomplishing his objective, and the Submerged Lands Act was passed, which gave rights to the submerged lands to the states.[12]

This legislation on the tidelands was the highlight of Daniel's career in the Senate. Although Daniel was seen as disloyal to the Democratic Party in supporting Eisenhower, most Texas state office-holders had also been disloyal, and many Texans in Congress had taken a very low-key approach in backing the Democratic ticket. Party disloyalty was, however, a major sin in the eyes of Speaker Sam Rayburn. Daniel recalled that there was a strained relationship between him and Rayburn on the tidelands issue because Rayburn had wanted to work out a compromise, and Daniel was the leading advocate for the states' rights position. That strained relationship, Daniel said, was greatest when Daniel supported Eisenhower. As Daniel recalled, "I know the first time I saw him when I was supporting Eisenhower he was out at Walter Hornaday's house (Hornaday was a Texas reporter who was well-liked by Rayburn and many in the Texas congressional delegation) at a January first black-eyed pea dinner that he had every year." Mr. Rayburn said to Daniel, "Get out of my way. I don't want to see you, I want to see Jean."[13] Rayburn, of course, was displaying his anger with Daniel for his party disloyalty, but by talking to Jean, Daniel's wife, he was not cutting off all relationship with him.

A bigger threat to loyal national Democrats and thus to House Speaker Sam Rayburn and Senate Democratic leader Lyndon Johnson was Governor Allan Shivers. Shivers had supported Eisenhower for the presidency, was a political threat to Lyndon Johnson, and had threatened to redistrict Sam Rayburn out of office. Rayburn did not trust Shivers who, he believed, had lied about supporting the national Democratic ticket. Shivers was a powerful figure in Texas politics with enormous financial backing. Ultimately, Rayburn and Johnson believed they had to take control of the state Democratic Party from Shivers. They succeeded in doing that, but only through an alliance with the liberal labor wing of the Democratic

Party in Texas, which, they quickly discovered, they could not control.[14] According to Daniel:

Well, after seeing that they couldn't lead this group who had helped them win control, then Johnson came over to me in the Senate to tell me all about it, that they went with the wrong people to beat old Shivers. They went with the wrong crowd. Told me about the disrespectful way they treated Mr. Rayburn and him and wanted to know would I work with him in trying to have a Democratic party that we could keep and a Democratic committee that would be friendly to him, one that wouldn't have his enemies on it, one that would be willing to work with him and I said, yes, I would be willing to do that. . . . Then we worked together at all the Conventions from then on. I kept them from having to depend on people who would not work with them. And we were friends, all three of us. Nobody was on our Democratic committee, hardly ever, that would have anything against and would be an enemy of either Johnson or Rayburn.[15]

Price Daniel campaigning for governor in downtown Houston.
Photograph from the Sam Houston Regional Library and Research Center, Liberty, Texas. Used by permission.

Daniel's dream, of course, was always to be governor of Texas, and he ran for that office in the Democratic primary in 1956, winning a closely contested race against liberal Ralph Yarborough. Daniel was governor for the next six years, but toward the end of his administration, he was faced with the seemingly insurmountable problem of finding sufficient revenue to run state government. From his early days in the Texas House of Representatives, he had been opposed to a sales tax, but fearing there would be insufficient state revenue, he allowed a sales tax to become law without his signature. Immediately he was criticized for the tax where merchants said, "Give a penny for Price," as they returned change to customers.[16] Additionally, the charismatic John Connally opposed him in 1962, and Daniel lost his bid for another term.

Daniel returned to legal practice and was soon appointed to head the State Library and Historical Association—Daniel was a devoted student of Texas history. In 1967, President Lyndon Johnson asked him to work on federal-state relations in his administration and to be director of the Office of Emergency Preparedness and a member of the National Security Council. Then, in 1970, Governor Preston Smith appointed Daniel to a vacant seat on the Supreme Court of Texas. He was elected to that seat for a full six-year term in 1972. The Supreme Court was not a retirement home for Daniel—he was an active member of the court and wrote seventy-three majority opinions. Many of his opinions dealt with land and mineral rights issues.[17]

Daniel retired from public life in 1979, and died in 1988. Price Daniel had an important position in Texas politics for thirty years, although his role in national politics was limited to the period from 1953, when he first assumed the office of US senator from Texas, until 1957, when he resigned from the Senate to become governor of Texas. His major accomplishment as a US senator was the tidelands legislation that gave ownership of offshore submerged lands to the states. The tidelands issue was Price Daniel's main concern, and he achieved his goal. Daniel was unusual in that he was, like Governor Allan Shivers, a conservative Texas Democrat who was willing to break party ranks and support a Republican for the presidency. Unlike Shivers, however, he did not alienate powerful Democrats like Lyndon Johnson and Sam Rayburn so much that he was unable to work with them. Indeed, after his support for the Republican ticket, he was able to align himself with Rayburn and Johnson to take control of the state Democratic Party, and the three of them—working as friends and political allies—went on to dominate the state party for their mutual benefit.

Well Done, Governor

Cartoon honoring the service of Price Daniel after Daniel's death in 1988.
Cartoon from Sam Nash, Tyler Courier-Times-Telegraph. Used by permission.

Bruce Alger's (center, holding sign) right-wing politics is well illustrated by this photograph of him at an anti-Lyndon Johnson demonstration in Dallas in 1960 near the Baker Hotel. Dallas Times Herald *photograph by John Mazziotta. Photograph in collection at Lyndon B. Johnson Library, Austin, Texas.*

17

Bruce Alger

US Representative 1955-1965

Bruce Alger was one of the early Texas Republicans to serve in the House of Representatives. First elected in 1954, Alger was defeated in the 1964 election. Claiming when he was elected to Congress that "My ignorance of politics couldn't be matched by anybody in politics,"[1] he was remarkably successful in defeating some of the most important names in Dallas politics. In 1954, Alger defeated former Dallas mayor Wallace Savage; in 1956, he beat famed Dallas County District Attorney Henry Wade; in 1958, Alger was victorious over state Senator Barefoot Sanders (later a highly respected federal judge); in 1960, Alger defeated well-known businessman and former state Representative Joe Pool; and in 1962, even in the wake of a nasty divorce, Alger was able to overcome state Representative Bill Jones. Earle Cabell, former Dallas mayor, finally crushed Alger by a 14 percent vote margin in 1964.[2]

Alger was able to win elections because he could mobilize conservative voters, especially voters in the affluent parts of Dallas. And, of course, in 1956, he greatly benefited from the strong support that Dallas County gave to Republican presidential candidate Dwight Eisenhower. In 1960, the Republican presidential candidacy of Richard Nixon again helped Alger. Alger had great political visibility because he was the lone Republican in the Texas congressional delegation, and his conservatism appealed to the Dallas business community that at least tacitly supported him. His rhetoric appealed to Dallas conservatives—he wanted to maintain traditional American values and was staunchly anti-communist. Government, in his view, had overstepped its bounds. He wanted to cut taxes, shift programs to the state level, reduce federal spending, and deregulate business. With enough freedom, Alger believed, a person could work hard and be successful in life.[3]

A draft of one of his speeches in his personal papers is titled "God in Our Government" and has as its theme that "God, not atheism or agnosticism is [the] basis for government and religious freedom." This lengthy, wandering outline combines biblical quotations with discussions of American history, the Federal Communications Commission, the Supreme Court, the views of a Wisconsin professor, and the views of Calvin Coolidge, among other topics. However, the point of his essay is clear. He wants to show that, "It is not enough to be protected by the Constitution, as neutralists, as agnostics, as atheists. We must be advocates. We must earnestly strive to advance God's Kingdom. To do less, it appears to me, or to practice or even tolerate agnosticism or atheism is to set in motion forces destructive of our God-fearing people."[4] It was not an unusual theme for Alger, whose views revolved around the Bible, the Declaration of Independence, and a strict interpretation of the Constitution.[5]

He was opposed to social security. To him, government did not belong in the pension business. He was also opposed to public housing, which, in his mind, was socialism that would destroy one's incentive to work for a home of one's own. A graduated income tax was socialistic as well, since Alger believed it was simply a redistribution of income. Unions were evil and were the agents of communism just as was big government. Walter Reuther, the president of the United Automobile Workers, was "communist trained," according to Alger. In addition, he was a fan of the communist-baiting Senator Joe McCarthy, and many of his views seemed to reflect those of the ultra-conservative John Birch Society.[6] Alger wrote a constituent about the John Birch Society, "Unfortunately, most of the news about John Birch Society is from enemies. If you judge people by their enemies they must be mighty fine folks!" But then Alger noted that he had chosen to put his work into the Republican Party.[7] When Reed Benson, a leader in the John Birch Society and the son of Eisenhower's Secretary of Agriculture, Ezra Taft Benson, wrote Alger, Alger responded telling him that "We conservatives are the front-line troops" to protect "our way of life."[8] However, the Birch Society troubled Alger. He claimed that he did not like organizations controlled by one person. He also said that he thought trying to impeach US Supreme Court Chief Justice Earl Warren—one of the most publicized efforts of the Birch Society—was "a waste of time."[9] There were other views as well that were too right wing even for Alger. When a constituent wrote that, "A Senate Subcommittee study reveals that 500 of the most active communists in this country are either foreign born, of foreign parentage, or married to foreign born" and asked for Alger's support for enforcement of immigration laws,[10] Alger responded in a way quite unexpected of someone holding such right-wing views:

I am enclosing a list of members of the last, or Eighty-Seventh Congress, and I would very much appreciate it if you would take pencil in hand and go through this list very carefully and mark every name that sounds foreign to our ears. As you do this, think carefully of what place these men have in American history, and what we would have done without such men had we barred their ancestors from our shores. I am in agreement with you, but I am very proud that this nation has grown to its present greatness by the efforts of brave and selfless men and women from all over the world, and that this has been a haven and a refuge for men and women who sought freedom, liberty and the greatness that is America.[11]

Such moderate and reasoned expressions were rare for Alger. He is instead remembered for being the only vote against the 1958 federal milk program for poor school children. Government, he thought, should not give children milk. Instead, that was the job of parents and providing free milk discouraged parents from caring for their own children. Once government provided milk to school children, he argued, "the government becomes the judge, the jury, the prosecutor of what you're going to eat, what you're going to drink, when you're going to do it. This will spill over through the whole system until someone else is running your school."[12]

A conservative group, the Americans for Constitutional Action, which rates members of Congress according to their support of conservative views, gave Alger its Distinguished Service Award for his voting from 1957-1959. In 1961, as an example, his Americans for Conservative Action (ACA) rating was 100 percent. John Dowdy, a conservative East Texas Democrat, had an ACA rating of 71 percent—the next highest rating in the Texas delegation. In contrast, Jim Wright, from nearby Fort Worth, had a rating of only 29 percent.[13]

Alger's extreme conservatism was never more visible than during the 1960 election. He considered John Kennedy a socialist and thought that his election would "end individual freedom in America."[14] After Kennedy was elected, Alger wrote a column wherein he claimed that Kennedy's three years in office was characterized by government by decree, and that Kennedy was governing with executive orders rather than congressional legislation. The result, wrote Alger, was a "pattern of dictatorship. . . ."[15]

When vice presidential candidate Lyndon Johnson came to Dallas shortly before the election to speak at a luncheon, he and Lady Bird were met with a jeering crowd at the Baker Hotel that included a sign-carrying Alger. The sign read, "LBJ sold out to the Yankee socialists." Johnson and Lady Bird then walked to the

Adolphus Hotel where they marched through another taunting crowd.[16] Historian Robert Dallek wrote that, "No single incident in the campaign involving Johnson did more to help the ticket than the public abuse of Lyndon and Lady Bird by right-wing opponents in Dallas. . . . Although Lyndon was genuinely outraged by the abuse, he immediately saw the political advantage in Texas and throughout the South in the televised pictures of a shrieking mob assaulting an unprotected vice-presidential candidate. . . ." Bill Moyers said of the incident that Johnson had not known how he was going to carry Texas. Said Moyers, "If he could have thought this up, he would have thought it up. Tried to invent it. But the moment it happened, he knew." The incident gave Johnson the opportunity to label the Republicans as extremists and it convinced conservative Southern Democrat Richard Russell of Georgia to do some last minute campaign efforts for the Democratic ticket in Texas and South Carolina.[17] Alger was not at the confrontation at the Adolphus; he was at the Baker Hotel. But the whole mob scene against Johnson and Lady Bird hurt the anti-Kennedy/Johnson forces and discredited Alger. Years later, when Jim Wright was talking of the incident, he said that he spoke to Alger about it and that Alger was just oblivious to the political harm that the incident had done to him and his conservative cause.[18] However, the negative reaction to the mob scene against Johnson eventually forced Alger to take out an ad in *The Dallas Morning News* in which he defended his actions. He was simply expressing his feelings, he explained, and the demonstration was spontaneous, with no harm coming to Johnson.[19]

Alger was an ideologue who, in spite of his skill in winning elections in Dallas, could not succeed within the House. When Alger was first elected to Congress, Speaker Rayburn made the friendly gesture of inviting him to the Speaker's office. After the meeting, Alger told reporters, "Rayburn is all right, but as I expected, he always puts his party ahead of his country." Rayburn was insulted and never again spoke to Alger.[20] Soon the regular luncheons of the Texas congressional delegation were changed to the Texas Democratic luncheons, effectively excluding the only Republican, Bruce Alger.[21] In Rayburn's last great political battle over the expansion of the size of the Rules Committee, Rayburn spoke to reporters and said that he had only lost four votes out of the twenty-two in the Texas delegation. A reporter corrected Rayburn, saying he had lost seven votes, "counting Alger." Rayburn immediately responded, "Hell, who counts Alger?"[22] One author described Alger as "an outcast among the Texas delegation. . . ."[23] An unidentified news clipping in the Alger papers has a comment from Congressman Jim Wright saying that Alger held

Bruce Alger campaign sticker. From the Guttery Collection, Poage Library, Baylor University, Waco, Texas.

"a holier than thou" attitude, and another representative was quoted as saying, "You can't discuss things with him, he preaches at you." [24]

Amazingly, Alger served on the Ways and Means Committee, the tax-writing committee, one of the most important in Congress. Still, he was unable to accomplish much in the House. In his ten years in Congress, he introduced ninety bills and resolutions and not one of them got out of committee, much less the House. Between 1959-1964, Dallas lost eight federal agencies. And for years Dallas city leaders had pushed for a new federal building, but Alger could not get the appropriation for the building. Alger had spoken against federal spending and Democrats in Congress took Alger at his word—no spending for a federal building in Dallas.[25] Years later, Alger said that the constant legislative losses were "destroy[ing] my outlook, my hope."[26]

In 1964, former Dallas Mayor Earle Cabell defeated Alger. Alger had gone through a difficult divorce and had lost his son in a traffic accident. *The Dallas Morning News* had backed Alger in 1956, 1958, 1960, and 1962, but it supported his opponent in 1964 and stressed his lack of legislative effectiveness. Alger continued to win in wealthier Dallas precincts, but by a close margin. In 1964, black voters turned out heavily against him. And, of course, underlying the election was the assassination of President Kennedy in Dallas in 1963. There was a reaction to the right-wing extremism in Dallas that had led to its label as "the city of hate."[27]

Alger returned to business interests in Florida and the Dallas area, never again entering politics. He was an early Republican—leaving office well over a decade before Texas elected its first Republican governor since Reconstruction. Bill Clements's 1978 election heralded the rise of the Republican Party in Texas. Alger's strength was in Dallas, the city that proved the core of Republican Party strength as they gained power in Texas politics. But Alger, like Martin Dies, left no real accomplishments. He was colorful, like Dies, but so much of an ideologue that he had no real policy impact in spite of having a wonderful stage—membership on the Ways and Means Committee. He is best remembered as a right-wing extremist who used that extremism to mobilize voters unhappy with the big government of the New Deal, the Fair Deal, and the New Frontier.

18

Jim Wright

US Representative 1955-1989
(Majority Leader 1977-1987,
Speaker 1987-1989)

JAMES CLAUDE "JIM" WRIGHT JR. served in Congress for more than a third of a century. His service spanned the time from Sam Rayburn's long service as Speaker of the House to the presidency of George H. W. Bush. During those years, Wright built a reputation for being one of the House's most able orators, craftiest legislators, and strongest leaders. His platform for gaining influence was the Public Works Committee, and, as he gained seniority, he moved through the ranks of leadership, ultimately serving as Speaker of the House from 1987-1989. His career ended in resignation when a series of ethics charges were levied against him. Even in resignation, though, Wright showed grace calling for an end to "mindless cannibalism" in the chamber he had made his political home.

Born in Fort Worth, Texas, on December 22, 1922, Wright was the only son and the eldest of three children of James Claude and Marie Lyster Wright. The Wright family moved frequently during Wright's formative years because of Mr. Wright's profession as a salesman and the challenges of the Great Depression. Young Jim Wright attended schools in Houston, Fort Worth, Dallas, and in Duncan, and Seminole, Oklahoma, before graduating from high school in Dallas. The Wrights were never destitute, but Wright remembers the year of 1931 as the "year we ate the piano" because they had to sell his mother's cherished instrument to feed the family.[1]

After high school graduation, Wright attended Weatherford College, where the family had eventually settled during 1939-1940, and The University of Texas from

Jim Wright showing off his cowboy boots with the Capitol in the background.
Jim Wright Collection, Texas Christian University, Fort Worth, Texas. Used by permission.

1940 to 1941. Wright never graduated from college, but has been a lifelong "bibliophile" and author of numerous books.

Immediately after the Japanese attack on Pearl Harbor, Wright left the university and enlisted in the Army Air Corps in December 1941, gaining a commission as an officer in 1942, and marrying Mary Ethelyn "Mab" Lemmons on Christmas day of that year. He gained combat experience flying missions in the South Pacific in B-24 bombers, earning the Distinguished Flying Cross. His outfit was known affectionately as the "flying circus" and saw a good deal of action.[2]

After the war, Wright returned to Weatherford and became the regional representative for the National Federation of Independent Business. Since high school, Wright had been interested in politics, and he took advantage of the opportunity to run for the Texas legislature in 1946. After election, he served in what he affectionately called the "carnival" under the "granite dome,"[3] earning a reputation as "the most liberal member of the House." Wright worked for the repeal of the poll tax, anti-lynching legislation, and the admission of African Americans to The University of Texas Law School.[4] This reputation led to the end of Wright's tenure in Austin after only one term. He was defeated by Floyd Bannister in the Democratic primary of 1948 by thirty-nine votes, after a mud-slinging campaign in which Wright was accused of being a communist and of favoring interracial marriage. After his defeat, he became partners with his father in a national trade extension and advertising firm.

These were family years as well, as the Wrights had five children and settled in to life in Weatherford. When the mayor resigned his office in 1949, Wright ran for the office, becoming the youngest mayor in Texas at the age of twenty-six. He served in that office, which he jokingly referred to as his highest office since he was "chief executive," until 1954. He was an effective, populist mayor, and became the president of the Texas Municipal League in 1953.[5]

A turning point came in 1954 when he decided to run for Congress—a brave decision, for he was taking on four-term incumbent Wingate Lucas who was backed by the Fort Worth business community and most importantly, Amon G. Carter, publisher of the *Fort Worth Star-Telegram*. Wright threw himself into the campaign, and when he noticed that many houses had antennas on their roofs, he purchased a full half-hour of time on the local NBC affiliate for $520, and found that he was soon known district-wide. Though Carter published a front page endorsement of Lucas, he allowed Wright to purchase a full page ad in the *Star-Telegram* the day before the election in which Wright promised he would be Carter's representative, but not his alone. Wright won the primary with 60 percent of the vote.[6]

Wright went to Washington and soon developed a close working relationship with Speaker Sam Rayburn. Though Wright initially wanted a seat on the Foreign Affairs Committee, Rayburn convinced him to accept assignment to Public Works instead, reasoning that Texas needed a representative on all major committees. Wright acceded to Rayburn's wishes, and the appointment allowed him to work on significant legislation—the Interstate Highway Act—in cooperation with President Dwight Eisenhower from the outset of his career. Importantly, it also enabled him to do favors for constituents, fellow Texans, and colleagues across the country.

After six years in Congress, Wright sought election to the United States Senate when Lyndon Johnson gave up his seat. In the special election of 1961, seventy-one candidates declared for the office, and Wright ran well, finishing third. But that was sufficient only to lose, and John Tower became the first Texas Republican in statewide office since Reconstruction. Wright would become a close ally of Johnson in the House, ultimately serving as the primary sponsor of Lady Bird Johnson's highway beautification bill.[7] That sealed a special relationship with Mrs. Johnson, and they often celebrated their birthdays together thereafter—she was ten years to the day Wright's senior. Wright incurred significant debt in his 1961 Senate race, and though he considered a rematch with Tower in 1966, he was unable to secure adequate funding for a statewide race.

Instead, Wright opted to build seniority in the House. President John Kennedy, in his last speech, said that with Wright's leadership, no city "is better represented in the Congress of the United States than Fort Worth."[8] And, as early as 1966, journalist Sarah McClendon speculated that Wright might be the next Speaker.

McClendon's report was ill-timed and had no real merit, but it demonstrated that Wright had been seen by some, including President Lyndon B. Johnson, as one of the future leaders in the House.[9] By 1976, *Texas Monthly* deemed Wright "a low-key, skillful technician, capable, when the need arises, of studied virtuoso showmanship." It also speculated, before Carl Albert's resignation, that Wright might attain House leadership, including majority leadership and eventually the speakership.[10]

Wright nurtured a record for innovative thinking in house politics, advocating strategies for peace with the Soviet Union, paying down the national debt, reforming campaign finance, promoting Latin American political development, and providing adequate water supplies for the Western United States.[11] Wright also wrote a well-received book, published originally in 1965 and in its third edition by 1976, about the relationship between citizens and their government.[12]

One of the House's strongest orators, Wright represented the center of the party ideologically. He served as deputy whip, appointed to the post by Tip O'Neill at the request of Speaker John McCormack.[13] His job was "persuading Southern Democrats to support the leadership" and "providing ideological balance to the leadership team."[14]

In 1976, when Carl Albert announced his retirement as Speaker of the House, making Tip O'Neill heir apparent as Speaker, the office of majority leader became vacant. In the past, the logical next majority leader would have been the majority whip, but in 1976, Whip John McFall was burdened by his role in the "Koreagate

*Jim Wright campaign poster from the 1961 special election that occurred when Lyndon Johnson
left the Senate to become vice president. John Tower won the election.
Jim Wright Collection, Texas Christian University, Fort Worth, Texas. Used by permission.*

Jim Wright with his old political ally, Lyndon Johnson.
Jim Wright Collection, Texas Christian University, Fort Worth, Texas. Used by permission.

Top: *Jim Wright would soon not smile in the presence of Phil Gramm who he came to believe betrayed him in reporting Democratic Budget Committee strategy to the Reagan administration. Wright had made a special effort to get Gramm on the Budget Committee. Gramm later changed parties and became a Republican. Jim Wright Collection, Texas Christian University, Fort Worth, Texas. Used by permission.*
Above: *Jim Wright attempts to lure his fellow Democrats to support him for majority leader. Etta Hulme cartoon from the* Fort Worth Star-Telegram. *Used by permission.*

scandal."[15] As a result, in addition to McFall, two other strong candidates emerged—liberal icon Phil Burton of California and resident House intellectual Richard Bolling of Missouri. When Wright entered the contest, it became a titanic struggle. In the four-way race, Wright staked out the ideological center of the Democratic Party and eventually defeated Phil Burton by one vote.[16]

Wright served as majority leader for ten years, working well in tandem with Tip O'Neill. O'Neill stepped down from the speakership when he did in part because he felt that Wright deserved a chance to be Speaker. Wright worked relatively well with President Jimmy Carter—he openly used their shared Southern heritage to his advantage. After all, he claimed, neither one spoke with an accent. He felt that Carter was too inflexible with Congress and that Carter's moralizing about the "pork barrel" could be a barrier to effective leadership. At one point, when they clashed over building reservoirs in the West, which Wright favored and Carter saw as boondoggles, Wright said in frustration, "Every time I see Carter he makes me feel like a political whore."[17] But if he occasionally differed with Carter, his difficulty in working with Ronald Reagan was even more profound. For six years, Reagan's leadership frustrated Democratic leaders in Congress, and their hopes for progressive reform were often stymied. Wright did occasionally flash a sense of humor in his relationship with Reagan. Once, when Reagan came to the Capitol to deliver his State of the Union address, Wright told the president that the teleprompter was not working and that he would have to improvise. Reagan immediately looked dismayed, and Wright couldn't go on with the joke. He told the president that he was just kidding, and Reagan went on to deliver his usual masterful speech.[18]

With Tip O'Neill's retirement as Speaker, Wright took office on January 7, 1987. Wright immediately sought to make Congress more vigorous, and he centralized party control over the Steering and Policy, Rules, and Budget Committees.[19] Though his leadership caused some to chafe as he tried to maintain party control, the years of his speakership were quite successful. Wright enhanced congressional authority over foreign policy, successfully building relationships with Soviet Premier Mikhail Gorbachev and Central American leaders.

Soon into his tenure as Speaker, he became the target of an ethics investigation led by Republican Representative Newt Gingrich of Georgia. Eventually, a number of ethics charges came forward and Wright became embroiled in controversy. The charges all had to do with two issues: Wright's publishing and sales of a book called *Reflections of a Public Man*,[20] and his business relationship with George Mallick, a Texas developer. The charges essentially were that Wright had sold his books in bulk to

Jim Wright's speech to the House of Representatives when he resigned the speakership.
Jim Wright Collection, Texas Christian University, Fort Worth, Texas. Used by permission.

interest groups to circumvent ethics rules banning speaker's fees. Wright argued that those charges were false, and that even had they been true, they would have fallen under the letter of House ethics rules that allowed earned royalties to be claimed by members of Congress. Investigators charged that he did not have a real business relationship with Mallick, and that their co-owned Malightco enterprise was a front for Mallick giving special gifts to Wright and his second wife Betty (he and Mab had divorced in 1970) in violation of House rules. Wright argued that the business relationship was real.[21] The ethics controversy soon became part of a "feeding frenzy" in Washington among media, and many of Wright's colleagues refrained from supporting him. The feeding frenzy had, months earlier, resulted in John Tower's defeat as a nominee for Defense Secretary, and Republicans saw Jim Wright's resignation as a perfect symmetry. Rather than getting an "eye for an eye" in retribution for Tower, they got a "Texan for a Texan."[22] Gingrich himself, having started the process moving, admitted that the ethics investigation against Wright was "never about ethics; it was always about power."[23]

In August of 1989, Wright resigned his congressional seat after thirty-five years. His resignation speech was masterful, befitting his oratory ability and his love of the House. He admitted that he had made mistakes, while vigorously denying any ethical wrongdoing. But he hoped that his resignation could serve as good faith payment for ending the "mindless cannibalism" that had characterized the last few years. He stepped down with grace.[24]

After retiring from Congress, Wright moved back to Fort Worth, his hometown. There, he taught a course in political science entitled "Congress and the Presidents" at Texas Christian University where he had an office stocked with furniture from his Speaker's office, and wrote columns for the *Fort Worth Star-Telegram*. He survived two major cancer surgeries, and continues to reside in Fort Worth.

19

Ralph W. Yarborough

US Senator 1957-1971

THE YARBOROUGH FAMILY hailed from the East Texas town of Chandler, in Henderson County. There, on June 8, 1903, Ralph Webster Yarborough was born as the seventh son of Charles Richard (C. R.) Yarborough and Nannie Spear Yarborough. Ralph's early years on the family farm instilled in him values that sustained him throughout his political career, a career in which he became known as "the patron saint of Texas liberals."[1]

The Yarboroughs were successful small farmers and ranchers, and Ralph's father had a large influence on him. C. R. served in several local offices, including mayor and justice of the peace.[2]

After graduating from Tyler High School as salutatorian, Ralph was admitted to West Point, where he studied only a year before returning home. Following a brief stint working at a flourmill in Enid, Oklahoma, he attended Sam Houston State Teacher's College for one semester, then traveled to Europe where he proofread letters for a Berlin newspaper. He soon returned home, however, for the same reason he left West Point—he missed Texas. He worked for a short time as a teacher, then enrolled in The University of Texas Law School in Austin, graduating with highest honors.[3]

Following admission to the Texas Bar, he married longtime sweetheart Opal Warren. "Next to being born," he said "that was really the most important event in my life." They had one son. At first, Opal claimed that she "didn't want a man in politics," but she gradually became his biggest supporter.[4]

His first job took them to El Paso, but he soon got an opportunity to work for the attorney general in Austin, and Yarborough made the move that resulted in his

Ralph Yarborough at the microphones and enjoying every minute of it.
From the collection at the Lyndon Baines Johnson Library, Austin, Texas.

lifelong friendship with Attorney General James Allred and an introduction to Texas Democratic politics.

Yarborough's reputation as a liberal reformer began during his four-year stint as assistant attorney general. During this time, he won a record million-dollar judgment in the Yates Oil field case and took on the Magnolia Oil Company, preserving the oil field rights for the Permanent School Fund in Texas.[5] These disputes helped him earn a reputation as a tenacious lawyer and a "man of the people." By 1935, Yarborough had left the attorney general's office and briefly entered into private practice before Allred appointed him to the Lower Colorado River Authority (LCRA), a position from which he embarked on his political career. During this time, he met Lyndon Johnson, then director of the National Youth Administration (NYA). The two men and their organizations cooperated in finding jobs for youth.

Yarborough resigned from the LCRA when Allred, now governor, appointed him to an unexpired term as judge in the 53rd Judicial District in Travis County. At thirty-two, Yarborough was one of the youngest men on the Texas bench. The first litigation he presided over was a gas case in which he overturned the jury's verdict and in doing so, showed that he was willing to take political risks and was always unafraid to stand up to the oil companies.[6]

Yarborough's first political campaign was for election to a full term in this judgeship, a battle he won on July 25, 1936. He focused on the fact that he was "a man who had to earn his own way" in politics, spoke in churches and schools, shook hands in the street, and developed a skill for remembering people's names. Yarborough was always more comfortable with a personal campaign style than he was with modern media-based campaigns, a preference that served him well through much of his career, but would be a part of his downfall at the end of it.

Soon after that victory, Allred promoted him to the position of presiding judge of the 3rd Judicial District in Texas. Yarborough used his new position to apply his liberal touch, including dismissing a few cases against blacks in a state still dominated by Jim Crow laws.[7] In 1938, Yarborough ran for Texas attorney general. He campaigned as the "people's lawyer," and in spite of a lack of funds, Yarborough believed he would win with hard work, thoughtful discussion of issues, and personal attention to voters. He placed third in the primary, but garnered 220,000 votes and statewide name recognition. Following his loss, Yarborough returned to his judgeship, but entered private practice in 1940, awaiting new political opportunities.[8]

Instead, the winds of war came and, at the age of thirty-eight, he served in the Army Judge Advocate General's office.[9] Yarborough went to Europe and witnessed the capture of the concentration camp at Flossenburg in the Bavarian forests, where the vision of "dead bodies stacked like cords of wood" left a lasting impression. After the war in Europe ended, and following the bombings of Hiroshima and Nagasaki, Yarborough became military governor of the Honshu Province in Japan, making his Ninety-seventh Infantry the only unit to have active duty in both the Atlantic and Pacific theaters. Having served under generals Dwight Eisenhower,

George Patton, and Douglas MacArthur, Yarborough returned home as a lieutenant colonel with a Bronze Star and a Combat Medal.[10]

After the war, Yarborough returned to private practice, aligning himself with the progressive wing of the Democratic Party in one-party Texas, where the winner of the party primary was guaranteed election in the fall general election. In that role, he campaigned for governor in 1952 and 1954 against conservative Governor Allan Shivers, and in 1956 against conservative US Senator Price Daniel, who wished to come home and serve as governor. These were harsh campaigns in which Yarborough railed against the big money interests and "political machine" in Texas, and his opponents accused him of being soft on communism and for unbridled labor unionism. True to his nature, Yarborough ran a grassroots campaign, frequently giving as many as twenty speeches per day, often at local gas stations and feed stores. His infectious grin earned him the nickname of "Smilin' Ralph."[11] Though his insurgent campaigns won an enthusiastic liberal following, the Democratic Party remained an entrenched conservative organization. Yarborough lost all three campaigns, but his followers were growing in numbers, and he was finding a support base among small factory and industrial workers, along with other blue-collar professions. After these three high-profile losses, many believed that Yarborough would retire from public life, but when Daniel resigned his Senate seat to assume the governorship, Yarborough stepped into the special election for that position.[12]

After nearly five years of uninterrupted campaigning, Yarborough had developed a political coalition and won with a plurality of 38 percent of the vote in a field of twenty-two candidates. One reporter noted that at the celebration following Yarborough's election, "there wasn't a big shot down there, it was just people." Just how Yarborough wanted it.[13]

On April 29, 1957, Yarborough entered the Senate, and Majority Leader Lyndon Johnson appointed him to the Interstate and Foreign Commerce, Government Operations, and Post Office and Civil Service committees. Yarborough immediately waded into the big issue of 1957, the passage of the first civil rights act since the Civil War. Both Yarborough and Johnson rejected the Southern Manifesto, a document signed by congressmen and senators in the South pledging resistance to integration of public schools. With Johnson's leadership, Yarborough and LBJ supported the Civil Rights Act of 1957, a bill that set the stage for rapid progress toward achieving equality in America.[14]

In 1958, when the regular Senate term expired, Yarborough defeated conservative oilman William Blakely, who ran with the backing of Shivers and Daniel. Yarborough countered with his famous campaign theme, "Put the jam on the lower

SENIOR SENATOR FROM SAXET

THIMK NEGATIVE

RALPH YARBOROUGH

Cartoon depicting Ralph Yarborough as out of step with Texas conservatives. Yarborough was often the target of criticism because of his outspoken liberalism. Harold Maples cartoon in the Fort Worth Star-Telegram. *Used by permission.*

shelf so the little man can reach it." Yarborough won the primary and general elections, taking the oath of office from his father, who made his son promise to "do a good job."[15]

Following the 1958 elections, Yarborough became chair of two subcommittees: the Civil Service Subcommittee and the Veterans Affairs Subcommittee. Yarborough pursued a number of other goals. He sponsored successful legislation, passed in 1962, to create the Padre Island National Seashore, which ultimately protected the barrier islands extending from Corpus Christi to the mouth of the Rio Grande. He later worked to establish the Guadalupe Mountains National Park in 1966. He also worked to pass the Cold War GI Bill.

As the presidential election of 1960 drew near, Lyndon Johnson vied for the

Democratic nomination. Though unsuccessful in his bid for the presidency, Johnson ran for vice president on the Kennedy ticket. With the Kennedy/Johnson team's election, Yarborough became the senior Texas senator.[16]

During the Kennedy presidency, the conflict between conservatives and liberals among Texas Democrats came to a head, with Governor John Connally and Yarborough as the leaders of the two camps. Kennedy came to Texas at least in part to help calm that conflict, and on November 22, 1963, he was mortally wounded while riding in a parade in Dallas. A published photograph taken shortly after the announcement of the president's death showed Yarborough, who had been riding behind Kennedy in the motorcade, with tears streaming down his face.[17]

Following the assassination, Johnson and Yarborough attempted to put aside what had become a personal feud for the sake of the nation. On Election Day in 1964, Yarborough easily won reelection. Since Yarborough had supported the Civil Rights Act of 1964, as he had every civil rights bill since 1957, and had the backing of George Meany and organized labor, Johnson could hardly work for his defeat. In the general election of 1964, Yarborough's opponent was Republican George H. W. Bush, a Yale graduate and oil millionaire, whose father had been a US senator from Connecticut. Bush ran a conservative campaign, but the Republican Party was still a minority in Texas, and Yarborough emerged victorious, winning easily—in part on the coattails of Johnson's landslide presidential election.[18]

Yarborough supported Johnson's Great Society legislation for civil rights and education, co-sponsoring the Elementary and Secondary Education Act of 1965, Higher Education Act of 1965, Cold War GI Act of 1966, and the Bilingual Education Act of 1967. His commitment to these laws earned him the title from fellow Senator Wayne Morse of "Mr. Education in the US Senate."[19]

As the 1960s progressed, the Vietnam War took center stage. Though Yarborough had been an early supporter of the effort, by the summer of 1965 he began to question the expansion of the war, and on March 1, 1966, Yarborough publicly raised his concerns during a Senate debate. His opposition was solidified when, in 1967, he concluded that Vietnam escalation had taken priority over Johnson's Great Society programs.[20]

Yarborough returned to the new Congress in 1969 with further prestige and influence. Now the chair of the Senate Labor and Public Welfare Committee, he felt that he should begin to focus on the lagging health care in America.[21] In the 1970 Senate primaries in Texas, it was expected that Yarborough would easily beat conservative opponent Lloyd Bentsen Jr., and early polls showed Yarborough with a solid lead. Bentsen released a series of television commercials linking Yarborough to riots and violence and targeting his opposition to the Vietnam War, effectively pushing Yarborough out of the mainstream in Texas. Yarborough blamed Bentsen's subsequent victory as using a "big lie technique" in the negative advertising.[22] Yarborough ran one more campaign, hoping to unseat Republican John Tower in the Senate in 1972. But he lost to Democrat Barefoot Sanders in the primary, and his political career was over.[23]

After leaving the Senate, Yarborough revived his law practice in Austin and stayed active in public affairs. He continued his efforts to make the Big Thicket a national preserve, making speeches and pushing the appropriate legislation. Passed in 1974, it established the Big Thicket National Preserve, ironically with the able support of his successor in the Senate, Lloyd Bentsen.[24]

After Yarborough's political career, he earned many accolades. As examples, The University of Texas named him a distinguished alumnus, and Governor Ann Richards honored Ralph and Opal for their accomplishments during their ninetieth birthday celebrations at the governor's mansion. On January 27, 1996, Yarborough died in his sleep. He is buried at the state cemetery in Austin. Perhaps the most notable Texas progressive leader of the twentieth century, Yarborough helped forge the way for social welfare and equality in Texas and throughout the nation.

Henry B. González.
Portrait in collection of Dolph Briscoe Center for American History, Austin, Texas. Used by permission.

20

Henry B. González

US Representative 1961-1999

IN THE SPRING of 1957, Henry B. González filibustered in the Texas Senate against ten segregation bills designed to circumvent the Supreme Court's landmark *Brown v. Board of Education* decision. González lashed out against the bills, declaring: "I seek to register the plaintive cry, the hurt feelings, the silent, the dumb protest of the inarticulate."[1] He spoke of the need for racial equality, invoking an array of classical sources including Herodotus, the Prophet Jeremiah, and John Donne. After twenty-two hours and two minutes, the filibuster ended. But it foreshadowed González's political career: stubbornness in his causes and a strong commitment to the downtrodden and forgotten.

For thirty-seven years, "Henry B." served the 20th Congressional District of Texas, following a fiercely independent path representing the downtrodden and showing a tendency to launch into lonely crusades against perceived injustices. He became the first Texan of Mexican American descent elected to Congress but later dropped out of the Hispanic Caucus, contributing to a feud between himself and some Latinos, among a group which had once considered him a savior. Though beloved in San Antonio, he was often considered an eccentric loner in Washington, where he would deliver long-winded speeches to an empty House chamber on an endless array of topics. As chairman of the House Banking, Finance, and Urban Affairs Committee, he was propelled into the national spotlight by leading the investigation of the savings and loan scandal of the 1980s and drafting bailout legislation for the savings and loan industry González was without question one of the most interesting and colorful men in Texas political history.

Born May 3, 1916, in San Antonio, Enrique B. González was the son of parents who fled to San Antonio in 1911 after revolutionary uprisings in their native

Mexico. His father, Leonides, became managing editor of *La Prensa,* a Spanish news-paper. As a result, the González home was a frequent stopping place for Hispanic intellectuals and Henry grew up around nightly discussions of "politics, religion, literature, art, music and life in general."[2]

From an early age, Henry joined his father's political discussions. "There seemed to be more communication between Papa and Henry than between Papa and the rest of us," his brother Joaquin recalled.[3] Like many Mexican Americans of his generation, Henry faced racial abuse on a regular basis and struggled with his identity. For instance, he needed to answer for himself whether he was Mexican or American. Eventually he wholly embraced the United States while feeling strong ties to his parents' native land.

After graduating from Thomas Jefferson High School, González took pre-engineering courses at San Antonio Junior College and then transferred to The University of Texas, where he stayed a year. It was during the Great Depression, and González worked odd jobs and cleaned rooms for a living. With barely enough money to eat, González developed anemia and had to move back home. His harsh life in Austin, which was also marred by racism, would haunt him for the rest of his life. Upon his return to San Antonio, he attended and graduated from St. Mary's University School of Law, though he never completed his bar examination. In 1940, he married Bertha, and the couple had eight children.

After working in military intelligence during World War II, González became assistant juvenile probation officer of Bexar County, where he earned the reputation of being "tough, but fair."[4] As a probation officer, González witnessed how politicians affected the lives of the poor. In 1945, one in twenty San Antonio Hispanics had tuberculosis, 53 percent lived in substandard housing, and 68 percent made less than $550 a year.[5]

By 1950, González had become a popular civic leader and was poised for a run at political office. When González announced he was going to run for the Texas House of Representatives in 1950, he was immediately written off by many observers. However, because he was well known on the west side, González successfully united the Latino vote and ran a credible campaign. Underfunded (his largest contributor gave $50), González nonetheless made the runoff for the Democratic nomination to face Stanley Banks Jr., a wealthy businessman, losing by only 2,000 votes.

González's strong showing in the election enhanced his stature and popularity. In 1953, he was asked to run with the "San Antonians," a slate of candidates challenging incumbents for city council. González readily agreed, and his ability to garner west side votes helped engineer a sweep for the challengers. In office, González showed his independent streak. Rather than being the "tame Mexican" his conservative running mates expected, he opposed calls to burn "Communist-tinged" books in the library as "Hitler tactics."[6] He fought a water rate increase and sponsored a law desegregating the city's recreational facilities. This independent streak stirred passions, and he was almost shot one night walking home.[7]

In 1956, González decided to run for the Texas Senate, a difficult task because he would have to defeat incumbent Ozzie Latimer. In this election, he overcame the landslide election of Republican Dwight Eisenhower to win and become the first Hispanic elected to the state Senate. He trailed Ike by a small margin in the district and far outpaced Democratic presidential candidate Adlai Stevenson. After this, a trend began that would last González's whole career: candidates on the top of the ticket rode his coattails, not vice versa, making him the most powerful politician in San Antonio. After his death, one observer wrote, "He was regarded as slightly less powerful than God and just as easy to offend."[8] He soon earned a reputation as a staunch populist, and showed his willingness to take on lost causes by becoming the liberal challenger to popular governor Price Daniel in the 1958 Democratic primary, losing badly. During that campaign, he traveled the state in his station wagon with two mariachi guitarists, one of whom could play the guitar while holding it on his head.[9]

In 1961, González joined many Texans in trying to fill Lyndon Johnson's seat in the Senate after LBJ became vice president. Though unsuccessful in that bid, he ran for a seat in the House after President John Kennedy appointed his predecessor Paul Kilday to the Court of Military Appeals. González defeated four opponents in a special election, winning 55 percent of the vote. Never again would González face a serious challenger.

In the House, González established himself as a New Frontier liberal, holding a copy of a draft bill to abolish the poll tax during his oath of office and introducing legislation supporting a variety of liberal causes, including civil rights, education, and the minimum wage. However, on a personal level, he became known for instigating personal quarrels, fighting verbally, and occasionally even physically. In 1963, González either punched or shoved, depending on who tells the story, Ed Foreman, a Texas Republican who called him a "pinko."[10]

A similar scenario would play out in San Antonio twenty-three years later, when González unapologetically punched a man for calling him a leftist.[11] González had

First term Congressman Henry B. González beams in this photo of him standing between President John F. Kennedy and Vice President Lyndon B. Johnson. From the collection at the Lyndon Baines Johnson Library, Austin, Texas.

an aversion to the appearance of impropriety, dropping out of the Hispanic Caucus because it sponsored a fund-raiser that allowed lobbyists to purchase tickets in his name.

González was one of the first congressmen to assert the assassinations of President Kennedy and Martin Luther King Jr. were caused by conspiracies. Appointed to head the House investigation, González got into a bitter squabble with the panel's chief counsel in 1977 and fired him. The rest of the panel was appalled, and González eventually resigned.

González was also known for his lonely stands in favor of various low salience causes. Using the technique known as the Special Order, which allows representatives to speak after the day's work is done, González would make "epic-length" speeches, often late at night with only C-SPAN cameras watching, on whatever his beefs were at the time.[12] He advocated the impeachment of Ronald Reagan (first in 1983, after the president's invasion of Grenada, and then in 1987, during the Iran-Contra scandal), asserted that organized crime was involved in the murder of federal Judge John W. Wood of San Antonio (which turned out to be true, and earned the thanks of FBI Director William H. Webster "for keeping the issue alive"),[13] and warned, to an empty chamber in the early 1980s "of the impending calamity of the savings and loan business."[14]

During the 1980s, Representative Ferdinand St. Germain seemed tyrannical in ruling the House Banking, Finance, and Urban Affairs Committee, but no attempts were made to oust him from his chair because the unpredictable González was next in line. But when St. Germain lost reelection in 1988, González assumed the position and immediately showed that he was no friend of big business or the banking industry. His successful six-year stint as chair ended with the Republican takeover of Congress in 1994. He presided with a fairness that won him praise from Republican Jim Leach, who opined: "If there were such a thing as chairman-of-the-year, Henry would be uncontested winner."

González's most productive years as a legislator occurred in his third decade in Congress when he became Banking Committee chair. He helped guide the country through the 1980s savings and loan debacle and pass legislation to bail out and reform the industry. This earned him a reputation as a congressional leader rather than just an iconoclastic maverick. González launched a massive investigation of the industry, which exposed a laundry list of excesses. His efforts led to a ten-year prison sentence for financier Charles Keating, who tried to buy the influence of five senators. González trotted the "Keating Five"—Democrats Alan Cranston, Dennis

DeConcini, John Glenn, and Donald Reigle and Republican John McCain—before his committee and berated them with unremitting hostility. As chair of the subcommittee on housing, González crafted landmark legislation on one of his pet issues. In 1990, he co-sponsored the Cranston-González National Affordable Housing Act, the first major overhaul of public housing since 1974. Included in the bill was a proposal by González to help first-time homebuyers make down payments and afford mortgage rates.

When Republicans won control of Congress in 1994, González lost his chair, and younger colleagues began to challenge him for the position of ranking Democrat. His allies stuck up for him, with Representative Joseph P. Kennedy II claiming "this guy defines the Democratic Party's values." González defended himself as well, giving an impassioned speech, which drew a standing ovation, in which he avowed "I have never failed myself, and I have never failed you." González kept his post.[15]

In 1997, when González retired because of failing health, his son Charles succeeded him in office. On November 28, 2000, González died in a San Antonio hospital at the age of eighty-four.

Though González sponsored little legislation that bears his name, his legacy is more wrapped up in what he symbolized. González fought for what he believed in, even if it meant doing so alone or subjecting himself to scorn. He believed in helping the poor and downtrodden, and worked hard to serve his constituents, answering all of his letters personally and possessing the ability to call many constituents by name. Constituents felt that he would help them if he could, and he often had success. His integrity was never questioned, and he claimed: "I've walked through the mud of San Antonio politics. I walked through the mud of state politics in Austin. And for thirty years, I've walked through the mud in Washington, DC, and I still haven't gotten the tips of my shoes dirty." The smell of corruption angered him, and he fought to rid the government of it every chance he got, often challenging his colleagues, and earning the reputation, said Jim Wright, of having "as much raw physical, intellectual and moral courage as anyone I know."[16]

21

John Goodwin Tower

US Senator 1961-1985

IN 1960, the winds of change began to blow across Texas. Lyndon Johnson set these changes in motion, running for reelection to his United States Senate seat and simultaneously for vice president. When John F. Kennedy and Johnson were elected president and vice president, Johnson had to resign from the Senate. His little-known Republican opponent that fall, John Goodwin Tower, ultimately filled that seat, becoming the first Republican to be elected to statewide office in Texas since Reconstruction and becoming the father of the modern GOP in the state. Tower spent the next twenty-four years in the Senate, becoming chair of the powerful Armed Services Committee. Because of his expertise in that field, he was nominated Secretary of Defense by President George H. W. Bush in 1988. Tower's political career ended with the rejection of his nomination by the Senate, but his legacy of leadership remains.

On September 29, 1925, in Houston, Texas, John Tower was born to Dr. and Mrs. Joe Z. Tower. Joe Tower was a Methodist minister who served churches across East Texas during John's childhood. Tower graduated from Beaumont High School and joined the Navy at age seventeen to fight during World War II. He saw action in the Western Pacific, and after the war returned home to attend Southwestern University, a school affiliated with the Methodist Church, in Georgetown, Texas.[1]

Tower held several jobs after graduating, even serving as a disc jockey on a local radio station in Central Texas. In that capacity, Tower honed his rhetorical skills, learning to express himself in few words. After several years, Tower enrolled at Southern Methodist University, where he earned a master's degree in economics. He continued his education at the London School of Economics, an experience that would change and mold his career path, and leave him with solidly conservative

Senator John Tower. John Tower Collection, Southwestern University, Georgetown, Texas. Used by permission.

leanings. He enjoyed his time in London, and gained an appreciation for English haberdashery—tailored suits, collared shirts, and elegant ties became Tower's "political uniform." He became known for his dapper dress, which, on his five-foot-five-inch frame, made him an easily recognizable figure in Washington.

Tower married Lou Bullington of Wichita Falls in 1952. They had three children, Penny, Marian, and Jeanne. Divorced in 1976, Tower married Lilla Cummings the next year. They, too, divorced a decade later. When elected to the Senate in a 1961 Texas special election, Tower was a political unknown whose victory was due to a combination of events. In the fall of 1960, Tower, then a political science professor from Midwestern State University in Wichita Falls, Texas, ran as a Republican against incumbent Senate Majority Leader (and vice presidential candidate) Lyndon B. Johnson. Johnson sought both positions under a Texas law passed specifically to allow him to pursue his ambitions for national office without forfeiting his Senate seat. At the time of the election, Tower was a political novice running as the nominee of a political party that had not elected anyone to statewide office since the end of Reconstruction. Despite this handicap, Tower garnered a respectable 41 percent of the vote.[2]

When Johnson resigned his Senate seat to assume the office of vice president, the Texas special election law dictated the process for choosing Johnson's successor. Under that law, anyone could declare as a candidate for public office and appear on the ballot by paying a nominal fee. If no candidate received a majority in the special election, the top two vote-getters, regardless of political party, would compete in a runoff election. In 1961, seventy-one individuals ran for the vacant Senate seat, with Tower as the only serious Republican candidate. Tower led the field in the April 4 election with 31 percent of the vote. The six serious Democratic candidates, led by the interim senator William Blakley, split the Democratic vote. Blakley was a conservative Democrat, believed by many to be as conservative as Tower. As a result, many Democrats either voted for Tower, thinking him to be more vulnerable than Blakley in the future, or opted out of the election completely. In any case, Tower won a very close election by a margin of about 10,000 votes out of nearly 900,000 cast.[3]

Tower soon earned a reputation as a member of the "far right of the political spectrum," and with Senator Barry Goldwater of Arizona was a leader of Republican conservatism.[4] He became a popular speaker for conservative causes and received a perfect 100 rating on the conservative Americans for Constitutional Action (ACA) voting index for 1961-1962. Over his career, Tower never dropped

OFFICIAL BALLOT

№ 7687

Vote for the candidate of your choice by scratching or marking out all other names.

SPECIAL ELECTION - UNITED STATES SENATOR - APRIL 4, 1961 (UNEXPIRED TERM)

WRITE-IN

DR. G. H. ALLEN of Bexar County	MRS. WINNIE K. DERRICK of Harris County	MARY HAZEL HOUSTON of Clay County	WESLEY ROBERTS of Gaines County
JIM W. AMOS of Van Zandt County	HARRY R. DIEHL of Harris County	BEN M. JOHNSON of Harris County	D. T. (DAVE) SAMPSON of Harris County
DALE BAKER of Travis County	HARVILL O. (TENNESSEE) EATON of Webb County	GUY JOHNSON of Harris County	ERISTUS SAMS of Waller County
DR. MALI JEAN RAUCH BARRACO of Harris County	REV. JONNIE MAE ECKMAN of Washington County	MORGAN H. JOHNSON of Harris County	A. DALE (AL) SAVAGE of Harris County
TOM E. BARTON of Grayson County	PAUL F. EIX of Dallas County	C. B. (TEX) KENNEDY of Bexar County	CARL A. SCHRADE of Karnes County
R. G. BECKER of Hidalgo County	BEN H. FABER of Leon County	H. SPRINGER KNOBLAUCH of Nueces County	ALBERT ROY SMITH of Maverick County
JACOB (JAKE) BERGOLOFSKY of Wichita County	DR. H. E. FANNING of Harris County	HUGH O. LEA of Orange County	HOMER HYRIM STALAROW of Dallas County
DR. TED BISLAND of Dallas County	CHARLES OTTO FOERSTER, JR. of Hidalgo County	V. C. (BUSTER) LOGAN of Collin County	FRANK STANFORD of Hill County
WILLIAM A. (BILL) BLAKLEY of Dallas County	HAROLD FRANKLIN of Cherokee County	FRANK A. MATERA of Bexar County	JOHN B. SYPERT of Dallas County
G. E. (ED) BLEWETT of Tarrant County	GEORGE N. GALLAGHER, JR. of Harris County	MAURY MAVERICK, JR. of Bexar County	JOHN G. TOWER of Wichita County
LAWRENCE S. BOSWORTH, JR. of Harris County	RICHARD J. GAY of Harris County	BROWN McCALLUM of Travis County	MRS. MARTHA TREDWAY of Grayson County
JOYCE J. BRADSHAW of Dimmit County	VAN T. GEORGE, JR. of Bexar County	JAMES E. McKEE of Galveston County	S. S. "CHEFE" VELA of Bexar County
CHESTER D. BROOKS of Travis County	ARTHUR GLOVER of Potter County	STEVE NEMECEK of Harris County	BILL WHITTEN of Hunt County
W. L. BURLISON of Tarrant County	HENRY B. GONZALES of Bexar County	GEORGE E. NOYES of Collin County	HOYT G. WILSON of Denton County
RONALD J. BYERS of Travis County	DELBERT E. GRANDSTAFF of Brazoria County	FLOYD PAYNE of Val Verde County	HUGH WILSON of Jefferson County
JOSEPH M. CARTER of Kendall County	CURTIS E. HILL of Dallas County	CECIL D. PERKINS of Travis County	WILL WILSON of Dallas County
GEORGE A. DAVISSON of Taylor County	WILLARD PARK HOLLAND of Harris County	W. H. (BILL) POSEY of Harris County	JIM WRIGHT of Tarrant County
	JOHN N. HOPKINS of Garza County		MARCOS ZERTUCHE of Bexar County

The 1961 special election ballot for US Senate where John Tower was elected the first Republican Senator from Texas since Reconstruction.
Jim Wright and Henry B. González were among the seventy candidates in the election.
Ballot in the John Tower Collection, Southwestern University, Georgetown, Texas. Used by permission.

below 72 and averaged 89 on the ACA index.

Tower's election to the Senate made him the founder of the modern Republican Party in Texas. Paul C. Eggers, a longtime Republican activist and onetime Republican gubernatorial candidate, remembered that Tower "became the Apostle Paul of Republicans" in the Lone Star State. One follower was Houston businessman George H. W. Bush. Bush was elected to the US House in 1966 and made

John Tower replaced Lyndon Johnson in the US Senate in 1961 when Johnson became vice president. Johnson's grin when shaking Tower's hand was no doubt insincere since Tower was both a Republican and an ultra-conservative replacement for Johnson. From the John G. Tower Papers, Southwestern University, Georgetown, Texas.

unsuccessful runs for the US Senate in 1964 and 1970. Through it all, one of his most ardent supporters was Tower. Tower even took time away from the Goldwater presidential campaign in 1964 to assist Bush. While the two were never close personal friends, Tower aide Ken Towery described their relationship as "a mutual respect and a very close political bond."[5]

On the major issue of civil rights, Tower stood firmly opposed to federal

John Tower with George H.W. Bush. John Tower Collection, Southwestern University, Georgetown, Texas. Used by permission.

involvement. He supported the Texas poll tax that disenfranchised those who did not pay to vote; he voted against making the Civil Rights Commission a permanent federal agency; and he joined Southern Democrats in filibustering, then voting agains,t the 1964 Civil Rights Act. His unabashed support for Barry Goldwater included supporting the hard-line opposition to the Civil Rights Act in the 1964 Republican Party platform. He joined Strom Thurmond as a Republican leader against the Voting Rights Act of 1965 and opposed the 1968 Civil Rights Act as well. Later in his career, he came to regret these votes.[6]

Tower's long tenure in the Senate did not come easily. Texas was still a Democratic state during his reelections in 1966, 1972, and 1978: testimony to his political skill on the one hand and the circumstances of his elections on the other. In 1966, Governor John Connally or Congressman Jim Wright probably could have defeated Tower, but he trounced Attorney General Waggoner Carr, a lackluster conservative Democrat with no national government experience. His 1972 reelection over his able opponent Barefoot Sanders probably had more to do with the weak presidential candidacy of liberal Democrat George McGovern than with anything Sanders did. Finally, the 1978 race against Robert Kreuger was a very narrow win despite Tower's outspending Kreuger by more than two to one. Good fortune no doubt played some role in Tower's career, but his ability to appeal to Texas voters and to shape his messages during campaigns secured his place as a dominant force in Texas politics for a quarter of a century.[7]

Tower became one of the Senate's leading experts on military and strategic defense policy, serving on the Armed Services Committee during his last twenty years on Capitol Hill. When Ronald Reagan was elected president in 1980, Tower openly coveted the office of defense secretary and was a serious candidate for appointment. Reagan ruled Tower out in part because he thought Tower's leadership in the Senate was needed. Instead of becoming secretary of defense, Tower served as chair of the Armed Services Committee during Reagan's first term. His leadership and voting record during his career exhibited a strong support for the military and a consistent desire to increase military spending. This did not abate as President Reagan argued for a balanced federal budget. "I don't think we put balancing the budget as our number one priority," Tower said of this period. "We put national security as our number one priority."[8] Tower won accolades for his effective chairing of the committee, but as was true throughout his whole Senate career, he was not terribly popular among his colleagues. He was an effective committee chair because of his intellect and preparation, but, as one pundit wrote: "Tower is not courtly, nor particularly congenial. He does not suffer fools. He does not sway other senators by charm or humor."[9]

Tower never forgot that he was the member of a strong Texas delegation. He came to Congress at the beginning of the sixties when Sam Rayburn still served as dean of the Texas delegation, and Tower learned early in his career that party politics, while important in the major issues of the day, would not mar the unity of the Texas delegation on issues affecting Texas.

In the years immediately following his Senate service, Tower engaged in two notable activities. First, he was selected by President Reagan to head an investigation of the Iran-Contra affair. The "Tower Commission" report was generally praised as balanced and appropriately critical of Reagan's lack of administrative control during the crisis.[10] Second, Tower became a consultant to many defense contractors, investigating on their behalf the political climate for defense spending in Congress. During the period between his retirement from the Senate and his nomination for secretary of defense, Tower earned $763,777 as a consultant.[11]

After the election of George H. W. Bush in 1988, President Bush tapped Tower for secretary of defense for several reasons. First, Tower certainly qualified as an expert in the arena of defense policy. He had been a key actor in the formulation of policy concerning America's military forces from the Vietnam War to Reagan's Star Wars initiative. Second, Tower and Bush had a long history as political friends. Third, the former senator was available and clearly wanted the job. Tower denied lobbying Bush for the position, but acknowledged that during the transition period he "arranged to meet with George Bush to discuss my ideas for managing the Pentagon."[12]

Tower's nomination soon encountered opposition from several fronts: questions concerning his conservative positions on defense policy; charges of conflicts of interest; allegations of inappropriate personal behavior, including excessive drinking and indiscretions with women; and personal differences with members of the Senate. Individually and as a group, these issues posed major obstacles to Tower's confirmation in a Senate controlled by Democrats. Tower's close associations with defense contractors became an issue immediately. With his record of supporting almost all defense contractor requests for funding of new weapons systems for almost a quarter of a century, Democratic senators doubted Tower could exercise skepticism about the many projects that came forward each year, with one observer noting that "John Tower has never seen a weapons system he did not like." A more titillating set of charges arose during Armed Services Committee hearings when

If It Walks Like a Hawk and Talks Like a Hawk but It Says...

John Tower, unsuccessfully nominated for secretary of defense by President George H.W. Bush, was considered to have a war-like, hawkish, foreign policy stance. Cartoon by Jeff Danziger, published in The Christian Science Monitor. *Used by permission.*

conservative lobbyist Paul Weyrich suggested that Tower lacked the "moral character" necessary to be secretary of defense. There were two aspects to the charges—that Tower had engaged in excessive drinking and in indiscreet activities with women. Tower pledged to abstain from drinking if confirmed as defense secretary, but the pledge seemed to have no impact on wavering senators. On March 9, 1989, the Senate voted 53-47 to reject Tower's nomination as secretary of defense.[13]

Tower wrote in his memoirs that the confirmation debate degenerated into partisan squabbling marked by unfairness and hypocrisy, but that overall "There is no simple, neat answer. The explanation is obviously a composite of many different factors."[14]

Tower, along with his daughter Marian, died on April 5, 1991, when his commuter plane crashed during a trip promoting his recently published memoir. Tower had left his mark on Texas politics; he left a state with a strong and growing Republican base that he had helped mold.

22

George H. W. Bush

US Representative 1967-1971;
President US Senate 1981-1989
US President 1989-1993

GEORGE HERBERT WALKER BUSH was a member of the Texas congressional delegation for two terms in the 1960s. Had that been his only public service, his role as a member of Congress would not have been remarkable. His rise to national prominence began, interestingly, when he lost an election to the US Senate, coming in second to another emerging Texas leader, Lloyd Bentsen. After that loss came a series of increasingly important positions in national government, culminating in his election as vice president for two terms and president for one. George H. W. Bush is one of Texas's most distinguished public servants, and his service began in Congress.

Bush was not native to Texas. He was born in Massachusetts and raised in Connecticut, where he lived a privileged life. His parents, Prescott and Flora Sheldon Bush, sent him to private schools, including Phillips Andover Academy. His father was a Wall Street banker who would later serve in the United States Senate from 1952-1963. After the December 7, 1941, attack on Pearl Harbor, Bush enlisted in the Navy, joining in 1942 immediately after high school graduation. Bush was a true World War II hero, flying fifty-eight missions as the youngest aviator in the US Navy and earning numerous medals for his service in the Pacific during the Second World War.

Upon his return from the war, he married his sweetheart Barbara Pierce in 1945, and their marriage was a strong one, producing six children, including the future governor of Florida, Jeb Bush, and the future governor of Texas and forty-third

George H.W. Bush campaigning for Congress in Houston. Photograph from collection at George Bush Library, College Station, Texas. Used by permission.

president, George W. Bush. The elder Bush had been accepted to Yale University before the war, and took the opportunity to finish his education after the war. He enrolled in an accelerated program, completing his degree in two-and-a-half years. At Yale, the tall and lanky left-hander played on the baseball team.

After graduating, Bush decided to get into the oil business, and after a brief time in California, in 1949 he moved his young family to Midland, Texas, where he worked initially for Dresser Industries before forming his own oil company, in part with the financial backing of his uncle George Herbert Walker.[1] By working long hours, he made his venture a success, and by the time he moved his oil company business from Midland to Houston, Texas, in 1958, he had become a millionaire in his own right.

Not surprisingly, given his family history, politics was never far from Bush's mind, and he became chair of the Republican Party of Harris County, Texas. With the urging of party leaders, he decided to run for the United States Senate in 1964 against Ralph Yarborough. He was encouraged by the success of John Tower in the special election in 1961, but Texas was still a Democratic state. Though Ralph Yarborough was a liberal in the conservative state, his populism and attraction among "yellow dog Democrats" was strong. With Lyndon Johnson running for president against the weak campaign of Republican Barry Goldwater, Bush had selected a really poor year to challenge the incumbent. However, his race garnered the highest vote total of any Republican ever in Texas, and he gained a great deal of national attention among Republicans even though Yarborough won the election.[2]

Bush had the political bug, and ran for a congressional seat in 1966, this time successfully. He was elected to represent Texas's 7th Congressional District, replacing John Dowdy, who had decided to move to the deep East Texas 2nd District (where he would be replaced by Charlie Wilson six years later). Upon entering Congress, Bush attained a coveted position on the House Ways and Means Committee, which set tax policy. This appointment was a sign that the GOP had big plans for the handsome and engaging young congressman.

Bush established a generally conservative voting record in the House.[3] He did sponsor ethics legislation, a bilingual education initiative, and environmental legislation. His most controversial act in the House was the support of the open housing provision of the Civil Rights Act. That vote was unpopular in the still race-conscious state, but Bush faced a relatively hostile audience in his district at one point and explained his vote, placating the crowd. He remembered that evening as one of his most rewarding in politics.[4]

From the beginning of his tenure in Washington, Bush was a strong supporter of the oil business. He was outspoken in his advocacy of continuing the oil depletion allowance, allowing oil companies to exclude 27.5 percent of their profits from taxes for the depletion of their resources, though he later voted for compromise legislation that reduced the rate to 20 percent. So strong was his support for those in the same business in which he had been so successful that when Treasury Secretary David Kennedy said to a Houston audience that Bush "bled and died for the oil industry," Bush wrote a letter thanking him for the characterization which, Bush noted, "might kill me off in the *Washington Post* but it darn sure helps in Houston."[5]

Of course, the major issue in politics at that time was the Vietnam War, and Bush became a staunch supporter of Presidents Johnson and Nixon on the war. He supported the war, though like many members of Congress, he had doubts about the conduct of it. And, at a Lincoln Day dinner in Houston, he expressed support for young protestors to express their views, reminding them "we in Texas certainly can't stand to be without the right to dissent."[6]

His colleague Bob Poage thought Bush "was a nice fellow and a reasonably efficient congressman. Very frankly, I didn't look upon George as particularly outstanding. . . I knew a good many that I thought showed, probably, more ability than George did."[7] Bush had only two terms as a Republican in a House of Representatives that was dominated by Democrats and a seniority system, so his lasting mark in politics would not come from that experience. But clearly, his early ventures in politics caught the eyes of national leaders and set him on a trajectory that would lead to the highest office in the land.

In 1970, with the backing of President Richard Nixon, Bush decided to give up his house seat and undertake another run for the United States Senate, thinking the run would be a rematch with Ralph Yarborough. But fate intervened, and when Lloyd Bentsen defeated Yarborough for the Democratic nomination, Bush found himself in a battle against a Texas moderate with ties to Texas business, rather than against the gadfly populist Yarborough. Though he ran a vigorous campaign, the state was still Democratic, and Bentsen proved to be a worthy opponent who was able to secure his advantage in the election. Bentsen won handily, and Bush was crushed by the loss, thinking that it might be the end of his career.[8]

Instead, the loss proved to be the beginning of Bush's rise to national prominence. After the Senate loss, Richard Nixon and other Republican leaders found another avenue for Bush—appointive offices with ever increasingly important responsibilities as Bush grew and proved his mettle. Nixon appointed him as ambassador to

'Remind me to congratulate the administration on turning out the vote'

George H. W. Bush faces defeat in his 1970 Senate race against Lloyd Bentsen who had defeated Ralph Yarborough for the Democratic nomination for US Senate. President Nixon had offered assistance to Bush, but to no avail in the state still dominated by Democrats. C.P. Houston cartoon from the Houston Chronicle. *Used by permission.*

the United Nations in 1971, where Bush served for two years. Bush then became chairman of the Republican Party during the difficult years of Watergate, and President Gerald Ford made him envoy to China during the critical years when the United States was normalizing its relationship with that nation. Ford made him director of the Central Intelligence Agency during the last year of his presidency. When Jimmy Carter won the election of 1976 and the Republicans became the minority party, Bush became a member of the Council on Foreign Relations, serving as its head from 1977-1979.[9]

Bush organized a national campaign to seek his party's nomination for president in 1980, losing to Ronald Reagan. Reagan, however, chose Bush as his running mate, and Bush served as vice president during the two terms of the Reagan presidency. He proved a loyal vice president, and used that position as a springboard for gaining his party's nomination for president in 1988. With the full backing of Ronald Reagan, Bush secured the GOP nomination and defeated Democratic

President George H. W. Bush dining with his old political rival, Senator Lloyd Bentsen.
Photograph from collection at George Bush Library, College Station, Texas. Used by permission.

standard-bearer Michael Dukakis and his old nemesis Lloyd Bentsen, the Democrat's vice presidential nominee. For Bush, becoming president seemed a fulfillment of a destiny. His long service and varied résumé seemed perfect for the job. Taking over from Reagan proved a bit of a balancing act; Reagan had always been a popular president but was more conservative than Bush. Bush wanted to be loyal to Reagan's legacy, but to establish his leadership in the presidency in his own right as well.[10]

As president, Bush served at a momentous time. The fall of the Soviet Union and Berlin Wall led to a reformulation of foreign policy in a post-Cold War world. Bush came forward with a plan he called the "New World Order" which was tested most strongly in the Persian Gulf War. That war was the greatest accomplishment of his presidency and led to high levels of support, which made him look invulnerable for reelection in 1992.[11] The fight over affirmative action "quota" systems led to passage of the 1991 Civil Rights Act, whicht he signed, but the act demonstrated that Democrats in Congress held sway on the issue.[12] Bill Clinton and the Democrats ran a campaign in 1992 arguing that Bush was out of touch with domestic policy, and critics within the Republican Party disliked the fact that he had acquiesced to a tax increase in the face of budget deficits. He lost a three-way election to Clinton, with the upstart candidacy of Ross Perot garnering nearly 20 percent of the vote.

Since his service as president, Bush has embraced his role as senior statesman, serving in a number of roles—helping raise funds for a number of humanitarian causes, often in the company of his successor as president, Bill Clinton, and serving as the loyal father of George W. Bush during the two terms his son served. Bush showed his resiliency and love for adventure during a parachute jump on his eightieth birthday, proving that his thirst for adventure continued unabated. Clearly, the public service of George H. W. Bush was not primarily defined by his congressional service, but the two terms in Congress were where he gained a first foothold in national politics, and the years in the House started him on the path to power.

Columnist Molly Ivins loved to make fun of George Bush as not a real Texan, and Texas Governor Ann Richards once said of Bush that he was "born with a silver foot in his mouth" for his occasional gaffes. But clearly, Bush was a formidable political leader in the great Texas tradition, and was one of the founders of the modern Republican Party in the state.

Republican Congressman Bill Archer from Houston.
Photo in collection of the Dolph Briscoe Center for American History, Austin, Texas. Used by permission.

176

23

Bill Archer

US Representative 1971-2001

BORN IN 1928, Bill Archer got his start in politics in 1955 as a city council member and mayor pro tempore of Hunters Creek Village. He served as a member of the Texas House of Representatives from 1967-1971. First elected as a Democrat, he received a plum assignment on the Appropriations Committee, but quickly became unhappy with the leadership of the legislature and the liberalism of the national Democratic Party. As a result, he changed from the Democratic to the Republican Party in 1967, becoming only the second Republican in the legislature.[1]

In 1970, he ran in a hard-fought campaign for the US House of Representatives from the Houston area. This was the seat being vacated by George H. W. Bush. Bush left that congressional seat to challenge Lloyd Bentsen (unsuccessfully) for the US Senate. Archer won the election to Bush's old seat and was appointed to the Banking and Currency Committee under the chairmanship of Democrat Wright Patman, who ran the committee autocratically. Archer's goal was the Ways and Means Committee, the tax-writing committee of the House of Representatives. George H. W. Bush had served on this committee and Archer, like Bush, could provide important input to the tax-writing committee on the interests of the oil industry, and especially the oil corporate centers in Houston. Archer was soon assigned to Ways and Means.

When Archer first served as a member of the Ways and Means Committee, Wilbur Mills was chair of the committee. Mills, a conservative Democrat from Arkansas, was a master of federal tax policy and tried, when possible, to run Ways and Means with consultation and input from all committee members. The style of another Democrat who chaired Ways and Means was more autocratic and partisan.

Bill Archer (left) and George Bush (right) with friends ready to play racketball. Used by permission of Bill Archer.

Dan Rostenkowski of Illinois gave Republicans little voice in the committee's work. Archer was to claim that serving under Rostenkowski ". . . certainly was the height of frustration for me."[2] One newspaper report described Archer as suffering "for years as the leader of the Ways and Means Committee's muzzled minority" and noted that he "was often the object of former Democratic Chairman Dan Rostenkowski's gruff and public rebuffs."[3] As an example of how Rostenkowski treated Archer and the Republican minority on the committee, on one occasion when Ways and Means began drafting President Clinton's tax proposals, Archer protested an effort to close the meeting to the public. Rostenkowski cut Archer off, called a vote, and "a stone-faced Archer was left staring ahead."[4]

For most of Bill Archer's lengthy career in the House of Representatives, he was in the minority and thus had limited policy-making power. However, with

Bill Archer (right) meeting with President Ronald Reagan (left). Used by permission of Bill Archer.

Republican control of the House after the 1994 elections, he himself became chairman of the Ways and Means Committee and continued as the chair until his retirement from the House in 2001. When Archer did become chair of Ways and Means, he had a difficult time because most of the Contract with America that the Republicans had signed and based their campaigns on involved issues in his committee. Additionally, the Republicans had committed to act on the contract in 100 days. Democrats were quick to respond to Archer's efforts to move the Republican agenda through Ways and Means. Democratic Representative Pete Stark of California claimed that the Republicans were using "Nazi tactics" in pursuing their agenda. And Democrat Sam Gibbons of Florida complained that Republicans were exploiting the poor to pay for tax breaks for the rich.[5] Democrats complained that Archer was inflexible.[6]

However, in pursuing his conservative economic agenda, Archer also had to battle the leadership of his own party in the House, most notably Speaker Newt Gingrich. When Archer tried to kill a $600 million tax credit that corn growers received for producing ethanol, Gingrich stacked the conference committee with ethanol supporters. It was a rare case of Archer letting his frustrations show. He said of the conference committee, "Politics will triumph over policy."[7] Overall, Gingrich worked to restrain Archer from implementing the conservative package that he desired. Archer, on the other hand, worked to prevent Speaker Gingrich from usurping the power of the Ways and Means Committee. Their relationship was described as "strained." Once, for example, at a meeting with House Republicans, Archer angered Gingrich when he said that a tax package had fallen short of Republican goals. Claimed a person who attended the meeting, "Newt just blew up."[8] When Archer tried to repeal the alternative minimum tax, it was too conservative a policy for even his Republican colleagues, who believed Democrats would use the proposal to attack them for supporting rich constituents.[9]

He retired because the Republicans imposed term limits that would have forced him to give up his chairmanship. After being chair of the Ways and Means Committee, of course, almost every other position in the House would have been a step down for Archer. He was, however, seriously considered for the speakership in 1998 after Newt Gingrich announced his departure from that office, though Archer withdrew from consideration, claiming, "I may be the right man for the job, but the job just isn't right for me at this time in my career." Archer had concluded that the job would be so time-consuming that it would keep him from his family.[10] For many, Archer was seen as the opposite of Newt Gingrich. Archer was "soft-spoken" and "mannerly." Gingrich, on the other hand, was a "firebrand" who gave the Democrats a "target to demonize." Archer, had he wished the position, would have been a more traditional and low-profile Speaker that other Republicans would not be embarrassed by in their districts.[11] But Archer was seventy years old, rather aged to begin the new role of Speaker. His chief competitors for the job, on the other hand, tended to be more than twenty years younger. Much earlier in Archer's political career, Senator John Tower had urged him to be his replacement when Tower retired from the Senate, but long years before he seemed to have a realistic chance, Archer's single goal was to chair Ways and Means.[12]

When Archer took over as chair of the Ways and Means Committee in 1995, he was described as:

A man of method.

Mr. Archer—straight-laced conservative, college fraternity man, Korean War veteran—is a meticulous man who can recite budget figures from memory. He never carries a balance on his credit cards. He does not accept campaign contributions from political action committees. He prepares his own income taxes. . . .

He is best-known as a serious-minded legislator who is fond of talking about restoring individual initiative through the tax code. But he also works with a homeless shelter and is proudest of his success during the 1970s in freeing 40 to 50 people from behind the Iron Curtain, including legendary gymnastics coach Bela Krolyl.[13]

Archer describes himself as a "common sense, real-life conservative." He is a believer in Frontier American values of self-reliance and individual initiative, remaining a traditional Republican without running afoul of the party's growing bloc of religious conservatives. On social issues being a conservative, tough-on-crime, anti-abortion rights Catholic has helped. With few challengers, Mr. Archer has steered clear of hot-button social issues, instead focusing on constituent services and economic issues that come before his committee.[14]

Conservative Democrat Charles Stenholm may have offered the most succinct description of Archer, "You do not put him in any box but very conservative."[15]

At the end of his career, he supported President Clinton's impeachment. However, most of his work in Congress dealt with economic matters. Archer helped to enact welfare reform, tax benefits for small businesses, health insurance reforms, tax credits for adoption, higher earnings limits on social security beneficiaries, income tax cuts, and reforms of the Internal Revenue Service.[16] Unlike his friend, Majority Leader Dick Armey of Texas, he did not support a flat tax, but instead was a supporter of a national sales tax as an alternative to the income tax, though that proposal never received serious attention by the Congress.[17]

When Archer retired, he took a position with Price Waterhouse. However, one of his strong interests throughout his public life was to inform young people about government. When he was a congressman, he would bring high school students from his district to Washington to meet with policy-makers. And, when he retired, he worked with The University of Texas to create the Archer Center, where students from University of Texas schools come to Washington for a semester, take courses in Washington, and work in internships in government or with interest groups.

Bill Archer was an early congressional Republican who chafed for years under Democratic control of the House of Representatives. While very conservative, unlike Bruce Alger, he was a gentlemanly, solid, low-key, hard-working congressman who worked within the constraints of being in the minority until the Republicans gained control of the House in 1995. For the remainder of his career, he was the chair of one of the most important committees and was one of the primary architects of Republican economic policies. He bore much of the Democratic attack on Republican control of Congress in the 1990s because of his efforts to implement the economic and tax policies of the Contract with America through the Ways and Means Committee. Representing a very conservative district that was one of the richest in the United States[18] and possessed of a very conservative economic philosophy, he believed Speaker Newt Gingrich's agenda was not sufficiently fulfilling conservative goals.

24

Barbara Jordan

US Representative 1973-1979

ORMER STATE SENATOR Max Sherman wrote that when Barbara Jordan was in the Texas Senate, she was called "the voice of God."[1] It is no wonder because Jordan had the richest, most powerful speaking voice a public figure could dream of having. Her voice was compelling and mesmerizing, and captured the nation during two keynote addresses at Democratic National conventions (1976 and 1992) and with her speech during the House Judiciary Committee hearings on the impeachment of President Nixon. When those who remember Watergate recall that era, it is likely they will remember Jordan speaking to them from a television screen and telling them what James Madison said about impeachment—"A President is impeachable if he attempts to subvert the Constitution." And, they are likely to remember Jordan telling the American people, "If the impeachment provision in the Constitution of the United States will not reach the offenses charged here, then perhaps that eighteenth-century Constitution should be abandoned in a twentieth-century paper shredder."[2]

Jordan's speeches could not only be serious, they could also be quite humorous. In her 1977 Harvard commencement address, she commented, "The invitation to be here today appeared designed either to challenge or intimidate. I quote an unedited paragraph from the letter of invitation. 'We invite you to speak on whatever topic you find suitable. A number of Harvard commencement speeches have been memorable. Perhaps, the most memorable was that of Secretary of State George C. Marshall, who used the occasion to announce the Marshall plan for Europe.' A Jordan plan to create, ameliorate, or eliminate will not be announced at this time. If I think of one at anytime during the remainder of my life, I will request a return visit."[3]

Congresswoman Barbara Jordan. Photo in collection of the Dolph Briscoe Center for American History, Austin, Texas. Used by permission.

Barbara Jordan was the first black woman in the Texas Senate and the first from a Southern state in the United States House of Representatives. Born in Houston, Texas, in 1936, she grew up in the era of segregation and had little exposure to whites. It was in high school where she discovered her speaking abilities and she excelled in debate. She decided she wanted to be a lawyer and attended Texas Southern University—originally known as Texas State University for Negroes, a state university that was originally designed to perpetuate segregation by complying with the separate-but-equal requirement of *Plessy v. Ferguson*. Again, she proved a superb debater. From Texas Southern, she went to Boston University for law school. Returning to Houston after law school, she opened a law practice, initially using her parents' home for office space.[4] Like many young lawyers, she was interested in politics and began registering black voters to help elect John Kennedy to the presidency in 1960. "Enamored" is how she described her feelings about John Kennedy and she was "devastated" when Kennedy was assassinated three years later.[5] But her involvement in the 1960 presidential campaign was not a temporary thing for Jordan. In 1962 and again in 1964, she was a candidate for the Texas House of Representatives. The problem for Jordan was that in those days all of Harris County (Houston) voted for the twelve at-large state representatives seats from the county. This was before the time when judicial decisions required single-member districts where smaller districts were drawn that elected one state representative. The at-large districts made it very hard for minority candidates to win elections, and Jordan lost both of her two first campaigns. By 1966, however, that had changed and there was massive reapportionment of electoral districts in Texas. In 1966, she ran in the new state senatorial district and won with 64.8 percent of the vote, although only 52 percent of her district was African American.[6] She was the first black senator elected to the Texas legislature since 1883 and the first black woman ever.[7]

The Texas legislature was ideologically conservative, Democratic, and male. Jordan managed to work with these Texas politicians, even those best described as "good ol' boys." She was approachable and friendly and learned to work within the legislative process. Senator (and later Congressman) Charlie Wilson of Lufkin showed her acceptance into the Texas legislative ranks when Jordan became the first woman ever invited on his yearly quail hunt. Rather than being radical or angry, Jordan was someone with whom the other legislators could work.[8]

A sign of her acceptance was that President Lyndon Johnson soon invited her to a meeting at the White House to discuss fair housing legislation. Jordan claimed that she was sitting in the Cabinet Room in the White House waiting for the president and thinking to herself, "Now Lyndon Johnson probably doesn't know who I am or what I am about, and my name probably just slipped in somehow and got into that [list]." Shortly thereafter the president came into the room and said, "Barbara, what do you think?" It was Jordan's first contact with Lyndon Johnson. There were to be a number of other meetings before Johnson's death, including a Houston fund-raiser to retire debt for Senator Ralph Yarborough where Johnson asked that Jordan be the person who introduced him. She had enough access to Johnson that he took her sorority on a tour of the Johnson Ranch. And, shortly before Johnson died, she appeared on stage with him at the Civil Rights Symposium at the LBJ Library.[9] It was clear that Jordan had arrived in Texas politics.

Although she did not get along with Governor John Connally, her greatest mentor was Senator Dorsey Hardeman, one of the oldest and most conservative members of the Senate. At the end of the term, she was voted Outstanding Freshman Senator.[10]

When the state was redistricted, senators drew either two- or four-year terms. Senator Jordan had drawn a two-year slot, so she had to run again in 1968 for an additional four-year term. She easily won again. She was instrumental in passing several laws, including a Fair Employment Practices Act that created the Fair Employment Practices Commission, a workmen's compensation reform package, unemployment compensation, and a liquor-by-the-drink law. She also succeeded in opposing the creation of a city sales tax to add to state sales taxes.[11]

She was politically ambitious and a close political ally of hers, Lieutenant Governor Ben Barnes, made her vice chair of the Redistricting Committee. That assignment was important because the 1970 census created the need to redistrict the state. Significantly, Texas received an additional seat in the US House of Representatives that, due to its growth, would be in Houston. Although there were claims that she allowed her senatorial district to be redistricted so that it was no longer a black district, Jordan got a congressional district that fit her political needs. Her victory in the 1972 congressional election was assured when Lyndon Johnson attended a fund-raiser on her behalf in the month before the election. With Johnson's endorsement, she was overwhelmingly elected to the US House and she became known as Lyndon Johnson's protégée. She requested a position on the Judiciary Committee. Johnson spoke to Omar Burleson, then a congressman from Abilene and a member of the House Ways and Means Committee, which was then the Committee on Committees for Democrats in the House, as well as with Wilbur Mills, the chair of the committee, to help her get the coveted spot.[12]

The 1973 Texas delegation. Jim Wright Collection, Texas Christian University, Fort Worth, Texas. Used by permission.

The Texas delegation stood with her at her swearing-in ceremony. Congressman Jim Wright recalled that there was a realization that Jordan's swearing as a member of Congress was a historical moment for Texas, and Congressman Ray Roberts suggested to the delegation that they should all show their support by standing with her at the ceremony. Congressman Jack Brooks responded that he was concerned that if all the delegation went to the well of the House, people would not be able to see who the new member was. Jordan replied to Brooks, "I am sure everyone will know it is me who is being sworn in."[13]

Jordan's style as a congresswoman was the same as it was as a state senator. She was determined to build a good relationship with other members of Congress, especially with the Texas delegation. She maintained a warm relationship with Congressman Charles Wilson, whom she had known in the Texas legislature,[14] and her connections to Lyndon Johnson helped her immensely.

The Judiciary Committee proved to be where the action was in 1974. First, Vice President Spiro Agnew resigned, and the committee dealt with confirming Gerald Ford as vice president. The Watergate scandal kept expanding, and the Judiciary Committee began examining the possible impeachment of President Richard Nixon. Members of the Judiciary Committee gave nationally televised speeches about the possible Nixon impeachment, and Jordan, with her extraordinary oratorical ability, suddenly was on the national stage.

Jordan made herself very busy in the House, focusing specifically on expanding minority rights. Perhaps her most significant legislative efforts were in passing key amendments to the Voting Rights Act and in setting up civil rights enforcement procedures for the Office of Revenue Sharing and for the Law Enforcement Assistance Administration.[15]

Jordan had become a sought-after speaker. She overwhelmed the audience with her keynote address at the 1976 Democratic Convention. There was talk of higher offices for her. However, her third term in the House (1977-1979) proved to be her last. She had been diagnosed with multiple sclerosis, which was significantly worsening by 1979 when she moved to Austin and began teaching at the LBJ School of Public Affairs.[16] But it was not only her health that caused her retirement from politics. She became disenchanted with congressional life, saying, "I did know that in Congress one chips away, one does not make shots, one does not make bold strokes. After six years I had wearied of the little chips that I could put on a woodpile."[17]

She was ethics adviser to Governor Ann Richards during the early 1990s. In 1992, she again gave the keynote address at the Democratic National Convention. President Clinton appointed her as the chairwoman of the United States Commission on Immigration Reform in 1994.[18]

However, her illness worsened, and she died in 1996 at the age of fifty-nine. Announcing her death, a *Houston Chronicle* headline said, "A voice for justice dies." [19] She is buried near the grave of the "Father of Texas," Stephen F. Austin, on the highest hill of the Texas State Cemetery in Austin.[20] Her political career was short, but important because of her exceptional speaking skills, her ability to work with other political figures, and the fact that she broke boundaries and became a pioneer for women and African Americans.

Barbara
Jordan

Famous keynote address by Representative Barbara Jordan at the Democratic National Convention, July 12, 1976. In the speech, often listed as one of the greatest hundred political speeches in history, Jordan used her strong oratory to ask, "who then will speak for the common good?" Photograph from the collection of the Library of Congress.

Charlie Wilson being entertained by belly dancers. Photograph from the collection of the East Texas Research Center,
Stephen F. Austin State University, Nacogdoches, Texas. Used by permission.

25

Charles Wilson

US Representative 1973-1997

CHARLES NESBITT WILSON was a Texas original who left a legacy as the epitome of a hard-partying yet effective member of Congress. One of the real "characters" of his time, "Good Time" Charlie was known for his taste for women and wine (and probably stronger intoxicants) during most of his twenty-four years in Washington. He gained fame after he left office for his incredible accomplishments, most of them done in secret, regarding support of Afghanistan rebels against the Soviet Union during the 1970s and 1980s, a rebellion that presaged the collapse of the Soviet Union.

Born on June 1, 1933, in the small town of Trinity, Texas, he attended three colleges before graduating from the US Naval Academy in 1956, having been a lackluster student who received a record-breaking number of demerits. After graduation, he was a surface fleet naval lieutenant monitoring the movements of Soviet submarines and later evaluating Soviet nuclear forces. He began earning what would be a career reputation—successful at work and a bad boy at play. His commanding officer remembered: "Charlie Wilson is the best officer who ever served under me at sea and undoubtedly the worst in port."[1]

Wilson often recounted the story of how he became interested in politics, relating that when he was thirteen, his dog strayed and a neighbor fed his dog something that contained crushed glass. Wilson first reacted by dousing the offender's garden with gasoline and setting it on fire. But, more productively, when he realized that the man who had injured his dog was a member of the local city council, he took action. Using his learner's permit, Wilson drove black voters to the polls, helping to defeat the incumbent by a narrow sixteen-vote margin.[2]

Wilson began his political career with election to the Texas House of Representatives in 1961, and after three terms, election to the Texas Senate in 1966. In 1971, he defeated Republican Charles O. Brightwell to succeed long-time incumbent John Dowdy in the US House of Representatives from the Second District of Texas. He was reelected eleven times before resigning in 1997, saying the job was no longer fun.[3]

Wilson married Jerry Carter in 1973 and divorced ten years later. They had no children. During his time in Congress, Wilson developed a reputation for three things: his carousing and drinking, his commitment to the local pork barrel to assure his reelection, and his work as a deal maker on the Foreign Affairs and Appropriations committees. In the opinion of some members of Congress, this did not add up to enough to make Wilson a productive member of Congress. His colleague Bob Poage remembered Wilson as "smart in many respects and obviously attractive to a great many people," but as someone "I wouldn't want to ride the river with."[4] But not all members shared Poage's perspective. When Jim Wright was embroiled in a race to be elected majority leader in 1977, he selected Wilson to give his nominating speech. If Wilson was not seen as one of the House's hardest workers, he was among its most popular and persuasive members.

Wilson's carousing was the stuff of legends because of his well-documented tendency to share drugs in hot tubs with cover girls and beauty queens. He was a hard drinker, an alcoholic, once smashing his Lincoln into a Mazda on Washington's Key Bridge, and then fleeing the scene to escape the police. And his on-the-edge lifestyle placed him on the edge of sanction by the House Ethics Committee—for cocaine use in 1983, for writing hot checks to the House bank in 1992, and for receiving illegal personal loans from his campaign account in 1995.[5] *The New York Times* dismissed him as "the biggest party animal in Congress."[6]

But his tendency to get in trouble was tolerated by his conservative and religious East Texas constituents for a couple of reasons. First, he was disarmingly honest about his shenanigans, often telling them that "The good Lord blessed me with the world's most tolerant and forgiving constituency, and I want to thank you for that."[7] Just as importantly, he consistently delivered generously to his district. He played pork-barrel politics very well, and spent a great deal of time traveling in a tour bus from small town to small town in his district to stay in touch with the folks back home. He was especially solicitous of the lumber industry, perhaps the most important in his district, which was largely shaded by the piney forest of deep East Texas. Famously, he once finagled a transportation bill to include funding for three

Charlie Wilson visiting with an Afghan child injured by a mine. Photograph from the collection of the East Texas Research Center, Stephen F. Austin State University, Nacogdoches, Texas. Used by permission.

American airports: Chicago's O'Hare, New York's LaGuardia, and Center, Texas's, Municipal.[8]

The source of his power in Congress was his positioning on two major commit-tees: Appropriations and Foreign Affairs. While he was thought of as a lightweight by many of his colleagues, his position on those two monster committees enabled him to do favors for his colleagues. While he was not diligent in his attention to detail, he certainly was not shy about using his well-placed committee assignments to secure favors for his constituency.

Wilson's career was pretty much summed up as that of a bright man who had maintained a high, if not dignified, profile, until 2003. In that year, George Crile published a book entitled *Charlie Wilson's War*, which contained a glamorized portrayal of Wilson's playboy tendencies combined with a historically correct account of Wilson's brilliant leveraging of his position on the Defense and Appropriations Committee to funnel hundreds of millions of dollars to the Mujahideen in Afghanistan, where they gradually bled the Red Army to death and helped cause the collapse of the Soviet Union. Wilson claimed that he convinced the Afghan fighters that "Kill the Commie Cocksuckers" was the famous Texas battle cry from the Alamo.[9] It was a very sympathetic portrayal of Wilson himself, warts and all.[10]

According to the story, Wilson was drawn into the superpower confrontation, through his relationship with a glamorous Texas socialite, Joanne Herring. Herring had socialized with kings, sheikhs, and politician,s and had entertained Houston through her own television show where she expounded her conservative, anti-communist message. She introduced Wilson to Pakistan's president, Mohammed Zia ul-Haq, for whom she became a trusted adviser.

When the Soviet Union invaded Afghanistan in 1979, Herring became a strong supporter of the Mujahideen resistance, which had very limited resources to combat the Soviet military. Herring persuaded Wilson to go to Pakistan and visit the huge Afghan refugee camps and hospitals filled with injured children from the Afghan conflict. Wilson embraced the cause and sought to enhance American funding of the Afghans by the CIA in order to counter the Soviets.

Over time, the budget for the CIA in Afghanistan grew to a robust half billion dollars a year, and Wilson persuaded Saudi Arabia to contribute a like amount to what became the largest clandestine CIA operation in history. Wilson realized that Russian helicopters provided an advantage that the Afghans could not counter, and secured funding for heat-seeking shoulder-launched Stinger missiles, weapons that changed the dynamics of the war.

The Stingers allowed the Afghans to take the offensive in the war, and with the Soviet economy on the precipice of collapse, Moscow withdrew its forces. Shortly after, the Soviet Union did collapse, in part because it had expended so much of its limited resources on the losing cause in Afghanistan. Wilson, literally riding on a white horse through Afghanistan, was cheered as the conquering hero. President Zia famously gave Wilson credit for coordinating the funding of the successful war, and summed up the victory in three short words on the CBS news show *Sixty Minutes:* "Charlie did it." For his efforts, Wilson was awarded an "Honored Colleague" award, something never before presented to anyone outside the CIA.

Of course, as with all operations, there were unintended side effects of the Afghan operation. After the victory by the Afghan rebels, the nation became a gath-

*Charlie Wilson riding a jackass in a parade back in the congressional district. Photograph from the collection of the East Texas
Research Center, Stephen F. Austin State University, Nacogdoches, Texas. Used by permission.*

ering place for militant Muslims from the Middle East and beyond, most significantly Osama bin Laden and Al Qaeda, and critics suggested this was the logical
outcome of Wilson's tactics. Wilson had an answer for the criticism that he had
unwittingly helped create the center of hatred of America. He had wrangled for
continued support to rebuild Afghanistan after the war, for US investment in food,
education, and help in modernizing the nation's economy. However, his requests,
made before other committees than his, fell largely on deaf ears. Famously, he
replied: "These things happened. They were glorious and they changed the world.
And the people who deserved the credit are the ones who made the sacrifice. And
then we fucked up the endgame."[11]

Wilson's reputation was enhanced further when he regained his glamorous reputation with the release of the 2007 movie, based on *Charlie Wilson's War*. In Tom
Hanks's portrayal of him, Wilson again emerged as the dashing figure he had been
in his heyday, and his friend Joanne Herring was appealingly played by actress Julia
Roberts. Both Hanks and Roberts were Academy Award winners for previous

movies. If the book had rehabilitated his reputation, the movie glamorized it. His friend and colleague, former Speaker Jim Wright, joked that his name was not even on a branch post office, but "Charlie had a whole war named after him."

In 1997, Wilson retired to Lufkin, Texas, and two years later he married Barbara Alberstadt, a former ballerina. He worked as a lobbyist in Washington for a time, but his post-Congress career was beset with health problems. During his last years in Congress, he had come to realize that his heavy drinking was a major health issue for him, and he quit drinking altogether, admitting that he was an alcoholic. He quipped: "I still miss it every day. But I guess I drank my share, and perhaps that of several others, before I quit."[12] In 2007, he had a heart transplant. He died of cardiopulmonary arrest on February 10, 2010, his career accomplishments enhanced greatly by the reputation he had first cultivated himself, but secured by a scenario that could only be the stuff of Hollywood.

26

Phil Gramm

US Representative 1979-1985;
US Senator 1985-2002

WILLIAM PHILIP GRAMM took an important role in both Texas and the national government. Elected to Congress first as a Democrat, Gramm became increasingly uncomfortable with his party and, at a critical point in his career, became a Republican. This change foreshadowed the changing of Texas from a Democratic state to a Republican one. In Congress, Gramm took his economic training and applied it to the Reagan revolution, using his economic conservatism to promote reductions in government spending and taxes and co-sponsoring legislation intended to balance the federal budget. He became a national leader among conservatives, and left a legacy of advocacy for limited government in the United States.

Gramm came to Texas from Georgia, where he had been born on July 8, 1942, the son of Kenneth and Florence Gramm. His father was disabled soon after Gramm's birth, and the family made do with his father's veteran's pension and the money his mother scraped together as a nurse.[1] Gramm attended the University of Georgia, earning undergraduate and PhD degrees. He came to Texas as an economics professor at Texas A&M University. At A&M, Gramm met his second wife, Wendy, during her interview for an economics position there. The two were married in 1970 and have two sons. Soon, Gramm began to be interested in Texas politics, and to seek public office.

His first run came in 1976, when he challenged Lloyd Bentsen in the Democratic primary for the Senate seat Bentsen had held for one term. Gramm claimed that the well-known centrist Bentsen had moved too far to the left for Texas.

GRAMM
U.S. CONGRESS ★ DEMOCRAT

Phil Gramm changed to the Republican Party, but was first elected to the House as a Democrat.
Bumper sticker in the Guttery Collection, Poage Library, Baylor University.

However, Bentsen won the primary handily, outpolling Gramm by 63.5 percent to 28 percent.[2] While that election campaign was unsuccessful, Gramm's next opportunity came two years later when he ran to succeed long-time Representative Olin "Tiger" Teague in Texas's 6th Congressional District, a sprawling constituency that stretched almost from Dallas to Houston through Gramm's hometown of College Station. Gramm ran as a conservative Democrat and was elected, defeating future member of Congress Chet Edwards in a close primary before winning the general election.[3] Soon after his election, Gramm became active in his attempt to enact President Ronald Reagan's economic policies through a bill that bore his name, the Gramm-Latta Bill. The Reagan budget called for increases in defense spending coupled with reductions in domestic spending for discretionary and entitlement programs. Gramm had been placed on the House Budget Committee through the sponsorship of his colleague, Majority Leader Jim Wright. Gramm had agreed to voice his conservative economic ideas on the committee, but to support the Democratic budget once a bill went to the floor.[4] In 1982, soon after voting for Reagan's budget as a leader of a group then called the "Boll Weevils," the Democrats ousted him from the committee because his Democratic colleagues had considered him a "spy" in their camp.[5] Gramm's response was to resign his House seat, quit the Democratic Party, and run for reelection to his seat in a special election. In his campaign, he framed the issue to his advantage, saying that he had to choose between representing liberal Massachusetts Speaker Thomas P. O'Neill or his constituents. Gramm said, "I decided to stand with y'all," and won the special election without a runoff. He immediately became a "player" in Republican politics.[6]

In 1984, when John Tower announced his retirement from the Senate, Gramm decided to seek Tower's seat. He outpolled Congressman Ron Paul and former gubernatorial candidate Hank Grover for the Republican nomination. In the statewide election that fall, Gramm defeated Lloyd Doggett, a state enator and future member of the House. The election began Gramm's three terms in the Senate, a period during which he gained a reputation as a spokesman for the idea that market forces should drive the economy without regulation. Former Senate colleague Peter Fitzgerald remembered that Gramm was "a true dyed-in-the-wool free-market guy. He is very much a purist, an idealist, as he has a set of principles and he has never abandoned them."[7]

In the Senate, Gramm took a seat on the Budget Committee and became a ceaseless worker for balancing the federal budget. Perhaps his most important act on that committee was the co-sponsorship of the Gramm-Rudman-Hollings Amendment with his colleagues Warren Rudman and Ernest Hollings, a measure designed to force the balancing of the federal budget.

Phil
Gramm

"..I GUESS THIS MEANS Y'ALL WON'T BE BACKIN' MY BID TO STAY ON THE BUDGET COMMITTEE..."

Democratic Congressman Phil Gramm was appointed to the Budget Committee, but betrayed Democratic plans to the Reagan administration, earning the enmity of Democrats in the House including the Texas Democratic delegation that had backed him for the Budget Committee assignment.
Cartoon by Scott Willis, printed in the Dallas Times Herald. *Used by permission of the artist.*

In the late 1990s, Gramm chaired the Senate Banking, Housing, and Urban Affairs Committee and worked to deregulate banking in the United States. The most important measure to accomplish that was the Gramm-Leach-Bliley Act of 1999, a measure that ended the separation of banking, insurance, and brokerage activities. The act later would be cited as one of the causes of the mortgage industry crisis in 2008, and Gramm was listed as one of *Time Magazine's* list of the twenty-five people most responsible for the crisis.[8]

Gramm was a good public works politician. He supported Texas projects such as the Houston Space Program, the "super-conducting supercollider" project near Waxahachie, Austin's Semitech research center, and a home base naval station at Ingleside. At a policy level, though, he advocated cuts in government spending and taxes, and pressed for a balanced budget amendment.[9]

For a period in 1996, Gramm was a candidate for the US presidency. He began the race with a sizable war chest of money, and hoped to capitalize on his conservatism and to frame the issues to conform with his free-market economics. His candidacy failed in early contests, and when he was defeated in Louisiana by Pat Buchanan, his race for the White House was effectively over. He withdrew from the campaign in favor of seeking reelection to a third term in the Senate.[10]

Gramm was never a popular member of Congress, and was seen as both ambitious and acerbic in his approach to office. One writer in Texas likened his personality to that of "a snapping turtle."[11] But one cannot argue that he didn't get results. Clearly, three pieces of legislation that bore his name—the Gramm-Latta, Gramm-Rudman-Hollings, and Gramm-Leach-Bliley measures—were three of the defining economic policies passed by Congress during his time there. They left a strong imprint on US policy, and one that has led to mixed reviews since he left Congress.

Gramm announced that he would not seek reelection to the Senate in 2002, and immediately there were those who thought that the reason was his close association with Enron. His free-market philosophy had meshed nicely with Enron's views, and he had received generous support from that company.[12] But Gramm said his association with Enron during the economic crisis caused by its excesses was not the reason for his retirement. Gramm explained: "The things that drove me into politics in the late 1970s were basically a commitment to balance the budget, to cut taxes, to reform welfare, and to roll back the borders of communism." He said, "And it sounds self-serving and inflated. But not only did I work for those things, not only did I play some leadership role in each and every one of them, but remarkably, they all happened. The things I came here to do were done."[13]

*Senator Phil Gramm, Dick Armey, and Tom DeLay discuss legislation. Photograph in Richard Armey Papers,
Carl Albert Library, University of Oklahoma. Used by permission.*

After he left Capitol Hill in 2002, Gramm went to work as an investment
banker and lobbyist for UBS, a Swiss bank that was hit very hard by the economic
downturn during the 2008 mortgage crisis. Gramm remained convinced that deregulation was a good economic principle, and that there was no evidence that the legislation he sponsored had a negative impact on the banking industry.

In 2008, Gramm served for a short period as a campaign adviser for his old
colleague in the Senate, John McCain. He resigned that position when public out-
cry came from his statement that Americans wrongly looked to government for bail-
ing them out in economic hard times, calling the US "a nation of whiners."[14] He
almost immediately withdrew from his advisory role, observing that he, rather than
the issues of 2008, had become the issue.

Gramm was in many ways a transformative member of the Texas delegation.
When he came to office as a conservative Democrat, Texas was still largely a part of
the old "solid South," still dominated by "yellow dog Democrats." His switch to the

Republican Party signaled a major change in the politics of Texas, and indeed of politics nationally. Democrats, up until his time, could hold widely diverse ideological positions. In the intervening years, both parties have become more ideological in their approaches to politics and the polarization of national politics is a consequence.

27

Richard Armey

US Representative 1985-2003
(Majority Leader 1995-2003)

RICHARD ARMEY was the first Republican majority leader from Texas. Not able to advance to the speakership, Armey left Congress to become a lobbyist and then to become chairman of FreedomWorks, which has taken a major role in opposing President Barack Obama's spending policies and especially President Obama's proposed reforms of the health-care system.

Armey is an economics professor turned politician. Born in North Dakota in 1940, he graduated from high school and began climbing power poles for the Rural Electrification Administration. While atop a power pole in the middle of the night in minus 30° weather, Armey concluded it was best to attend college. He went to Jamestown College in North Dakota for his bachelor's degree, then received his master's degree from the University of North Dakota, and his PhD in economics from the University of Oklahoma. From there he taught at the University of Montana, West Texas State, Austin College, and the University of North Texas. It was at the University of North Texas that he settled in and became chairman of the Department of Economics.[1]

It is claimed that one night in 1984 Armey was watching C-SPAN with his wife and turned to her saying that the congressmen on television sounded "like a bunch of damned fools." His wife agreed and told him that he "could do that."[2] Shortly thereafter, Armey entered the 1984 congressional race in the 26th District of Texas. He ran as a Republican against incumbent Democrat Tom Vandergriff. The 1984 election was a banner year for Republicans in Texas because of the extraordinary popularity of Ronald Reagan in the state. However, Vandergriff was an incumbent and a well-known community leader, and as a result, the election was close. Armey was aided by a last-minute campaign boost from Vice President George H. W. Bush, who gave a campaign speech on his behalf the night before the election. Still, the election was so close that it was not possible for Armey to claim victory until midday on the day after the election.[3] Because of the rapid movement of Texas into the Republican column, Armey never again had serious opposition in an election—something that, no doubt, helped him immensely in his pursuit of leadership in the Republican Party in the House of Representatives.

Armey was a proponent of free-market economics and an advocate for Ronald Reagan's economic policies. However, as a new congressman he was best known for his personal thrift. Rather than get an apartment in Washington, DC, Armey first slept in the house gymnasium. After House Speaker Tip O'Neill evicted Armey from the gymnasium, Armey slept on a couch in his congressional office rather than rent an apartment. Armey received much publicity for his sleeping habits, but he claimed he did this not for any political reason, but because he was not wealthy and needed to save money since, at the time, he had four boys in college.[4]

It was early in his career that Armey began to attack government spending—first with a plan to bombard appropriations bills with amendments to cut spending and, in his second term, with a major reform of public housing. He showed an ability to work in a bipartisan fashion with legislation to close military bases that were seen as unnecessary. He also worked with Democrats to reform agricultural policies.[5]

It was, however, a challenge to a Republican president—George H. W. Bush, the man who had helped Dick Armey win his first election by a hair's breadth—that positioned Armey for leadership in the House of Representatives. President Bush had promised in his presidential campaign not to raise taxes; however, he had decided to break that promise to the dismay of Armey and many other conservative Republicans. Armey proposed a resolution opposing new taxes that was passed by the Republican Conference by a three-to-one margin. Soon Armey was the ranking Republican on the Joint Economic Committee.[6] In 1992, Armey ran for chair of the Republican Conference, won, and became a leading critic of President Bill Clinton.[7] With the 1994 elections, Republicans saw an opportunity to retake control of the House of Representatives for the first time in forty years. Public opinion polls of Congress were low, and there was immense unhappiness with the Clinton administration's health care proposals, of which Armey was a major critic.

*Dick Armey signing copies of the Republican Contract with America which was the Republican congressional campaign
platform in the 1994 election. Photograph in Richard Armey Papers, Carl Albert Library,
University of Oklahoma. Used by permission.*

Working with Republican Whip Newt Gingrich, another leader of the increasingly
influential conservative younger generation in the Republican Party, Armey wrote a
conservative agenda of limited government known as "The Contract with
America." Armey and scores of Republican House members stood on the steps of
the Capitol to introduce the contract to the American people. It was seen as a turning point for the Republican Party in the House of Representatives. With the 1994
elections, Republicans gained control of the House of Representatives, and
Democratic Speaker Tom Foley was defeated—the first time in almost 150 years
that an incumbent Speaker had been defeated for reelection.[8]

With Republican control of the House of Representatives in 1995, Richard
Armey was elected majority leader, and Newt Gingrich of Georgia was elected
Speaker. In his position, Armey worked to pass many of the promises of the
Contract with America. By 1997, however, a number of leading Republicans had

Congressman Dick Armey (left) in an in-flight meeting with President George H.W. Bush. To Armey's right is Republican Congressman Steve Bartlett of Dallas. In front of Bartlett is Clayton Williams, a wealthy businessman who was the Republican candidate for Texas governor defeated by Ann Richards. Behind Williams is Andrew Card, a Bush senior staffer. Photograph in Richard Armey Papers, Carl Albert Library, University of Oklahoma. Used by permission.

become unhappy with the leadership of Speaker Gingrich. Although Armey denied it, others claim he was part of the plot to oust Gingrich from his position by presenting him with an ultimatum that he either resign as Speaker or be removed by a formal vote. Armey backed out of the plan when he became aware that he would not be the choice to replace Gingrich. Several Republicans ridiculed Armey's denials of his involvement and his credibility suffered, although he remained majority leader.[9]

Armey later spoke of his relationship with Speaker Gingrich, saying that they had worked well together with Gingrich developing ideas and Armey handling operational matters. However, Armey stated that he and Gingrich were never close and that their relationship grew strained when he learned that Gingrich had been having an extramarital affair at the same time that President Clinton was being impeached. That may have been the final split between Armey and Gingrich. Said Armey, "He put our whole conference at risk. He wasn't just cheating on his wife. He was cheating on us too."[10]

Armey was one of the major critics of the Clinton administration and was a strong advocate of President Clinton's impeachment. President Clinton jokingly spoke of his attitude toward Armey when he spoke of Senator John Glenn's trip on the space shuttle. Said Clinton, "I met with Senator John Glenn recently to decide who should be the next distinguished member of Congress hurled into the far reaches of the universe. Godspeed, Dick Armey."[11]

Armey announced his retirement from Congress saying that he was exhausted and that family concerns influenced his decision as well.[12] He served from January 3, 1985, to January 3, 2003. Armey was majority leader from January 3, 1995, until his retirement from Congress. He became a lobbyist and chair of FreedomWorks, an organization that seeks lower taxes and greater economic freedom.

Armey was never able to achieve some of his major policy goals—perhaps the most important being the flat tax, which would be a tax with a constant rate, rather than the current progressive rate that varies with income.[13] Armey was known for his lack of diplomatic speech. When Hillary Clinton testified on behalf of her health reform bill, Armey told her that reports of her charm were overstated.[14] When answering a question about a controversial and lucrative book deal that was being criticized by Democratic Congressman Barney Frank, who is gay, Armey referred to Congressman Frank as "Barney Fag."[15] Armey later made an even more offensive comment about Congressman Frank.[16] In 2009, on a television show, he was debating President Obama's economic policies with reporter Joan Walsh and interrupted Walsh by saying, "I'm so damn glad you can never be my wife because I surely wouldn't have to listen to that prattle from you every day."[17]

In spite of these and other verbal gaffes, he played a major role in Republican economic policies during his years in Congress and especially during his years in the leadership. Now playing a major role in constructing grass-roots opposition to President Obama's policies, Armey also has reflected on why the Republican Party lost its majority in the House of Representatives in 2006. In Armey's view, prior to the rise of Newt Gingrich to the position of minority whip, the Republican leadership in the House had grown too accustomed to being in the minority and were too accommodating toward the Democrats. He and Gingrich and other Ronald

Reagan conservatives set as their goal the retaking of the House by the Republican Party. The Contract with America was their platform. Armey says the success of that aggressive strategy and that platform in the 1994 elections was why the Republicans took control of the House and the Senate—gaining fifty-four seats in the House and eight seats in the Senate. However, Armey stated that in spite of such successes as welfare reform, Republicans did not learn the right lesson. Republicans were outmaneuvered by President Clinton with the shutdown of the federal government in 1995 and, claims Armey, that was the first step on the road away from the Reagan revolution. Politics began to supersede policy and principle, and the use of earmarks to bring pork projects to congressional districts became an avalanche. Spending went out of control and huge expenditures occurred, such as the Medicare prescription drug benefit and a growth in non-defense discretionary spending that is growing twice as fast as during the Clinton administration. At the same time, notes Armey, social security is collapsing, rogue nations are going nuclear, and the Middle East problems continue. Yet, instead of focusing on these issues, Republicans have made issues of flag burning, the death of Terri Schiavo (a famous case involving the right to die), and same-sex marriage. In the view of Armey, the problem for the Republican Party is that it lost its roots as the party of limited government and Reagan era conservatism—roots planted to a great degree by Richard Armey of the 26th District of Texas.[18]

28

Tom DeLay

US Representative 1985-2006
(Majority Leader 2003-2006)

O F ALL OF THE TEXANS who have served in leadership positions in
Congress, the one with the most controversial reputation is Tom
DeLay. Elected to Congress from a suburban district near Houston,
DeLay soon established himself as a leading voice among conservatives. Rising first to the position of majority whip and then to majority leader,
DeLay was proudly partisan in his approach to politics. He masterminded a redistricting of Texas congressional districts in 2003, bringing the Republican Party and
its congressional delegation to a zenith in influence, but then found himself
embroiled in controversy and legal complications within just a couple of years. His
resignation from the House under the pall of ethics investigations reflected the partisan approach he had himself fostered.

DeLay was born on April 8, 1947, in Laredo, Texas. His father was an oil and
gas man, and the family spent many of DeLay's formative years in Venezuela before
returning to Texas where DeLay graduated from high school in Corpus Christi.[1] He
attended Baylor University for two years, and earned a reputation as a prankster—
ending his time on the Waco campus with an expulsion for painting a building on
the Texas A&M campus Baylor green. He finished his undergraduate career at the
University of Houston, receiving a biology degree in 1970. In 1972, he and his
wife, the former Christine Furrh, had a daughter, Danielle, who grew up to be a
professional dancer.

Upon graduation, DeLay began his career in the pest control industry. He first
worked for a pesticide manufacturer and then bought an extermination business
that he built into a successful operation. While he was in business, DeLay began to

harbor a distrust for government decision-makers, having difficulty with the Internal Revenue Service over issues of failure to pay payroll and income taxes, and with the Environmental Protection Agency for the use of a banned pesticide. These conflicts helped form DeLay's views that government should be less intrusive in American life.

In 1978, DeLay ran successfully for the Texas House of Representatives, the first Republican to represent Fort Bend County in the fledgling days of Republican success in Texas. In Austin, he became known as a hard-partying member of the House, and earned the nickname "Hot Tub Tom."[2]

By 1984, he ran successfully for Congress, replacing Ron Paul in the chamber when Paul sought the presidency as the Libertarian nominee for that position. DeLay's reputation for partying only grew, and by his early congressional service, he was drinking "eight, ten, twelve martinis a night at receptions and fundraisers." He soon realized that his habits were making life spin out of control and became a born-again Christian, giving up hard liquor and refocusing his life. By 1985, his conviction that government was too large, along with his conservative Christian theology, made him a natural for the rising power of the "new right" in Congress. He became a major critic of the National Endowment for the Arts and the Environmental Protection Agency, among other government entities.

When the Republican Party took control of the House in 1994, ending nearly forty consecutive years of control by the Democrats, DeLay was in position to take a leadership role. His passionate conservatism and aggressive style meshed well with a new majority intent on making major changes in the nation's through their Contract with America. He was elected third in command in the new Congress, the majority whip. Though DeLay was not the first choice of his two superiors in the House—Speaker Newt Gingrich and fellow Texan and Majority Leader Dick Armey, he became an effective leader, earning a reputation as a very tough taskmaster for the conservative agenda. He did not always get along well with Armey and Gingrich, and at one point in 1997 he and a group of Republicans tried unsuccessfully to oust Gingrich as Speaker.[3] His hard-line tactics led to his nickname, "The Hammer," a moniker that DeLay relished. One classic example of his strident leadership was the role he took in ushering the impeachment of President Bill Clinton in the House. He first called for Clinton's resignation, but then led the crusade for Clinton's impeachment.

Speaker Newt Gingrich resigned from Congress soon after the elections of 1998, when the GOP lost ground in part because of the unpopularity of the impeachment of Clinton, and DeLay looked to be in line for election to a higher post in the House, perhaps even the speakership. But DeLay realized that his strident partisanship had alienated a number of members within the Republican Party and had made it difficult for him to work with Democrats across the aisle, so he sponsored the election of Dennis Hastert—a low-profile moderate who was well-liked by members of both political parties—as Speaker, and he retained the position of whip. But DeLay was widely seen as the power behind the throne in Congress, and as the most powerful Republican in the House.

DeLay was consistently among the most conservative members of the US House, opposing tax increases, government regulation of business, labor unions, environmental regulation, and gun control. He referred to the Environmental Protection Agency as the "Gestapo of Government." He favored restrictive immigration laws and was rigidly pro-life on abortion policy. In foreign policy, DeLay was strongly anti-Fidel Castro with regard to Cuba and pro-Israel in Middle East politics. In 2005, he sponsored congressional action to intervene in the case of Terry Schiavo, a woman in a persistent comatose state whose husband and parents were locked in a struggle over whether her life support should be removed. DeLay's intervention to require life support to be continued was, in his words, "one of my proudest moments in Congress."[4] Altogether, he consistently was among the members of Congress with "perfect" conservative scores of zero from the liberal Americans for Democratic Action group.[5]

Dick Armey's resignation from the House in 2003 allowed DeLay to move up the ladder to become majority leader, and he had visions of a dominant Republican majority reminiscent of the Democratic era that had preceded the 1994 Republican takeover. Accordingly, DeLay became active in fundraising for the Republican Congressional Committee and began to seek ways to use redistricting as a mechanism for increasing GOP power. He took the redistricting fight home to Texas, arguing that a Republican-dominated state with a majority of Democrats in the congressional delegation was unfair.

The fight to redistrict Texas actually began in 2001, when DeLay tried to make certain that a Republican majority could be elected in the Texas legislature. Among other issues, DeLay felt that new party control would allow redistricting the congressional lines in Texas. A Washington-based public interest group called "Democracy 21" collected data showing that to accomplish his objective, DeLay was able to raise $12.6 million dollars for the 2002 elections. He did so through a group of political action committees, each with slightly different objectives, so that the same contributors could give to multiple committees—PACs that included "Americans for a Republican Majority," "Texans for a Republican Majority,"

Cartoon about the pro-Republican redistricting orchestrated by Tom DeLay in 2003.
Gary Oliver cartoon from the Big Bend Sentinel. *Used by permission.*

"Republican Majority Issues Committee," and "DeLay for Congress."[6]

With the Republicans in control in the Texas legislature, DeLay then worked hard to pass a major redistricting plan that would "blow up" the districts of a number of Democratic incumbents so that they would not have the incumbent advantage in the elections of 2004. DeLay's explanation was direct: "I'm the majority leader, and we want more seats."[7]

As negotiations came to a head during the summer of 2003, DeLay brokered a deal between agricultural and oil Republicans, groups that were at odds regarding the redistricting plans in West Texas, to pass the new plan. Though it is highly unusual for a member of the US House of Representatives to be involved directly in the writing of a state legislative bill, DeLay's involvement marked the turning point in negotiations.[8] In the fall of 2004, as a consequence of the redistricting, the Republican Party picked up six seats in the Texas delegation, going from a 17-15 deficit to a 21-11 majority.

It turned out that the redistricting was the high point of DeLay's career. After that, a series of legal and ethical issues overtook him. On September 30, 2004, the House Ethics Committee unanimously admonished DeLay for endorsing Representative Nick Smith's son to succeed him in office in exchange for Representative Smith's vote in favor of a Medicare bill, and for misusing the Federal Aviation Administration in an attempt to locate Democratic legislators who had fled from Austin to avoid voting during the redistricting fight in the Texas legislature.[9]

On October 3, 2005, a Texas grand jury indicted Delay on a felony, charging that he moved $190,000 in corporate donations to Republican candidates in the state legislature in 2002 against state law.[10] DeLay was convicted on these charges by an Austin jury on November 24, 2010, although he avowed his innocence and promised to appeal his conviction. DeLay charged that his conviction was nothing more than "the criminalization of politics." However, the prosecutor, Rosemary

Tom DeLay (far left) watching as President George W. Bush signs legislation.
Photograph from the George W. Bush Library collection.

Lehmberg, convinced the jury that the charges were not politically motivated and were about "holding public officials accountable" and demonstrating that "no one is above the law."[11] On January 10, 2011, Judge Pat Priest rejected arguments that DeLay's conviction was a political vendetta by the Austin district attorney and sentenced him to three years in prison. DeLay vowed to appeal.[12]

In 2006, DeLay suffered from his close association with Jack Abramoff, a corrupt Washington lobbyist. DeLay had a close relationship with Abramoff, receiving gifts, including paid golfing holidays to Scotland and a number of concert tickets.[13] Additionally, two of DeLay's former political aides and Abramoff himself pleaded guilty in 2006 to charges relating to an influence-peddling scandal, though charges against DeLay were eventually dropped in August of 2010.[14]

As the ethics and legal charges mounted, Delay found it to be necessary to step down as majority leader.[15] Then, DeLay resigned from the House on April 4, 2006, when it looked increasingly unlikely that he could be reelected that fall. Ironically, he was not allowed to take his name off the ballot as the Republican nominee for the district, and Nick Lampson, one of the Democrats who had lost his seat to DeLay's redistricting in 2004, was elected to replace him (though Lampson's tenure proved to be limited to only one term).

After his resignation from the House, DeLay continued to support conservative causes. He has remained committed to quality foster care, including sponsorship of a "Christ-centered" foster community called Rio Bend in Richmond, Texas. He has continued a schedule of public speaking and fund-raising for conservative political causes and has founded a political consulting firm called First Principles, LLC.[16] He wrote a political memoir, befitting his well-earned reputation as a pugnacious politician, entitled *No Retreat, No Surrender: One American's Fight,* coauthored with Stephen Mansfield.[17] In it he vigorously defended himself against the legal charges he faced, and compared his opponents to Nazis: "I believe it was Adolf Hitler who first acknowledged that the big lie is more effective than the little lie, because the big lie is so audacious, such an astonishing immorality, that people have a hard time believing anyone would say it if it wasn't true. You know, the big lie—like the Holocaust never happened or dark-skinned people are less intelligent than light-skinned people. Well, by charging this big lie liberals have finally joined the ranks of scoundrels like Hitler."

In 2009, he came back into the public sphere in a light-hearted way. Following his daughter's profession of dancing, DeLay agreed to join in the made-for-television competition *Dancing with the Stars.* Though he eventually dropped out of the competition because of injury, he placed himself back in the public sphere and demonstrated he was still willing to take on opponents—whether on the dance floor or in the public arena.

Tom DeLay

Long before her distinguished career as a US senator, Kay Bailey Hutchison was a Texas cheerleader. She is the second to the right on the front row. Photo in collection of the Dolph Briscoe Center for American History, Austin, Texas. Used by permission.

29

Kay Bailey Hutchison

US Senator 1993-

ORN IN 1943, Kay Bailey Hutchison has been a successful political figure in Texas for over thirty years. She is the first woman from Texas to be a United States senator and is one of the most popular elected officials in Texas. Hutchison grew up in La Marque, Texas, attended The University of Texas and The University of Texas Law School, graduating in 1967 as one of only seven women in her class. Unable to find a job as a lawyer in Houston because of discrimination against women in the legal profession, she went to work for a television station where she covered local politics. She was the first female television reporter on the air in Texas.[1]

One of her news assignments was to interview Anne Armstrong, who was co-chair of the Republican National Committee, and soon after, Armstrong hired Hutchison as her press secretary. Armstrong was to become her lifelong friend and supporter. She served as the chair of all of Hutchison's political campaigns. Until Armstrong's death in 2008, Hutchison never made a major decision without consulting her.[2]

In 1972, at the age of twenty-nine, Hutchison ran and won a seat in the Texas House of Representatives where she served two terms. Hutchison was the first Republican woman elected to the Texas legislature. It was while she was in the Texas legislature that she met her future husband, Ray Hutchison, who also was serving in the legislature and was then the Texas Republican Party Chair.[3]

In 1976, Hutchison was appointed by President Gerald Ford to the National Transportation Safety Board where she served for two years. In 1978, she moved to Dallas and married Ray Hutchison. She then ran for the US House of Representatives in 1982, but lost that election to Steve Bartlett who later was to serve as mayor of Dallas. In private life in Dallas, she worked as the senior vice president and general counsel of Republic Bank. She cofounded Fidelity National Bank and owned McCraw Candies.[4]

In 1990, she re-entered electoral politics with a campaign for the office of State Treasurer. Democrat Ann Richards had held that position, but successfully ran for governor and Hutchison took advantage of the open seat to successfully run for that office.

In 1993, President Bill Clinton appointed the US senator from Texas, Lloyd Bentsen, to be secretary of the treasury. Robert Kreuger was appointed by Governor Richards to replace Bentsen, and then he ran against Hutchison (and numerous other candidates) in a special election. Kreuger, a former English professor and university administrator, had previously been an unsuccessful senatorial candidate, running in a close election against Republican Senator John Tower in 1978. He had then been named US Ambassador-at-Large and coordinator of Mexican affairs by President Carter. Running again for the US Senate in 1984, he failed to make the Democratic primary runoff. He had been elected to the US House of Representatives in 1974 and reelected in 1976. On paper, Kreuger seemed a formidable candidate. However, he only got 29 percent of the vote in the special election. Hutchison actually got ninety-nine votes more than Kreuger, but neither of them was close to a majority and so a runoff election was required. In that election, Hutchison overwhelmed Kreuger, getting 67.3 percent of the vote. This special election was to fill the remainder of Lloyd Bentsen's term; but then Hutchison had to run for a full term in 1994.[5] It was in the period between her election in the special election and the 1994 election that Hutchison faced her greatest political crisis. No Texas senator had ever been indicted while in office, but the Travis County district attorney began a felony investigation of Hutchison. Essentially, there were allegations that as state treasurer, Hutchison had used state resources and state employees for personal and political use and then had tried to remove the evidence. Hutchison insisted that, "This is clearly political and designed to bring me down. We've been totally honest. The people of Texas understand this is political."[6] Hutchison was acquitted when prosecutors would not go forward with their case after the judge ruled against the admissibility of evidence the prosecution considered crucial to their case. The judge then ordered jurors to find the senator not guilty of the four felony charges and one misdemeanor. The vindicated Hutchison spoke of the trial, "I stood and fought because I knew that I had done nothing

Kay Bailey Hutchison was the first woman elected to the US Senate from Texas.
Campaign flyer in the Guttery Collection, Poage Library, Baylor University.

wrong. I fought because I knew the charges were political . . . and I fought because I knew there was only one way to keep this from ever happening again to someone who goes against the political insiders like I did."[7] Her acquittal seemed to make her defeat in the 1994 general election an impossible task. The winner of the Democratic primary and primary runoff was Richard Fisher. Fisher had run in the 1993 special election and had finished fifth among the twenty-four candidates. A wealthy financier and advisor to Ross Perot, Fisher had defeated US Representative Mike Andrews and Attorney General Jim Mattox for the Democratic nomination. With Hutchison's acquittal, Fisher's chances were hopeless. Hutchison won the election with 60.8 percent of the vote. From then on, Hutchison faced no serious reelection threat. In 2000, she won the election against Democrat Gene Kelly, a perpetual candidate whose main strength was a name shared with a well-known movie star. Hutchison garnered 65 percent of the votes. And, in 2006, Hutchison got 61.7 percent of the vote against Barbara Radnofsky, an obscure candidate who was far from the highly visible opponents that Hutchison had attracted in 1993 and 1994.[8]

Like Price Daniel before her, Hutchison grew tired of Washington—though it took her far longer than it did Daniel. Her goal in 2010 was to return to Texas as its governor. The problem for her was that Governor Rick Perry had no interest in yielding the office. The result shaped up to be a major Republican primary fight. Perry maintained popularity among the most conservative and dominant wing of the party, and the race developed into a battle over who could claim the most conservative credentials. Interestingly, Texas has become such a conservative state that the battle for control of the state's executive branch was within the Republican Party. No Democratic candidate could mount a serious challenge for the office in that election season.

Hutchison's lengthy political career meant that she had a record to attack, and there are two matters that have long caused concern with conservative Republicans in Texas. One is that in 1976, she and her husband supported Gerald Ford for president against Ronald Reagan, who unsuccessfully challenged Ford for the Republican nomination. Reagan, of course, has become a Republican hero and the criticism of being a Ford supporter has haunted Hutchison. Indeed, supporting Ford in 1976 may be one reason that Ray Hutchison lost his try for the governorship in 1978. Additionally, although Kay Bailey Hutchison has voted to curtail the funding and the availability of abortion, to make fetuses eligible for healthcare coverage, and to make it a crime for anyone other than a parent to accompany a minor to an out-of-state abortion provider, Hutchison believes that abortion should remain legal with some limits. Pro-life advocates cannot forgive her for that viewpoint. As John Gizzi, the political editor of *Human Events,* a conservative magazine, has said, "Overall, she's very conservative, but she is pro-choice. She would never overturn *Roe v. Wade.*"[9]

Her voting behavior in the Senate does indicate a very conservative ideology. For example, anti-tax and gun-rights interest groups give her nearly perfect favorable ratings. The American Conservative Union gives her an 89.4 percent conservative rating. The National Abortion Rights Action League Pro-Choice America which advocates abortion rights, has rated her zero in the past four years. Gay rights groups also give her ratings of zero. The *National Journal* rates her the twentieth most conservative in the US Senate. Her problem in the Republican primary with conservative Governor Rick Perry was that she left the impression that she is less than a solid conservative. Hutchison has explained that impression by saying, "Because I speak in civil tones, some want to try to label me a moderate. My voting record is one of the most conservative in the US Senate. . . . We can't expect to remain the majority

*From left: Majority Leader Bill Frist, controversial nominee to the 5th Circuit Court of Appeals Priscilla Owen,
President George W. Bush, Senator Kay Bailey Hutchison, Senator John Cornyn.
Photograph from George W. Bush papers.*

party in Texas if we drive out voters that support Republican principles but might not agree on every single issue."[10]

Hutchison has an intense work ethic, has tried to project an image as a fighter, and has a reputation for a quick temper.[11] However, in public she presents a reasoned voice, and she has great popularity with local officials in Texas because of her efforts to protect military bases and bring funds to Texas for such things as bridges and scientific research. And the state's Democrats have praised her for her willingness to work across party lines. Indeed, it is that pragmatic streak that may be at the core of her social conservative opposition—she is a conservative, but without the profound ideological commitment.[12]

She was given consideration for the Republican vice-presidential nomination in 2008. However, as with John McCain, social conservatives were not completely comfortable with her—primarily because of her abortion views. That factor may have kept her from the nomination in spite of her generally conservative record and lengthy political career. On the other hand, Sarah Palin had the support of social conservatives and did not have a Washington political career. These characteristics

222

gave her acceptance within a wing of the party where McCain needed support and gave her the appearance of being a "fresh face" in politics.[13]

Hutchison is clearly a pioneer. She was one of the few women in her University of Texas Law School graduating class, was the first woman Republican in the Texas legislature, and was the first woman US senator from Texas. Like Barbara Jordan, Hutchison has also broken barriers. She appears to understand her role as a pioneer—in 2009, she met with Secretary of State Hillary Rodham Clinton at the Dallas Women's Museum and the two women "spoke to each other like close sisters, rather than political adversaries who share almost nothing in common." They spoke of life lessons to young women and talked of their own successes, defeats, and frailties.[14] In spite of criticism from the social conservative wing of the party, this pioneer in Texas politics has successfully practiced the art of pragmatic conservative politics for decades.

On January 13, 2011, Hutchison announced that she would not seek another term in the Senate when her current term expires in 2013. She announced that the last two years of her service had been difficult, and that she wanted to spend more time with her adopted nine-year-old children, Bailey and Houston. She planned to work in the private sector and do volunteer work "because I want to change the direction of our country."[15]

Opposite: *Senator Kay Bailey Hutchison. Official US Congress portrait.*

Notes

CHAPTER 2: Joseph Weldon Bailey

1. Alwyn Barr, *Reconstruction to Reform* (Austin: University of Texas Press, 1971), 210; Sam Hanna Acheson, *Joe Bailey: The Last Democrat* (New York: Macmillan, 1932), 30-31, 37.

2. Acheson, 47-48, 55.

3. Champ Clark, *My Quarter Century in American Politics,* Volume 2 (New York: Harper and Brothers, 1920), 9-10, 343.

4. Seth S. McKay and Odie B. Faulk, *Texas after Spindletop* (Austin: Steck-Vaughn Company, 1965), 18.

5. David Graham Phillips, "The Treason of the Senate," *Cosmopolitan Magazine* (July 1906): 627-36.

6. "The Laborer and His Hire—Another Standard Oil Lesson," *Hearst's Magazine* (February 1913): 174-88.

7. Alfred Henry Lewis, "The Hon. (?) J.W. Bailey," *Cosmopolitan Magazine* (April 1913): 601-05.

8. David Graham Phillips, "The Treason of the Senate," *Cosmopolitan Magazine* (July 1906): 627-36, esp. 627.

9. Joe B. Frantz, *Texas Bicentennial: A History* (New York: W.W. Norton, 1984), 153.

10. Acheson, 175; Phillips, 627-36.

11. Alfred Steinberg, *Sam Rayburn: A Biography* (New York: Hawthorn Books, 1975), 8.

12. Clark, vol. 1, 9-10.

13. D.B. Hardeman and Donald C. Bacon, *Rayburn: A Biography* (Austin: Texas Monthly Press, 1987), 27.

14. Chauncey M. Depew, *My Memories of Eighty Years* (New York: Charles Scribners' Sons, 1924), 183.

15. Claude G. Bowers, *Beveridge and the Progressive Era* (Boston: The Literary Guild, 1932), 184-85; Claude Bowers, *My Life* (New York: Simon and Schuster, 1962), 69.

16. Thomas Fleming, *Around the Capital with Uncle Hank,* (New York: Nutshell Publishing Company, 1901), 54-55.

17. Acheson, 12, 15.

18. Ronnie Dugger, *The Politician* (New York: W.W. Norton, 1982), 58.

19. Escal F. Duke, "The Political Career of Morris Sheppard, 1875-1941" (PhD dissertation, University of Texas, 1958), 184-86.

20. Ibid., 131; Bob Charles Holcomb, "Senator Joe Bailey, Two Decades of Controversy" (PhD dissertation, Texas Technological College, 1968), 497.

21. Joseph W. Bailey telegram to O.B. Colquitt, March 4, 1911, Joseph Weldon Bailey Papers, Dallas Historical Society.

22. Holcomb, 497; Acheson, 297.

23. Ibid.; George P. Huckaby, "Oscar Branch Colquitt: A Political Biography" (PhD dissertation, University of Texas, 1946), 331-32.

24. Duke, 273; Huckaby, 425.

25. Acheson, 389; Norman D. Brown, *Hood, Bonnet, and Little Brown Jug* (College Station: Texas A&M University Press, 1984), 16-17.

26. Steinberg, 76.

CHAPTER 3: Morris Sheppard

1. "Sen. Sheppard's Body to Lie In State Today: Dean of Congress Dies in Walter Reed of Brain Hemorrhage," *Washington Post*, April 10, 1941.

2. Richard Bailey, "Morris Sheppard," in Kenneth E. Hendrickson Jr., Michael L. Collins, and Patrick Cox (eds.), *Profiles in Power: Twentieth-Century Texans in Washington* (Austin: University of Texas Press, 2004), 28-41.

3. "Morris Sheppard," *Biographical Directory of the United States Congress, 1774-Present;* Richard Bailey, "John Morris Sheppard," *The Handbook of Texas Online.*

4. Bailey, *Profiles in Power,* 28-29.

5. "Young Texan Fervid: Mr. Sheppard Pays Glowing Tribute to Democracy," *Washington Post,* January 17, 1907.

6. Richard Bailey, "Morris Sheppard of Texas: Southern Progressive and Prohibitionist" (PhD diss., Texas Christian University, 1980), 53-54.

7. Bailey, *Profiles in Power,* 30-31.

8. "Sheppard Predicts His 'Dry' Bill Will Pass the Senate Tomorrow: Country-Wide Prohibition With Five or Six Years Also Forecast—Expects Favorable Action by the House," *Washington Post,* July 31, 1917.

9. Bailey, *Handbook.*

10. "Sen. Sheppard's Body. . . ."

11. Former Speaker Jim Wright has an amazing storehouse of recollections about members of Congress. The Sol Bloom-Morris Sheppard story is one of them.

12. Bailey, *Profiles in Power,* 31.

13. Ibid., 33.

14. Bailey, *Handbook.*

15. William E. Leuchtenburg, *The White House Looks South* (Baton Rouge: Louisiana State University Press, 2005), 82.

16. "Suffrage Wins in Senate; Now Goes to States," *The New York Times,* June 5, 1919.

17. Bailey, *Handbook.*

18. Morris Sheppard, "The Work of the League of Nations," speech before the United States Senate, October 5, 1921.

19. Bailey, *Handbook.*

20. "Senator Sheppard," *Washington Post,* April 10, 1941.

CHAPTER 4: John Nance Garner

1. Joe B. Frantz, *Texas: A Bicentennial History* (New York: W.W. Norton, 1984), 178.

2. Neil MacNeil, *Forge of Democracy* (New York: David McKay, 1963), 80.

3. This discussion is largely from Patrick Cox, "John Nance Garner," in Kenneth E. Hendrickson Jr., Michael L. Collins, and Patrick Cox, *Profiles in Power: Twentieth-Century Texans in Washington* (Austin: University of Texas Press, 2004), 42-52.

4. John McDuffie to John Nance Garner, May 18, 1949, John McDuffie Papers, W.S. Hoole Special Collections, University of Alabama, Montgomery, Alabama.

5. Allan A. Michie and Frank Ryhlick, *Dixie Demagogues* (New York: The Vanguard Press, 1939), 27.

6. Ibid., 28.

7. D. B. Hardeman and Donald C. Bacon, *Rayburn: A Biography* (Austin: Texas Monthly Press, 1987), 137.

8. Arthur M. Schlesinger Jr., *The Crisis of the Old Order, 1919-1933* (Boston: Houghton Mifflin Company, 1956), 227.

9. Hardeman and Bacon, 70, 115, 136.

10. Jordan A. Schwarz, "John Nance Garner and the Sales Tax Rebellion of 1932," *Journal of Southern History* (1964): 162.

11. Jordan A. Schwarz, *The Interregnum of Despair* (Urbana: University of Illinois Press, 1970), 236.

12. Schwarz, "John Nance Garner and the Sales Tax…," 165.

13. Rexford G. Tugwell, *The Democratic Roosevelt* (Garden City: Doubleday and Company, 1957), 226.

14. Anthony Champagne, "Sam Rayburn: Achieving Party Leadership," *Southwestern Historical Quarterly* (1987): 373-392.

15. Lionel V. Patenaude, *Texans, Politics, and the New Deal* (New York: Garland Publishing, 1983), 35-36.

16. Ibid., 36.

17. Michael J. Romano, "The Emergence of John Nance Garner as a Figure in American National Politics, 1924-1941" (PhD diss., St. Johns University, 1974), 237.

18. Ibid., 238.

19. Ibid., 247.

20. Ibid., 307.

21. James Farley to Claude Bowers, February 8, 1940, Box 9, folder "Feb. 1940", James Farley Papers, Library of Congress, Washington, DC; See also, Ibid., 293-294.

22. James Farley to Claude Bowers, December 21, 1939, Box 8, folder "Dec. 1939", James Farley Papers, Library of Congress, Washington, DC.

CHAPTER 5: Sam Rayburn

1. Quoted in H.G. Dulaney, Edward Hake Phillips, and MacPhelan Reese, *Speak, Mr. Speaker* (Bonham: Sam Rayburn Foundation, 1978), 478.

2. D. B. Hardeman and Donald C. Bacon, *Rayburn: A Biography* (Austin: Texas Monthly Press, 1987), 28-58.

3. Anthony Champagne, *Congressman Sam Rayburn* (New Brunswick: Rutgers University Press, 1984), 16-18.

4. Ibid., 95-136.

5. Ibid.

6. C. Dwight Dorough, *Mr. Sam* (New York: Random House, 1962), 110-121.

7. Hardeman & Bacon, 66-67.

9. Ibid., 145-199.

10. Ibid.

11. Anthony Champagne, "Sam Rayburn: Achieving Party Leadership," *Southwestern Historical Quarterly* (1987): 380-392.

13. Especially in the aftermath of the 1946 elections, Rayburn was quite insistent that he did not wish to be the minority leader. He wrote F. Edward Hébert, a Democratic congressman from Louisiana, "I have thought about this matter even long before the election, and I came to the definite conclusion that I could, in all probability, be of more service to my country and my party by not being tied to this official position. I feel that I would be freer and more effective to take the Floor on the larger questions than otherwise and that the Membership on both sides would probably listen to me as well, and I think better, if I were not in the position of minority leader. I feel this very deeply." Sam Rayburn to F. Edward Hébert, November 29, 1946, F. Edward Hébert Papers, Tulane University, New Orleans, Louisiana.

14. On the presidential boomlet in 1952, see, Hardeman & Bacon, 357-374. On Rayburn's desire to be vice president in 1956, see, Hale Boggs interview by T. H. Baker, early draft of an interview for the LBJ Library, March 13, 1969, 5, Hale Boggs Papers, Tulane University, New Orleans, Louisiana. Earlier in his life, Rayburn hoped to become vice president under Franklin Roosevelt in either 1940 or in 1944. See Hardeman & Bacon, 230-242.

15. Hardeman & Bacon, 358.

16. Carl Albert interview with Ron Peters, May 25, 1979, 40-41, The Carl Albert Papers, The Carl Albert Center, University of Oklahoma, Norman, Oklahoma.

17. Robert Caro writes that Lyndon Johnson told William O. Douglas in the 1940s that if one wanted to be President, "you've got to do it through Sam Rayburn." Robert Caro, *The Path to Power* (New York: Alfred A. Knopf, 1982), 759.

18. For the importance of mentor-protégé relationships in politics as well as Sam Rayburn's mentor-protégé relationships see, Anthony Champagne, et al., *The Austin-Boston Connection* (College Station: Texas A&M University Press, 2009).

19. Said Rayburn, "You can't really say how you lead. You feel your way, receptive to those rolling waves of sentiment. And if a man can't see and hear and feel, why then, of course, he's lost." Quoted in Dulaney, et al., 108.

Chapter 6: Hatton W. Sumners

1. Elmore Whitehurst, "Hatton Sumners—His Life and Public Service," Hatton W. Sumners Papers, Dallas Texas, 4.

2. Ron C. Law, "Congressman Hatton W. Sumners of Dallas, Texas: His Life and Congressional Career, 1875-1937" (PhD diss., Texas Christian University, 1990), 3-5.

3. Raymond Moley and Celeste Jedel, "The Gentleman Who Does Not Yield: Hatton Sumners, Dallas Diogenes," *Saturday Evening Post*, May 10, 1941, 13.

4. Mary Catherine Monroe, "A Day in July: Hatton W. Sumners and the Court Reorganization Plan of 1937" (Master's thesis, University of Texas at Arlington, 1973), 22.

5. Law, 17.

6. Monroe, 26-27.

7. Moley and Jedel, 99.

8. Law, 26.

9. Monroe, 28.

10. Dewey W. Grantham Jr., "Texas Congressional Leaders and the New Freedom, 1913-1917," *Southwestern Historical Review,* Vol. 53 (1949): 35.

11. Law, 79.

12. Monroe, 33.

13. Ibid., 44-45.

14. Lionel V. Patenaude, "Garner, Sumners, and Connally: The Defeat of the Roosevelt Court Bill in 1937," *Southwestern Historical Quarterly,* Vol. 74 (1970): 38-51.

15. Hatton W. Sumners, *The Private Citizen and His Democracy,* (Dallas: Southwestern Legal Foundation, 1959), 29.

CHAPTER 7: Thomas Connally

1. George N. Green, "Thomas Terry Connally," *Handbook of Texas;* see generally, Tom Connally as told to Alfred Steinberg, *My Name is Tom Connally* (New York: Thomas Y. Crowell, 1954).

2. "National Affairs: New Team," *Time,* August 11, 1941.

3. Green; Connally, 103-109.

4. Connally, 117-129.

5. Ibid., 130-146. Connally wrote, "Although I didn't have much hope that John would get the nomination, I agreed to line up delegations for him." See, Connally, 139.

6. Ibid., 138-146.

7. Ibid., 160

8. Ibid.

9. *Schechter Poultry Corp. v. United States,* 295 U.S. 495 (1935).

10. Connally, 163-164.

11. Ibid., 164.

12. Ibid., 184-195.

13. Ibid., 194.

14. Ibid., 194-195.

15. Ibid., 195.

16. Green.

17. Ibid.

18. George Norris Green, *The Establishment in Texas Politics* (Westport: Greenwood, 1979), 7. (Hereinafter, Green, *Establishment*).

19. Green.

20. Ibid.

21. Ibid.

22. See generally, Connally.

23. Ibid.

24. Ibid., 298.

25. Ibid., 358-359.

26. Green, *Establishment,* 148.

27. Ibid., 148-149.

Chapter 8: Wright Patman

1. Quoted in, Nancy Beck Young, *Wright Patman: Populism, Liberalism, & the American Dream* (Dallas, TX: Southern Methodist University Press, 2000), 301.

2. Ibid., 16-24; Philip A. Grant Jr., "John William Wright Patman," *The Handbook of Texas Online.*

3. Ben R. Guttery, *Representing Texas* (Charleston, SC: BookSurge, 2008), 234-275.

4. Young, 125-132; 163-167.

5. Ibid., 300.

6. Robert Dallek, *Lone Star Rising* (New York: Oxford University Press, 1991), 211-212.

7. Young, 6-7.

8. Ibid., 270

9. Lewis E. Weeks, Oral History, C. Rufus Rorem: A First-Person Profile by Lewis E. Weeks, Health Services Research (1983), 17.

10. Young, 64-65.

11. Ibid., 83-86.

12. Ibid., 218-219.

13. Ibid., 172.

14. Bill Archer interview by Edward J. Harpham and Anthony Champagne, May, 2009.

15. Young, 221.

16. Young, 271-288.

Chapter 9: Martin Dies Jr.

1. John Connally with Mickey Herskowitz, *In History's Shadow: An American Odyssey* (New York: Hyperion, 1993), 107.

2. George N. Green, "Martin Dies," *Handbook of Texas Online.*

3. Martin Dies, *Martin Dies' Story* (New York: Bookmailer, 1963), 139.

4. "Ex-Rep. Martin Dies, 71, Is Dead; Led Un-American Activities Unit," *The New York Times,* November 15, 1972.

5. Dies, 78.

6. Don E. Carleton, *Red Scare* (Austin: Texas Monthly Press, 1985), 94.

7. Ibid.

8. Dies, 130.

9. Carleton, 94.

10. Dies, 79.

11. Ibid.

12. Robert Dallek, *Lone Star Rising* (New York: Oxford University Press, 1991), 210.

13. Dies, 81.

14. Dies, 83.

15. Carleton, 93.

16. Dies, 83.

17. Dallek, 307.

18. Carleton, 94.

19. "Papers of Rep. Martin Dies: Texas congressman famed for warning of communist dangers," Sam Houston Center, Texas State Library and Archives Commission.

20. Carleton, 94.

21. Green.

22. Ibid.

23. Papers of Rep. Martin Dies.

CHAPTER 10: George Mahon

1. Lawrence L. Graves, "George Herman Mahon," *The Handbook of Texas Online.*

2. Wanda Webb Evans, *One Honest Man: George Mahon A Story of Power, Politics and Poetry* (Canyon, TX: Staked Plains Press, 1978), 44-47.

3. See generally, Evans, *One Honest Man.*

4. Dillon S. Myer, Oral History by Helen S. Pryor, University of California at Berkeley Bancroft Library, July 7, 1970, 306-307.

5. Evans, 45-46.

6. Ibid., 224.

7. Ibid., 183.

8. Ibid.

9. Ibid., 48, 63.

10. George Mahon interview with Richard F. Fenno Jr., U.S. National Archives and Records Administration, June 8, 1959.

11. Evans, 63-64, 185-191.

12. Jim Wright interview with Clay Avery, March 4, 2002.

13. Evans, 216.

14. Ibid., 218.

15. Ibid., 218-219.

16. Ibid., 219.

17. Graves.

18. Evans, 140.

19. Ibid., 141.

20. "The Nation: Scenario of the Shake-Up," *Time,* November 17, 1975.

21. Ben Guttery, *Representing Texas* (Charleston, SC: BookSurge, 2008), 275.

22. Ibid., 104-105.

23. Charles Wilson interview with James Riddlesperger and Anthony Champagne, September 3, 2008.

CHAPTER 11: Lyndon Baines Johnson

1. Robert Dallek, *Lone Star Rising* (New York: Oxford University Press, 1991), 78.

2. Robert Caro, *The Path to Power* (New York: Random House, 1981), 213-214.

3. Ronnie Dugger, *The Politician: The Life and Times of Lyndon Johnson* (New York: W.W. Norton, 1982), 183.

4. Joanne Connor Green, Donald W. Jackson, and James W. Riddlesperger Jr., "Lyndon Johnson and the 1957 Civil Rights Act," paper presented at Jim Wright Symposium, Texas Christian University, April 19, 2002.

5. Robert A. Caro, *Means of Ascent* (New York: Knopf, 1990), 44.

6. Garry Wills, "Monstre Désacré," *New York Review of Books* (April 26, 1990).

7. Gilbert C. Fite, *Richard B. Russell: Senator from Georgia* (Chapel Hill: University of North Carolina Press, 1991), 266-268.

8. Ibid, 310.

9. Richard H. Rovere, *Senator Joe McCarthy* (New York: Meridian, 1959), 137.

10. Robert A. Caro, *Master of the Senate,* (New York: Knopf, 2002), 555-556.

11. George Reedy, *Lyndon Johnson: A Memoir* (New York: Andrews and McMeel, 1984), 117.

12. Randall B. Woods, *LBJ: Architect of American Ambition* (New York: Free Press, 2006), 330.

13. Kenneth G. Hendrickson, "Lyndon B. Johnson," in Kenneth G. Hendrickson, Michael L. Collins, and Patrick Cox, eds, *Profiles in Power: Twentieth-Century Texans in Washington* (Austin: University of Texas Press, 2004), 131.

CHAPTER 12: William Robert "Bob" Poage

1. William Robert Poage, *My First 85 Years* (Waco, TX: Texian Press, 1985), 60.

2. Ibid., 1-5.

3. Ibid., 39.

4. Ben R. Guttery, *Representing Texas* (Charleston, SC: BookSurge, 2008), 123.

5. Cindy Van Auken, "The Texas Legacy of Mr. Agriculture," *Waco Herald-Tribune*, December 12, 1999, A1.

6. Laura W. Duggan, "William Robert Poage," *The Handbook of Texas Online.*

7. Poage, 56-57.

8. Duggan, 2.

9. Poage, 93.

10. Poage, 59.

11. Darrell Dunn, "Poage Gave His Life for this Area," *Waco Tribune-Herald*, January 4, 1987.

12. Oliver Talley, "Former Rep. Bob Poage Dies in Temple at Age 87," *The Dallas Morning News,* January 4, 1987, 37A.

13. Dunn.

14. Jim Wright, *You and Your Congressman* (New York: Capricorn, 1965), 82.

15. Anne Millet, "W. R. Poage: Democratic Representative from Texas," *Ralph Nader Congress Project Citizens Look at Congress* (Washington, DC: Grossman, 1972), 2.

16. Ibid., 12.

17. Fowler West, *He Ain't No Lawyer!: Memories from My Years with Congressman Bob Poage* (Waco, TX: Fowler West, 2009), 75-76.

CHAPTER 13: W. Lee O'Daniel

1. C. Dwight Dorough, *Mr. Sam* (New York: Random House, 1962), 397.

2. Ibid.

3. John Mark Dempsey, *The Light Crust Doughboys are on the Air!: Celebrating Seventy Years of Texas Music* (Denton: University of North Texas Press, 2002), 27.

4. George Green, "O'Daniel, Wilbert Lee Pappy," *The Handbook of Texas Online*.

5. Robert Caro, *The Years of Lyndon Johnson: The Path to Power* (New York: Alfred Knopf, 1982), 696-97.

6. Ibid., 697.

7. Ibid., 698.

8. Ibid.

9. Ibid., 699.

10. Ibid., 702; Bill Crawford, *Please Pass the Biscuits, Pappy: Pictures of Governor W. Lee "Pappy" O'Daniel* (Austin: University of Texas Press, 2004), 30.

11. Caro, 702.

12. Green.

13. Crawford, 71.

14. Caro, 703;

15. Green; Crawford, 45-46.

16. Crawford, 177.

17. Caro, 734-740.

18. Robert Dallek, *Lone Star Rising: Lyndon Johnson and His Times, 1908-1960* (New York: Oxford University Press, 1991), 230.

19. Dallek, 295.

20. Ron Stone, "August 4, 1941," *Book of Texas Days* (Fredericksburg, TX: Shearer, 1984).

21. James Reston Jr., *The Lone Star: The Life of John Connally* (New York: Harper & Row, 1989), 124.

22. Green.

23. Ibid.; Crawford, 48.

CHAPTER 14: Lloyd Bentsen

1. Christian Davenport, "Bentsen Honored in political tribute: Legendary leader's accomplishments are recalled at fundraiser," *Austin American-Statesman*, December 14, 1999.

2. Michael L. Collins, "Lloyd Bentsen," in *Profiles in Power: Twentieth-Century Texans in Washington*, Kenneth E. Hendrickson Jr., Michael L. Collins and Patrick Cox, eds. (Austin: University of Texas Press, 2004), 256.

3. James Fallows, "Lloyd Bentsen: Can Another Texan Apply?" *Atlantic Monthly* (December 1974): 86-90.

4. Collins, 257.

5. Ibid, 257-258.

6. Fallows.

7. Collins, 261-262.

8. Ibid., 264-266.

9. Lloyd M. Bentsen Jr., *The Handbook of Texas Online*.

10. Gary Klott, "Senate Begins Work on $9 Billion of Tax Rises," *The New York Times*, December 2, 1987, D2.

11. Susan F. Rasky, "Rule of Thumb for Negotiating a Budget: Don't Tax Friends," *The New York Times,* October 14, 1990, A21.

12. Michael Barone and Grant Ujifusa, *The Almanac of American Politics, 1990,* (Washington, DC: National Journal, 1989), 1156.

13. "The Democrats in Atlanta: Bentsen's Acceptance: Protect the Dream," *The New York Times,* July 22, 1988, A13; Margorie Randon Hersey, "The Campaign and the Media," in Gerald M. Pomper, *The Election of 1988* (Chatham, NJ: Chatham House, 1989), 92.

14. "Facing a Skeptical America: Clinton's Hard Sell, President Takes NAFTA on the Road," *Los Angeles Times,* September 16, 1993, A18.

15. Christian Davenport, "Bentsen honored in political tribute," B1.

16. Joe Holley, "Lloyd Bentsen, Texas Senator, Vice Presidential Candidate," *Washington Post,* May 24, 2006, B06.

17. Collins, 269.

CHAPTER 15: Jack Brooks

1. Michael Wines, "The 1994 Campaign: Democrats; Bringing Home Bacon Isn't Protecting Veterans," *The New York Times,* November 6, 1994.

2. Susanna McBee, "The Gospel According to Jack Brooks; Texas Congressman Preaches Against Revenue Sharing to a Tough Audience," *Washington Post,* March 13, 1979.

3. Mike Robinson, "Crusty Texan Takes Over Judiciary Committee," *Associated Press,* January 29, 1989.

4. Ibid.

5. Ibid.

6. Ibid.

7. Ruth Marcus, "Rep. Brooks is Expected to Head Judiciary Committee; Outspoken Texan Says It Would Be 'an Honor and a Privilege' to Succeed Rodino," *Washington Post,* March 16, 1988.

8. Kenneth J. Cooper, "Obstacle Still Stands in the Path of the Ban on Assault Weapons; Texas Democrat Jack Brooks Likely to Play Hardball in Conference," *Washington Post,* May 7, 1994.

9. "The Other Members: 14 Representatives Selected to Serve on the Iran Panel," *The New York Times,* December 18, 1986.

10. Jack Brooks conversation with Anthony Champagne, October 1995, Bonham, Texas.

11. Robinson.

12. Jack Brooks conversation.

13. Alan Ehrenhalt (ed.), *Congressional Quarterly's Politics in America—Members of Congress in Washington and at Home, 1986* (Washington, DC: CQ Press, 1985), 1495.

14. Ibid., 1494.

15. Bill Archer interview with Edward J. Harpham and Anthony Champagne, May, 2009.

16. Cooper.

17. Robinson

18. "Jack Bascom Brooks," *Biographical Directory of the United States Congress.*

19. Robinson.

20. Jimmy Carter, Beaumont, Texas—Remarks at Dedication Ceremonies of the Jack Brooks Federal Building, June 24, 1978.

21. Wines.

22. Marcus.

23. Leslie Carpenter, "Washington Beat: Brooks Becomes Key LBJ Confidant," *Washington Post*, April 4, 1964.

24. McBee.

25. Ibid.

26. Anthony Champagne, Douglas Harris, James Riddlesperger, and Garrison Nelson, *The Austin-Boston Connection* (College Station: Texas A&M University Press, 2009), 233.

27. Judith Graham (ed.), *Current Biography Yearbook* (New York: H.W. Wilson Company, 1992), 87.

28. Phillip C. Duncan and Christine C. Lawrence (eds.), *Politics in America 1996: The 104th Congress* (Washington, DC: Congressional Quarterly, 1996), 1273.

29. Ibid.

30. Sue Anne Pressley, "The Comeuppance of Texas Icon Mirrors National's Political Revolt," *Washington Post*, December 7, 1994.

31. Ibid. See also, Wines.

CHAPTER 16: Price Daniel

1. See generally, *Dan Murph, The Life of Price Daniel: Texas Giant* (Austin: Eakin Press, 2002).

2. George Norris Green, *The Establishment in Texas Politics* (Westport: Greenwood Press, 1979), 4.

3. Ibid., 201.

4. Murph, 3-68.

5. Price Daniel interview by Anthony Champagne, January 10, 1979.

6. Murph, 44-68.

7. Ibid., 78-84.

8. Ibid., 74-92.

9. D.B. Hardeman and Donald C. Bacon, *Rayburn: A Biography* (Austin: Texas Monthly Press, 1987), 351-355.

10. Green, 148.

11. Ibid., 146.

12. Murph, 128-129.

13. Daniel interview.

14. Ibid.

15. Ibid.

16. Murph, 210-211.

17. Ibid., 234-240.

CHAPTER 17: Bruce Alger

1. Ben R. Guttery, *Representing Texas* (Charleston, SC: BookSurge, 2008), 15.

2. Carolyn Carney, "Bruce Alger: The Voice of Cold War Politics in Dallas," *Legacies* (2003): 50-62.

3. Ibid.

4. Box 13, Folder 26, Bruce Alger Papers, Dallas Public Library.

5. Carney, 52.

6. Ibid., 53-54.

7. Bruce Alger to Donald G. Berry, March 31, 1964, Box 28, Folder 3, Bruce Alger Papers, Dallas Public Library.

8. Bruce Alger to Reed A. Benson, June 18, 1964, Box 28, Folder 3, Bruce Alger Papers, Dallas Public Library.

9. Robert J. George to Bruce Alger, April 6, 1961, Box 10, Folder 1, Bruce Alger Papers, Dallas Public Library. George is commenting on statements that Alger made "in an interview where he talked about the John Birch Society."

10. Mrs. Philip L. Collins to Bruce Alger, February 7, 1963, Box 22, Folder 16, Bruce Alger Papers, Dallas Public Library.

11. Bruce Alger to Mrs. Phillip L. Collins, February 18, 1963, Box 22, Folder 16, Bruce Alger Papers, Dallas Public Library.

12. Carney, 53.

13. "ACA Ratings, 1961," Box 10, Folder 23, Bruce Alger Papers, Dallas Public Library.

14. Carney, 57.

15. Bruce Alger, "Where is Government by Decree Leading Us?," Box 13, Folder 26, Bruce Alger papers, Dallas Public Library.

16. Carney, 57-58.

17. Robert Dallek, *Lone Star Rising* (New York: Oxford University Press, 1991), 587-88.

18. Jim Wright interview by Anthony Champagne and Jim Riddlesperger, July 9, 2008.

19. Carney, 58.

20. D.B. Hardeman and Donald C. Bacon, *Rayburn: A Biography* (Austin: Texas Monthly Press, 1987), 417.

21. Guttery, 14-15.

22. C. Dwight Dorough, *Mr. Sam* (New York: Random House, 1962), 15.

23. Guttery, 14-15.

24. Box 38, Folder 3, Bruce Alger Papers, Dallas Public Library.

25. Carney, 60.

26. Ibid.

27. Ibid., 60-61.

CHAPTER 18: Jim Wright

1. Ben Procter, "Jim Wright," in Kenneth E. Hendrickson Jr., Michael L. Collins, and Patrick Cox, eds., *Profiles in Power: Twentieth-Century Texans in Washington* (Austin: University of Texas Press, 2004), 229.

2. Jim Wright, *The Flying Circus: Pacific War 1943 as seen through a Bombsight* (Guilford, CT: Lyons Press, 2005).

3. Procter, 235.

4. Bruce Oppenheimer and Robert L. Peabody, "How the Race for Majority Leader Was Won—By One Vote," *Washington Monthly*, November 1977, 50.

5. Mark W. Beasley, "Jim Wright: Mayor of Weatherford, Texas, 1950-1954," in *Jim Wright, Weatherford Days . . . A Time of Learnin'*, (Fort Worth: Madison Publishing, 1996), 113-122.

6. Jim Wright, *Balance of Power*, (Atlanta: Turner Publishing, 1996), 32.

7. Procter, 242.

8. "Remarks at the Breakfast of the Fort Worth Chamber of Commerce, November 22, 1963," *Public Papers of the President* (1963), 888.

9. Sarah McClendon, "Jim Wright To Be Next House Speaker," *El Paso Times*, March 10, 1966, 1.

10. Griffin Smith Jr. and Paul Burka, "The Best, the Worst, and the Fair-to-Middlin'," *Texas Monthly*, May 1976, 109.

11. See, "The Jim Wright Slant on Washington," December 22, 1958, Jim W. Wright Papers [Hereafter JWP]; "The Jim Wright Slant on Washington," February 16, 1959, JWP; Jim Wright, "Clean Money for Congress," *Harper's Magazine*, April, 1967, n.p., JWP; "The Wright Slant on Washington," February 18, 1965, JWP; Jim Wright, *The Coming Water Famine* (New York: Coward-McCann, 1966).

12. Jim Wright, *You and Your Congressman* (New York: Coward-McCann, 1965).

13. Tip O'Neill with William Novak, *Man of the House* (New York: Random House, 1987), 226.

14. Barbara Sinclair, *Majority Leadership in the U.S. House* (Baltimore: Johns Hopkins University Press, 1983), 33.

15. "Koreagate" had to do with charges that McFall had accepted illegal contributions from Korean lobbyists, charges that were never proven but crippled McFall's congressional career.

16. For a full description, see Anthony Champagne, Douglas B. Harris, James W. Riddlesperger Jr., and Garrison Nelson, *The Austin-Boston Connection* (College Station: Texas A&M Press, 2009), 219-250.

17. Bob Woodward, *Shadow: Five Presidents and the Shadow of Watergate* (New York: Simon and Schuster, 1999), 55.

18. Paul Boller, *Congressional Anecdotes* (New York: Oxford University Press, 1991), 320-321.

19. John Barry, *The Ambition and the Power: The Fall of Jim Wright, a True Story of Washington* (New York: Viking Press, 1989).

20. Jim Wright, *Reflections of a Public Man* (Fort Worth: Madison Publishing, 1984).

21. Michael Wines, "Wright Lawyers Ask Panel To Dismiss Ethics Charges," *The New York Times*, May 11, 1989, D28.

22. Jim Wright, *Balance of Power*, 485.

23. Procter, 242.

24. Jim Wright, *Balance of Power*, 490.

CHAPTER 19: Ralph W. Yarborough

1. Patrick Cox, *Ralph W. Yarborough: The People's Senator* (Austin: University of Texas Press, 2001), 2.

2. Ibid., pp 5-12.

3. Ibid., 11.

4. Ibid., 11-13.

5. William G. Phillips, *Yarborough of Texas* (Washington, DC: Acropolis Books, 1969), 21.

6. Cox, 47-50.

7. Cox, 63.

8. Cox, 74-80.

9. Mark Odintz, "Ralph Webster Yarborough," *The Handbook of Texas Online.*

10. Ibid.

11. Ibid.

12. Cox, 130-137.

13. Ibid., 142-143.

14. Robert A. Caro, *The Years of Lyndon Johnson: Master of the Senate* (New York: Knopf, 2002), 996.

15. Ibid, 158-160.

16. Ibid., 163.

17. William Manchester, *The Death of A President* (New York: Harper and Row, 1967).

18. Phillips, 73.

19. Cox, 230.

20. Cox, 240-243.

21. Phillips, 73-75.

22. Cox, 267.

23. Ben Guttery, *Representing Texas* (Charleston, SC: BookSurge, 2008), 163.

24. Cox, 273-275.

CHAPTER 20: Henry B. González

1. Ronnie Dugger, "The Segregation Filibuster of 1957," *Texas Observer,* December 27, 1974, 46-47; Molly Ivins, "The Late Henry B. was a boxer, not a saint," *Fort Worth Star-Telegram,* November 30, 2000.

2. Eugene Rodriguez Jr., *Henry B. Gonzalez* (New York: Arno Press Inc., 1976) 30.

3. Ibid., 35.

4. Ronny Dugger, "Gonzalez of San Antonio, Part III: The South Texas Cauldron, Guns, Disease, Politics, Victory," *Texas Observer,* May 9, 1980, 16.

5. Ibid., 19.

6. Rodriguez, *Gonzalez,* 63.

7. Ibid., 70.

8. Jan Russel, "Henry B. Gonzalez," *Texas Monthly,* January 2001, 204.

9. Ron Hutchison, "Rep. Henry B. Gonzalez is One of Texas' Most Colorful Politicians," *Fort Worth Star-Telegram,* September 8, 1997.

10. Joe Patrick Bean, "Henry B. one of the last giants," *The Dallas Morning News,* December 3, 2000.

11. Hutchison, "Rep. Henry B. Gonzalez is One of Texas' Most Colorful Politicians."

12. Christopher Hitchens, "No Fool on the Hill: Henry B. Gonzalez is Different. Constitutionally," *Harpers Magazine,* October 1992, 84.

13. Congressional Quarterly, *Politics in America 1990.*

14. Hitchens, 84.

15. Catalina Camia, "Henry B. Gonzalez dies at 84: Democratic congressman was a trailblazer in Texas, *The Dallas Morning News,* November 29, 2000, 1A.

16. Interview with Jim Wright, March 4, 2002.

CHAPTER 21: John Goodwin Tower

1. John Goodwin Tower, *The Handbook of Texas Online.*

2. John R. Knaggs. *Two Party Texas: The John Tower Era, 1961-1984* (Austin, TX: Eakin Press, 1986), 3-7.

3. Gladwin Hill, "Tower is Elected Senator in Texas," *The New York Times,* May 29, 1961, 1.

4. *Current Biography,* 1962, 426.

5. Andrew Rosenthal, "Politics, Not Affection, Is the Bond," *The New York Times,* February 9, 1989, B10.

6. George N. Green, and John J. Kushna, "John Tower," in Kenneth E. Hendrickson Jr., Michael L. Collins, and Patrick Cox, eds., *Profiles in Power: Twentieth-Century Texans in Washington* (Austin: University of Texas Press, 2004), 204-205.

7. Ibid., 206-214.

8. Alan Ehrenhalt, *Politics in America, 1982* (Washington, DC: Congressional Quarterly Press, 1981), 1147.

9. Barone, Michael and Grant Ujifusa, *Almanac of American Politics, 1984* (Washington, DC: National Journal, 1983), 1114.

10. John G. Tower, *Consequences: A Personal and Political Memoir* (Boston: Little, Brown, 1991), 286-287.

11. "Tower Nomination Spurned by the Senate," *Congressional Quarterly Almanac, 1989* (Washington, DC: Congressional Quarterly Press, 1989), 404.

12. Tower, *Consequences,* 25-26.

13. James D. King and James W. Riddlesperger Jr., "The Rejection of a Cabinet Appointment: The Senate and John Tower," in Meena Bose and Rosanna Perotti, eds., *From Cold War to New World Order: The Foreign Policy of George H.W. Bush* (Westport, CT: Greenwood Press, 2002), 379-383.

14. Ibid., 323.

CHAPTER 22: George H. W. Bush

1. Dorothy DeMoss, "George Bush" in Kenneth E. Hendrickson Jr., Michael L. Collins, and Patrick Cox, eds., *Profiles in Power: Twentieth Century Texans in Washington* (Austin: University of Texas Press, 2004), 276.

2. Herbert S. Parmet, *George Bush: The Life of a Lone Star Yankee* (New York: Scribner, 1997), 113-115.

3. Ibid., 123.

4. DeMoss, 278.

5. Parmet, 127.

6. Parmet, 130.

7. Oral memoirs of William Robert "Bob" Poage, Baylor University Institute for Oral History, 1985, 14.

8. Parmet, 145.

9. DeMoss, 279-282.

10. Parmet, 357-380.

11. Bob Woodward, *The Commanders* (New York: Simon and Schuster, 1991).

12. W. Gary Fowler, Donald W. Jackson, and James W. Riddlesperger Jr., "Symbolic Politics Revisited:

The Bush Administration and the 1991 Civil Rights Act," in Richard Himelfarb and Rosanna Perotti, eds., *Principle over Politics?: The Domestic Politics of the George H. W. Bush Administration* (Westport, CT: Greenwood, 2004), 183-202.

CHAPTER 23: Bill Archer

1. Robert Dodge, "Archer tackles dream job—He leads House GOP charge on tax package, welfare reform," *The Dallas Morning News*, March 19, 1995.

2. Ibid.

3. Robert Dodge, "Archer steps out of shadows with proposals for tax cuts—Ways and Means chairman pursues ambitious agenda," *The Dallas Morning News*, June 13, 1997.

4. Robert Dodge, "2 learn how it is on other side—New roles of Archer, Andrews reflect presidential politics," *The Dallas Morning News*, May 10, 1993.

5. Robert Dodge, "Living a dream—Archer's rise to top of key House committee makes him central figure in GOP's strategy," *The Dallas Morning News*, March 19, 1995.

6. Dodge, June 13, 1997.

7. Catalina Camia, "Archer, Gingrich rift over corn is making waves," *The Dallas Morning News*, May 10, 1998.

8. Dodge, June 13, 1997.

9. Robert Dodge, "Archer steps up as leader in tax debate," *The Dallas Morning News*, June 12, 1997.

10. Robert Dodge, "Still Focused on Change—With retirement approaching, Congressman Bill Archer continues to try to overhaul Social Security, tax system," *The Dallas Morning News*, October 10, 1999.

11. Richard Whittle and Catalina Camia, "GOP ready for low-profile House speaker—Texan Archer takes name off list," *The Dallas Morning News*, November 8, 1998.

12. Dodge, March 19, 1995.

13. Ibid.

14. Ibid.

15. Ibid.

16. Dodge, October 10, 1999.

17. Ibid.

18. Dodge, June 13, 1997.

CHAPTER 24: Barbara Jordan

1. Max Sherman (ed.), *Barbara Jordan: Speaking the Truth with Eloquent Thunder* (Austin: University of Texas Press, 2007), xi.

2. Ibid., 31.

3. Sandra Parham (ed.), *Barbara Jordan: Selected Speeches* (Washington, DC: Howard University Press, 1999), 53-54.

4. Barbara Jordan and Shelby Hearon, *Barbara Jordan: A Self-Portrait* (Garden City: Doubleday, 1979), 3-110.

5. Barbara Jordan interview by Roland C. Hayes, March 28, 1984, LBJ Library.

6. Jordan and Hearon, 107-136.

7. PJ Pierce, *Let Me Tell You What I've Learned: Texas Wise Women Speak* (Austin: University of Texas Press, 2002), 14.

8. Jordan and Hearon, 137-142.

9. Barbara Jordan interview by Roland C. Hayes, March 28, 1984, LBJ Library.

10. Jordan and Hearon, 149-151.

11. Vista McCrosky, "Barbara Jordan," in Kenneth E. Hendrickson Jr., Michael L. Collins, and Patrick Cox (eds), *Profiles in Power* (Austin: University of Texas Press, 2004), 182-185.

12. Ibid., 187.

13. Jim Wright interview by Anthony Champagne and Jim Riddlesperger, July 9, 2008.

14. George Crile, *Charlie Wilson's War: The Extraordinary Story of How the Wildest Man in Congress and a Rogue CIA Agent Changed the History of Our Times* (New York: Atlantic Monthly Press, 2003), 79-80.

15. Parham, xii.

16. McCrosky, 191.

17. Barbara Jordan special interview by Liz Carpenter, February 5,1985, LBJ Library.

18. McCrosky, 191-192.

19. Sherman, 89.

20. Ibid., 8-9.

CHAPTER 25: Charles Wilson

1. "Charlie Wilson: The Times Obituary," *The Times of London Online,* February 10, 2010.

2. Doug Martin, "Charlie Wilson, Texas Congressman Linked to Foreign Intrigue, Dies at 76," *The New York Times,* February 11, 2010, B19.

3. Ben R. Guttery, *Representing Texas,* (Columbia, SC: BookSurge, 2008), 158.

4. Oral Memoirs of William Robert "Bob" Poage, Baylor University Institute for Oral History, 1985, vol 5, 136.

5. John Spong, "The Rehabilitation of Charlie Wilson," *Texas Monthly,* June 2004.

6. "Charlie Wilson: The Times Obituary," *The New York Times,* February 11, 2010.

7. Spong.

8. Ibid.

9. Molly Ivins, "Blowback? What Blowback?: Charlie Wilson's adventures in Afghanistan," *Texas Observer,* July 31, 2003.

10. George Crile, *Charlie Wilson's War: The Extraordinary Story of the Largest Covert Operation in History* (New York: Atlantic Monthly Press, 2003).

11. "Charlie Wilson: The Times Obituary."

12. Charlie Wilson interview with James Riddlesperger, September, 2008, Fort Worth, Texas.

CHAPTER 26: Phil Gramm

1. Eric Lipton and Steven Labaton, "Deregulator Looks Back, Unswayed," *The New York Times,* November 16, 2008.

2. Ben R. Guttery, *Representing Texas,* (Columbia, SC: BookSurge, 2008), 201.

3. Michael Barone and Grant Ugifusa, *The Almanac of American Politics,* 1996, (Washington, DC: National Journal, 1995), 1260.

4. Jim Wright, *Balance of Power* (Atlanta: Turner, 1996), 351.

5. Alan Ehrenhalt, ed., *Politics in America: The 100th Congress* (Washington, DC: CQ Press, 1987), 1436.

6. Michael Barone and Grant Ugifusa, *The Almanac of American Politics, 1998* (Washington, DC: National Journal, 1997), 1335.

7. Lipton and Labaton.

8. *Time*, http://www.time.com/time/specials/packages/article/0,28804,1877351_1877350_1877330,00.html, accessed March 21, 2010.

9. Michael Barone and Grant Ugifusa, *The Almanac of American Politics, 1996* (Washington, DC: National Journal, 1995), 1260.

10. Michael Barone and Grant Ugifusa, *The Almanac of American Politics, 1998* (Washington, DC: National Journal, 1997), 1337.

11 Lipton and Labaton.

12. Jeff Gerth and Richard J. Oppel Jr., "Enron's Collapse: The Power Couple," *The New York Times*, January 18, 2002.

13. Philip Shenon, "Public Lives: An Unyielding Texan Leaves his Brand on Capitol Hill," *The New York Times*, September 10, 2001.

14. Larry Rohter, "McCain Co-Chairman, Under Fire, Steps Aside," *The New York Times*, July 19, 2008.

CHAPTER 27: Richard Armey

1. "About FreedomWorks: Chairman Dick Armey," FreedomWorks, www.freedomworks.org.

2. "Biographical Sketch of the Creator of the Collection," Richard K. Armey Collection, University of Oklahoma, Norman, Oklahoma.

3. David Flick, "Vandergriff, Armey Fight Dow to Wire for Last Possible Votes," *The Dallas Morning News*, November 6, 1984.

4. "About FreedomWorks: Chairman Dick Armey."

5. Carolyn Barta, "Armey's Army: 'Commandos' to Mount Budget Attacks," *The Dallas Morning News*, February 3, 1986; Richard Whittle, "Armey says he's ready to lead House majority—Republican congressman prepares to 'speak for the party,'" *The Dallas Morning News*, November 20, 1994.

6. "About FreedomWorks: Chairman Dick Armey."

7. "National Briefing—Armey Defeats Lewis," *National Journal*, December 8, 1992.

8. Dick Armey, "Where We Went Wrong," *Washington Post*, October 29, 2006.

9. Steven Erlanger, "Paxon Says He Doesn't Want Speaker's Post Despite Revolt," *The New York Times*, July 21, 1997; James Carney and Karen Tumulty. "Ready, aim, misfire," *Time*, July 28, 1997; Sandy Hume, "Armey of one," *Texas Monthly*, September 1997.

10. Andrew Malcolm and Johanna Neuman, "News Shocker: Dick Armey now admires Bill Clinton," *Los Angeles Times*, September 11, 2009.

11. Ibid.

12. Suzanne Gamboa, "Armey Says He Will Retire, Saying He Is 'Pretty Exhausted,'" *Lubbock Avalanche Journal*, December 12, 2001.

13. Richard Armey, *The Flat Tax: A Citizen's Guide to the Facts on What It Will Do for You, Your Country, and Your Pocketbook* (New York: Ballentine, 1996).

14. Malcolm and Neuman.

15. Michael Ross, "Armey Remark About Democrat Sparks Furor-Politics: House majority leader says he merely mispronounced Rep. Frank's name in an interview. But some think it was not an accident," *Los Angeles Times,* January 28, 1995.

16. "Armey Makes Anti-Gay Joke," *St. Petersburg Times,* August 4, 2000.

17. Sam Stein, "Armey to Joan Walsh: I'm So Glad You Can Never Be My Wife," *The Huffington Post,* January 28, 2009.

18. Armey, "Where We Went Wrong."

CHAPTER 28: Tom DeLay

1. Michael Barone and Grant Ujifusa, *The Almanac of American Politics, 1996* (Washington: DC: National Journal, 1995), 1317.

2. Peter Perl, "The Gospel According To Tom Delay," *Washington Post Magazine,* May 14, 2001.

3. Alison Mitchell, "Gingrich Emerging From Self-Exile, Humbler, Wary and Thinner," *The New York Times,* October 27, 1997.

4. Jeffrey Goldberg, "Party Unfaithful," *The New Yorker,* June 4, 2007.

5. See, for example, Americans for Democratic Action Scores for 2005, http://www.adaction.org/media/votingrecords/2005.pdf.

6. Juliet Eilperin, "Fundraising Focus Earns DeLay Wealth of Influence," *Washington Post,* July 22, 2003, A01.

7. David M. Halbfinger, "Across U.S., Redistricting as a Never-Ending Battle," *The New York Times,* July 1, 2003.

8. Jay Root and John Moritz, "GOP tentatively agrees to remap," *Fort Worth Star-Telegram,* October 9, 2003, 1, 14A.

9. Sheryl Gay Stolberg, "After Ethics Rebukes, DeLay's Fortunes May Lie With His Party's," *The New York Times,* October 8, 2004.

10. Philip Shenon, "DeLay is Indicted Again in Texas, Money Laundering is Charge," *The New York Times,* October 4, 2004.

11. James C. McKinley Jr., "DeLay Convicted in Donation Case by Texas Jury," *The New York Times,* November 25, 2010, A1, A26.

12. James C. McKinney Jr., "DeLay Sentenced to 3 years in conspiracy and money-laundering case," *The New York Times,* January 11, 2011.

13. Carl Hulse and Adam Nagourney, "Lobbyist's Guilty Plea Seen as Threat to DeLay Return," *The New York Times,* January 5, 2006.

14. Juan A. Lozano, "Ex-Rep. Tom DeLay Unsurprised after DOJ Ends Probe," *Fort Worth Star-Telegram,* August 16, 2010.

15. David Stout, "DeLay is Indicted and Forced to Step Down as Majority Leader," *The New York Times,* September 28, 2005.

16. See TomDeLay.com, http://www.tomdelay.com/meet-tom/.

17. Tom Delay and Stephen Mansfield, No Retreat, *No Surrender: One American's Fight* (New York: Sentinel HC, 2007).

1. "Biography," Kay for Governor, April 26, 2009.

2. PJ Pierce, *Let Me Tell You What I've Learned: Texas Wise Women Speak* (Austin: University of Texas Press, 2002), 120; "1927 Anne Armstrong 2008/ Texan remembered as political trailblazer," *Houston Chronicle*, July 31, 2008; Jennifer O'Shea, "10 Things You Didn't Know About Kay Bailey Hutchison," *U.S. News & World Report*, July 24, 2008.

3. Karen Foerstel, *Biographical Dictionary of Congressional Women* (Westport: Greenwood, 1999), 130; O'Shea.

4. Pierce, 117; O'Shea.

5. Ben R. Guttery, *Representing Texas* (Columbia, SC: BookSurge, 2008), 97; 202-204.

6. George Kuempel, "Hutchison is issued subpoena—Senator denies claims of treasury misdeeds," *The Dallas Morning News*, September 4, 1993.

7. George Kuempel and Selwyn Crawford, "Hutchison acquitted of all charges—DA's move to drop case spurs ruling—Judge declines to decide if evidence is admissible," *The Dallas Morning News*, February 12, 1994.

8. Guttery, 202-204.

9. Todd J. Gillman, "Hutchison still faces skeptics—in battle over who's more conservative, some Texans not sure she's the real deal," *The Dallas Morning News*, June 7, 2009.

10. Ibid.

11. Wayne Slater, "Hutchison says work ethic, determination shaped career—Senate candidate has often gone against stereotypes," *The Dallas Morning News*, April 28, 1993.

12. Todd J. Gillman, "Hutchison easily wins 3rd Senate term," *The Dallas Morning News*, November 8, 2006.

13. Todd J. Gillman, "Hutchison's VP potential debated—Some see her as good 'counterpunch'; others question appeal to base," *The Dallas Morning News*, February 12, 2008.

14. Gromer Jeffers Jr., "Rivals engender life lessons—Clinton, Hutchison share inspirational stories at Dallas Women's Museum gathering," *The Dallas Morning News*, March 28, 2009.

15. Anna Tinsley and Maria Recio, "Race to replace Hutchison may draw a crowd," *Fort Worth Star-Telegram*, January 14, 2011, p. 1B.

Index

abandoned property act, 122
abortion issues, 110, 181, 211, 220, 221
Abramoff, Jack, 214
Abrams, Elliott, 115
adoption, 181
affirmative action, 175
Afghanistan, 4, 191, 194-95
African Americans, 4, 6, 82, 133-34, 137, 185
Agnew, Spiro, 188
agricultural interests and reforms, 42, 43, 89, 93
Al Qaeda, 195
Albert, Carl, 38, 138
Alger, Bruce, 4, 114, 128-34, 182
Allen, Robert, 27
Allred, James, 52, 104, 146
American Hospital Association, 59
Americans for Constitutional Action, 131, 161-62
Americans for Democratic Action, 94, 211
Andrews, Mike, 219
Anti-Ballistic Missile Treaty, 110
anti-lynching legislation, 137
anti-Semitism, 59
anti-trust laws of Texas, 10
Appalachia, federal aid to, 76
Archer, Bill, 4, 6, 61, 176-82
Arizona statehood, 14
Armey, Richard, 3, 6, 181, 203-208, 210, 211
arms sales embargo, 53
Armstrong, Anne, 217
Army-McCarthy hearings, 83
at-large districts, 185
atomic bomb, 76

Bacon, Donald C., 27
Bailey, Joseph Weldon, 3, 4, 9-15, 17, 33, 38, 49, 82
Bankhead, William, 5, 35
banking, deregulation, 200
Banks, Stanley Jr., 154
Bannister, Floyd, 137
Barkley, Alben, 22-23, 29
Barnes, Ben, 186
Bartlett, Steve, 217
Beall, Jack, 43
Benson, Ezra Taft, 130
Benson, Reed, 130

Bentsen, Lloyd Jr., 5, 6, 105-112, 151, 169, 172, 173, 177, 197-98, 218
Berlin Wall, 175
Bethune, Mary McLeod, 82
Beveridge, Albert, 12-14
Biden, Joe, 113
Big Thicket, 151
bin Laden, Osama, 195
Black, Eugene, 57, 60
blacks, see African Americans
Blakely, William, 148, 161
Bloom, Sol, 20
Boggs, Hale, 38
Bolling, Richard, 38, 142
Bowers, Claude, 12
Brightwell, Charles O., 192
Brooks, Jack, 3-4, 113-19, 187
Brown v. Board of Education, 104, 116, 122, 123, 153
Bryan, William Jennings, 9, 17
Buchanan, James, 3, 82
Buchanan, Pat, 200
budget, federal: balancing, 110, 197, 199, 200; deficit spending, 29; national debt, 138; non-defense discretionary spending, 208
"Bureau of Education," John Nance Garner's, 27, 28, 108
Burgess, Jack, 92
Burleson, Omar, 186
Burton, Phil, 142
Bush, George H.W., 169-75; campaign against Ralph Yarborough, 150; as Republican congressman from Houston, 5, 108, 177; support from John Tower, 162-63, as US president, 3, 6, 110, 112, 135, 159, 166; as US vice president, 204
Bush, George W., 169, 175
Bush, Jeb, 169
Byrns, Joseph, 28

C-SPAN, 157, 203
Cabell, Earle, 129, 133
campaign contribution limits, 110
Canada, 112
Cannon, Clarence, 74, 76
Cannon, Joseph, 12, 18
Caribbean, military intervention in, 49
Carleton, Don, 66
Carr, Waggoner, 165

Carter, Amon G., 137

Carter, Jimmy, 110, 115, 142, 173, 218

Catholics, 21, 50, 181

Central America, military intervention in, 49

Central Intelligence Agency, 173, 194

China, 173

Christian Coalition, 118

civil rights: Civil Rights Act of 1957, 37, 83, 84, 148; Civil Rights Act of 1964, 87, 116, 150, 165; Civil Rights Act of 1968, 165; Civil Rights Act of 1991, 175; for Latinos, 4; opposition to, 34, 53, 58, 76, 122, 165; support for, 110, 148, 155, 171, 188

Civil War, 148

Clark, Champ, 9, 12, 43

Clark, Tom, 123

Clements, Bill, 134

Clinton, Hillary Rodham, 207, 223

Clinton, William Jefferson, 105, 112, 175, 178, 181, 188, 204, 207, 208, 210, 218

Cold War GI Bill, 149, 150; see also veterans

Cold War, 55, 175

Collum, John, 43

Combs, J.M., 68

Commodity Exchange Authority Act, 92

communism: Bruce Alger, 129; Lloyd Bentsen, 108; Martin Dies, 66, 68, 69; Henry B. González, 155; Phil Gramm, 200; Joanne Herring, 194; House Un-American Activities Committee, 4, 63, 65; Joe McCarthy, 83, 130; W. Lee O'Daniel, 95, 100, 104; Jim Wright, 137; Ralph Yarborough, 148

Connally Hot Oil Act, 52, 54

Connally, John B., 49, 63, 107, 108, 110, 121, 126, 150, 165, 186

Connally, Thomas, 5, 22, 48-55, 121, 123

Contract with America, 179, 182, 205-206, 208, 210

Cooley, Harold D., 90

Coolidge, Calvin, 27, 130

Cornyn, John, 7

cotton industry, 43

Coughlin, Charles E., 59

court-packing plan of 1937, 21-22, 29, 39, 43, 47, 52, 64; see also Supreme Court

Cranston, Alan, 157-58

Crile, George, 193-94

Cross, Oliver, 90

Cuba, 211

Culberson, Charles, 14

Cullen, Hugh Roy, 68

Dallek, Robert, 132

Daniel, Price, 54, 68, 120-27, 148, 155, 219

death penalty, 108

DeConcini, Dennis, 157-58

defense, national, 35, 66, 74, 76, 78, 198; see also military and strategic defense policy

DeLay, Tom, 3, 6, 209-15

Depew, Chauncey, 12

Dies, Martin Jr., 4, 63-70, 74, 79, 100, 134

Doggett, Lloyd, 199

Dowdy, John, 131, 171, 192

Dukakis, Michael, 110, 112, 173

Eckhardt, Bob, 118

education: bilingual, 171; federal aid to, 76; integration of public schools, 148; see also Brown v. Board of Education, Plessy v. Ferguson

Edwards, Chet, 198

Eggers, Paul C., 162

Eighteenth Amendment (Prohibition), 17, 18-20

Eisenhower, Dwight D.: events in administration, 5, 54, 130, 155; as sponsor of civil rights bill, 84; support from Dallas voters, 129; support of conservative Democrats, 93, 113, 121, 124, as general, 148; working relationships with Texas congressmen, 74, 137

England, 23

Enron, 200

environmental legislation, 171

Environmental Protection Agency, 210, 211

Equal Rights Amendment, 93

ethanol, 180

ethics policies, 171, 192, 209, 213

Evans, Wanda, 74

expansionism, American, 10

Fair Deal, 134

farm to market roads, 34

Farmer's Alliance, 9

Fascism, 65

Federal Aviation Administration, 213

Federal Communications Commission, 35, 116, 130

Federal Reserve, 26, 58, 61, 62

Fenno, Richard, 76

Fisher, Richard, 219

Fitzgerald, Peter, 199

flat tax, 181, 207

Foley, Tom, 94, 205

food stamp legislation, 94

Ford, Gerald, 74, 78, 92, 173, 188, 217, 220

foreign policy, 53, 77, 142, 175

Foreman, Ed, 155

Frank, Barney, 207

Frantz, Joe, 25

free market, deregulation, 199, 200, 201, 204

futures market reform bill, 42

gambling, 42, 43, 123

Garner, John Nance, 3, 4-5, 12, 22, 24-31, 34, 35, 38, 44, 50, 82

gay rights, 220

GI Bill, 149, 150; see also veterans

Gibbons, Sam, 179

Gingrich, Newt, 142, 144, 180, 182, 205-207, 210

Gizzi, John, 220

Glenn, John, 158, 207

Goldwater, Barry, 87, 161, 165, 171

González, Charles, 158

González, Henry B., 4, 6, 152-58

Gorbachev, Mikhail, 142

Gramm, William Philip "Phil," 6, 197-202

Great Depression, 27, 50, 54, 63, 76, 95, 99-100, 135, 154

Great Society, 59, 76, 87, 116, 150

Green, George Norris, 54

Greenspan, Alan, 112

Grenada invasion, 157

Grover, Hank, 199

Guadalupe Mountains National Park, 149

gun control, 118, 211, 220

Hardeman, Dorsey B., 27, 186

Harding, Warren G., 49

Hare, Silas, 9

Harrison, Pat, 22-23, 29

Hastert, Dennis, 211

Hastings, Alcee, 115

health care, health insurance, 150, 181, 203, 204, 207

Hébert, F. Edward, 61, 78

Herring, Joanne, 194-95

highway beautification, 138

Hillbilly Boys, 98, 100

Hispanic Caucus, 153, 157

Hollings, Ernest, 199

Hoover, Herbert, 5, 27, 50

Hornaday, Walter, 124

House Committee on Un-American Activities, 4, 63, 64-66, 68; see also communism, Joe McCarthy

housing, 95, 130, 185, 204

Houston, Andrew Jackson, 100

Hutchison, Kay Bailey, 4, 6, 7, 216-23

Hutchison, Ray, 217, 220

immigration laws and policies, 43, 76, 130, 211

income tax, 10, 130, 181, 210

integration of public schools, 148

Internal Revenue Service, 181, 210

Interstate Commerce Commission, 34-35

Interstate Highway Act, 137

Iran-Contra investigation, 115, 157, 166

isolationism, American, 23, 49, 104

Israel, 211

Ivins, Molly, 175

John Birch Society, 130

Johnson, Claudia Alta "Lady Bird," 82, 131-32, 138

Johnson, Lyndon Baines, 80-87, 138, 155, 172; relationship with Lloyd Bentsen, 108; relationship with Jack Brooks, 113, relationship with Price Daniel, 121, 122, 125, 126; relationship with Barbara Jordan, 185, 187; relationship with George Mahon, 76, 77; relationship with Wright Patman, 57, 58, 61; relationship with Bob Poage, 92, 94; Senate race against W. Lee O'Daniel, 66, 100, 101; as presidential candidate, 171; as US president, 3, 116; as protégé of Sam Rayburn, 5, 38; relationship with Allan Shivers, 124; as vice presidential candidate, 131-32, 150, 159, 161; as US vice president, 110-11; relationship with Ralph Yarborough, 147, 148

Johnson, Sam, 57

Jones, Bill, 129

Jones, Marvin, 3, 44

Jordan, Barbara, 4, 6, 76, 119, 183-89, 223

Keating, Charles, 157

Kelly, Gene, 219

Kennedy, David, 172

Kennedy, Jacqueline Bouvier, 116

Kennedy, John F., 37, 131, 138, 155, 185; assassination, 5, 49, 76, 87, 116, 134, 157, 185; partnership with Lyndon Johnson, 84, 110-12, 132, 150, 159

Kennedy, Joseph P. II, 158

Kilday, Paul, 155

Kilgore, Joe, 107

King Ranch, 81

King, Martin Luther Jr., 157

Kleberg, Richard, 81

Koreagate, 142

Korean War, 108

Kreuger, Robert, 165, 218

Ku Klux Klan, 50, 57

labor issues and unions, 14, 29, 67-68, 95, 104, 110, 124, 130, 148, 150, 211

Lampso, Nick, 214

Latimer, Ozzie, 155

Latinos, 4, 6, 153, 154; see also Mexicans, Mexico

Leach, Jim, 157

League of Nations, 14, 23, 49

Leath, Marvin, 93

Lehmberg, Rosemary, 214

Lemmon, Walter S., 42

Lend-Lease Act, 23, 53

Lewis, John L., 25
liquor by the drink law, 186
Long, Russell, 110
Longworth, Nicholas, 27
Louderback, Harold, 43
Lower Colorado River Authority, 147
Lucas, Wingate, 137
lumber industry, 192

MacArthur, Douglas, 148
Mahon, George, 3, 71-79, 119
Mallick, George, 142-44
Manhattan Project, 76
Mann, Gerald, 66, 100
Mansfield, John, 3
Mansfield, Mike, 110
Mansfield, Stephen, 214
Marshall, George, 76
mass media in political campaigning, 95
Mattox, Jim, 219
Mayfield, Earle, 50
McCain, John, 158, 201, 221
McCarthy, Joseph, 66, 83, 130
McClendon, Sarah, 138
McCormack, John, 138
McDuffie, John, 26, 28
McFall, John, 142
McGovern, George, 92, 165
Meany, George, 150
Medicaid and Medicare, 76, 110, 208, 213
Mexicans, Mexico, 12, 23, 25, 50 112, 153, 155, 165
military and strategic defense policy, 23, 35, 49-50, 165, 166; see also defense
milk for schoolchildren, 131
Mills, Roger Q., 4
Mills, Wilbur, 77, 177, 186
minimum wage, 93, 155; see also labor issues and unions
Molotov, Vyacheslav, 53
Moody, Dan, 50
Morse, Wayne, 150
mortgage industry crisis, 200-01
motor vehicle licensing, 90
Moyers, Bill, 132
Mujahideen, 194
Muslims, 195
Myer, Dillon, 74

National Aeronautics and Space Act of 1958, 84
National Archives, 18
National Democrats, 17
National Endowment for the Arts, 210
National Industrial Recovery Act, 50, 52

National Rifle Association, 118
National Security Council, 126
National Youth Administration, 82, 147
natural resources tax, 99, 100
Nazism, Nazis, 65, 100, 214
Neff, Pat, 14-15
New Deal: Bruce Alger, 134; James Allred, 104; Martin Dies, 63-64, 66; John Nance Garner, 27-29; Lyndon Johnson, 81, 82; George Mahon, 76; Wright Patman, 58, 59; Sam Rayburn, 5; Morris Sheppard, 23; Hatton Sumners, 44; attempts at majority in Supreme Court, 21-22, 52 (see also court-packing); Texans as committee chairs during era, 3
New Frontier, 134, 155
New Mexico statehood, 14
New World Order, 175
Nixon, Richard M., 74, 77, 92, 113, 115, 129, 172; impeachment, 6, 116, 183, 188
Nixon, Walter, 115
North American Free Trade Agreement (NAFTA), 112
North Atlantic Treaty Organization (NATO), 49, 53

O'Connor, John, 28, 35
O'Daniel, W. Lee (Pappy), 4, 53, 58, 66, 79, 82, 95-104, 122
O'Neill, Thomas P. "Tip," 138, 139, 198, 204
Obama, Barack, 203, 207
oil and gas industry: depletion allowance, 171-72; large East Texas field, 50, 52; decline in prices during Depression, 54; Permanent School Fund, 146; submerged lands off Texas coast, 121, 123; tax breaks for, 110, 177; Ralph Yarborough and big companies, 147
old age pensions, 100

Padre Island National Seashore, 149
Palin, Sarah, 221
Panic of 1893, 39
Parr, George, 83, 107
Parten, J. R., 66
Passman, Otto, 77
Patinaude, Lionel V., 28
Patman, Wright, 3, 6, 56-62, 78, 177
Patton, George, 148
Paul, Ron, 210
Pearl Harbor, 23, 104, 136, 169; see also World War II
Penfield, W.L., 12, 14
Perot, Ross, 175, 219
Perry, Rick, 219-20
Persian Gulf War, 175
Pierce, Henry Clay, 10
Plessy v. Ferguson, 122-23, 185
Poage-Aiken Act, 92
Poage, Bob (William Robert), 3, 6, 61, 78, 88-94, 172

Poage, Scott T., 93

Poindexter, John, 115

political action committees, 211

poll tax, 53, 98, 108, 137, 155, 165

Pool, Joe, 129

poverty, war on, 87

prayer in schools, 108

prenatal and neonatal care, 110

Priest, Pat, 214

Progressives, 17, 18, 20, 23

Prohibition, 4, 14, 17, 18, 21, 50, 57, 100-101

prostitution, 57

public housing, 130, 204

public works projects, 26, 34, 200

Quayle, Dan, 111-12

racial issues and racism, 122, 154

Radnofsky, Barbara, 219

railroad regulation, 10, 34-35

Rainey, Henry, 28

Rayburn Stock and Bond Bill, 34

Rayburn, Sam (Samuel Taliaferro), 32-38, 43, 44, 50, 123, 166; relationship with Bruce Alger, 132; protégé of Joseph Weldon Bailey, 12, 15; relationship with Lloyd Bentsen, 107; mentor to Jack Brooks, 113; and civil rights, 84; relationship with Price Daniel, 121, 122, 124, 125, 126; relationship with Martin Dies, 65-66, 70; 58, 61, 65-66, 70, 71, 74, 81, 82, 84; protégé of John Nance Garner, 4, 26, 27, 28; mentor to Lyndon Johnson, 81, 82; relationship with George Mahon, 71, 74; as New Deal supporter, 5; relationship with Wright Patman, 58, 61; relationship with Bob Poage, 90; as Speaker of US House of Representatives, 3, 135; relationship with Jim Wright, 137

Raymond, Mannie, 107

Reagan, Ronald, 6, 110, 173; Contract with America, 207-08; economic policies, 197, 198; impeachment threat, 157; popular with Texas voters, 204; relationships with Texas congressmen, 142, 165, 166

Reconstruction, 37, 39, 134, 138, 159, 161

redistricting in Texas, 211-13, 214

Reed, Thomas, 9

Reedy, George, 84

Reese Air Force Base, 77

Reese, Jim, 78

Reigle, Donald, 158

Republican-Southern Democrat conservative coalition, 53

Reuther, Walter, 130

revenue sharing, 116-117, 118

Richards, Ann, 105, 151, 175, 188, 218

Ritter, Halsted L., 43

Roberts, Ray, 187

Roe v. Wade, 220

rogue nations, 208

Roosevelt, Franklin D., 21, 35, 52-53, 65, 76, 82, 104; court-packing plan, 43, 64; relationship with Martin Dies, 63, 66, 67, 70; John Nance Garner as vice president, 25, 26, 28-29, 31, 50; relationship with Lyndon Johnson, 58, 81, 100; relationship with Morris Sheppard, 17, 21, 22-23; relationship with Hatton Sumners, 39, 44; Texans' influence during administration, 5, 34

Rorem, Rufus, 59

Rostenkowski, Dan, 178

Rudman, Warren, 199

Rural Electrification Administration, 35, 203

rural electrification, 34, 82, 90, 92, 95

Rural Telephone Act of 1949, 90, 92

Russell, Richard, 83, 132

sales tax, 98-99, 121, 122, 126, 181, 186

Sam Rayburn dam and reservoir, 115

Sanders, Barefoot, 129, 151, 165

Sanger, Alexander, 43

Saudi Arabia, 194

Savage, Wallace, 129

savings and loan scandal and bailout, 153, 157-58

Schiavo, Terri, 208

Schlesinger, Arthur Jr., 27

Schlesinger, James, 77-78

School Milk Act, 92

Schwarz, Jordan, 27

Securities and Exchange Commission, 35

securities, regulation of, 35

segregation, segregationists, 37, 58, 84, 104, 121, 122-23, 153, 155, 185

Selective Service, 23

seniority system in Congress, 35-37, 61, 78, 82, 83, 90, 94, 172

Sheppard, John, 17

Sheppard, Morris, 4, 5, 16-23, 63, 66, 82, 95, 100

Sherman, Max, 183

Shivers, Allan, 93, 122, 123-24, 126, 148

Silver Democrats, 9, 10

single-member districts, 185

Smith, Al, 20-21, 50

Smith, Howard, 37

Smith, Preston, 126

Smoot-Hawley Tariff, 26

Social Security, 130, 181, 208

socialism, 130, 131

soil conservation programs, 34

Southern Manifesto, 116, 148

Soviet Union, 65, 138, 191, 194

space, competition for dominance in, 83

Spanish-American War, 49

Spence, Brent, 60

Sputnik, 84

St. Germain, Ferdinand, 157

Star Wars initiative, 166

Stark, Pete, 179

states' rights, 121, 124

Stenholm, Charles, 181

Stevenson, Adlai, 93, 155

Stevenson, Coke, 83, 101

Stimson, Henry, 76

Stockman, Steve, 118

Strategic Defense Initiative, 110

strikes, sit-down, 29, 64; see also labor issues and unions

Submerged Lands Act, 124

Sullivan, Leonor K., 93

Sumners, Hatton, 22, 39-47

Supreme Court, 43, 44, 50, 52, 68, 104, 122, 123, 130, 153; packing of, 21-22, 29, 47, 64

Sweatt, Heman, 122

Taft, William Howard, 43

Tammany Hall, 21, 35

tariffs, 18, 23, 26

taxes: flat, 181, 207; income, 10, 130, 181, 210; natural resources, 99-100; oil and gas industry, 110, 177; poll, 53, 98, 108, 137, 155, 165; sales, 98-99, 121, 122, 126, 181, 186

Taylor, Walton D., 52

Teague, Olin "Tiger," 198

Tennessee Valley Authority, 95

term limits, 118, 180

Terrell, Alexander, 42

Texas Monthly, 138

Texas Railroad Commission, 52

Texas Regulars, 104

Thornton, Robert L., 43

Thurmond, Strom, 165

tidelands of Texas, 54, 121, 122, 123, 124, 126

Tower, John Goodwin, 5, 138, 144, 151, 159-68, 171, 180, 199, 218

Towery, Ken, 163

trade barriers, 112

Truman, Harry S., 34, 38, 54, 108, 123

Tugwell, Rexford, 27

US v. Texas, 123

United Nations, 49, 53, 54, 172

urban renewal, 87

utility holding companies, regulation of, 35

Vandergriff, Tom, 203-04

Versailles, Treaty of, 23

veterans, 95, 149-50

Vietnam War, 87, 92, 116, 150, 151, 166

Vinson, Fred, 108

voting irregularities, 42

Voting Rights Act, 165, 188

Wade, Henry, 129

Wages and Hours Bill, 29; see also labor issues and unions

Walker, George Herbert, 171

Walsh, Joan, 207

Warren, Earl, 130

water issues and projects, 34, 122, 138

Watergate, 5-6, 61, 94, 172, 183, 188

Waters-Pierce Oil Company, 10-11

Watershed Protection and Flood Prevention Act, 92

weapons reduction, 50; see also defense

Webb Air Force Base, 77

Webster, William H., 157

welfare reform, 200, 208

Wells, Jim, 12, 25

West, Milton, 107

Weyrich, Paul, 167

Whitten, Jamie, 77

Wilson, Charles Nesbitt "Charlie," 4, 78, 171, 185, 187, 190-196

Wilson, Woodrow, 4, 17, 18, 23, 26, 34, 35, 43, 49, 54

Witt, Edgar, 90, 92-93

women: in Congress, 4, 6, 183-89, 223; discrimination against, 217; suffrage for, 14, 23

Wood, John W., 157

Woodmen of the World, 20

workman's compensation insurance, 186; see also labor issues and unions

World War I, 49, 90, 105

World War II, 18, 23, 35, 76, 82, 107, 115, 122, 147-48, 154, 159, 169

Wozencraft, Alfred P., 41

Wright, Jim, 135-44, 165; Americans for Constitutional Action rating, 131; race for majority leader, 118, 192; relationships with other congresspeople, 47, 77, 93, 132, 158, 187, 192, 196, 198; as Speaker of House, 3, 6

Yarborough, Ralph W., 5, 63, 68-69, 85, 108, 126, 145-51, 171, 172, 186

Zia ul-Haq, Mohammed, 194